Democratic Values
in the Muslim World

Democratic Values in the Muslim World

Moataz A. Fattah

LYNNE
RIENNER
PUBLISHERS

BOULDER
LONDON

Paperback edition published in the United States of America in 2008 by
Lynne Rienner Publishers, Inc.
1800 30th Street, Boulder, Colorado 80301
www.rienner.com

and in the United Kingdom by
Lynne Rienner Publishers, Inc.
3 Henrietta Street, Covent Garden, London WC2E 8LU

First hardcover edition published in 2006 by Lynne Rienner Publishers, Inc.

ISBN: 978-1-58826-545-6

Printed and bound in the United States of America

 The paper used in this publication meets the requirements
of the American National Standard for Permanence of
Paper for Printed Library Materials Z39.48-1992.

5 4 3 2 1

Contents

Tables and Figures

Acknowledgments

Many people contributed hours of their time to help me in my pursuit of the data, information, opinions, and experiences that form the central elements of this work. Sadly, I cannot mention the names of several people who have been extremely helpful. Some, however, can be thanked openly or by reference to the aliases they chose for themselves.

I must thank some of the most dedicated Arab professors who encouraged me to pursue this endeavor. Atop the list are Mustapha Kamel al-Sayyid, Kamal al-Monouffi, Saif El-deen Abdlefattah, Hassan Nafa'a, Nazli Mou'awad, Hazem Hussni, and Nadia Mostapha of Cairo University; Ahmad Yossef Ahmad and Nevin Moussa'd of the Arab League's Institute of Arab Studies; Wadoda Badran and Ola Abu Zaid of the Arab Women Organization, all of whom contributed time and effort to this project. I am also highly appreciative of the great intellectuals and scholars, such as Bahgat Korany, Mohamed Omara, Tareq al-Bishri, Mohamed Salim al-'Awa, Ref'at al-Sa'eed, Sa'eed al-Ashmawi, Iqbal Baraka, and Hassan Hanafi, among many others, who were generous with their time, responded to my questions, and examined my work.

Moreover, I wish to acknowledge and give special thanks to the professors, intellectuals, researchers, and employees of thirteen academic and Islamic research centers in Egypt, Iran, Turkey, Sudan, Libya, Saudi Arabia, United Arab Emirates, Malaysia, Pakistan, and Bangladesh who worked so hard in helping me administer the surveys, conduct the focus-group discussions, and interview intellectual and religious elites. Most notably, I am indebted to the staff and researchers of the Middle East Research Council in Beirut, the Institute of Arab Studies of the Arab League, and the Center for the Study of Developing Countries and the

Center for Political Research and Studies (Cairo University). Thank you for your generous financial and academic support.

For their extensive and detailed suggestions for improving the initial survey and reviewing the final versions, my special thanks go to K. Radi and five anonymous professors and researchers at Tehran University; Fahd Mahrani, M. al-Omair, and eleven anonymous scholars and intellectuals in Saudi Arabia; Abdulhaq al-Jundi and two Syrian intellectuals; Marawan Tabara of Lebanon; No'aman Rahim, Khaled Jamil, and six anonymous scholars and intellectuals in Pakistan; Mohamd al-Ameen, Abu Bakr Sokkho, and Jebreil Safair of Senegal; Safi Moeyn and Hamid Yassein of Morocco; and Anees Sobah, Karim Galil, and Sa'eed Salim of Algeria. Many friends and colleagues deserve credit for their moral and logistical support, such as Ahmad Shrief, Mohamed al-Mahdi, Ashraf Eid, and Mohamad Gaber.

At the Department of Political Science, Western Michigan University (WMU), I found an extremely helpful and healthy academic environment that enabled me to explore difficult questions and serious issues about the relationship between Islam and democracy. I want to acknowledge Kevin Corder, the chairperson of the department, who was the first to introduce me to quantitative analysis. I was honored to benefit from his thorough and deep review of the methodological aspects of this project. In terms of the theoretical and philosophical discussions of democratic norms and praxes, I am indebted to Emily Hauptmann's discussions and comments on my work. I really appreciate everything she does for all the graduate students in the Department of Political Science at WMU. I am very thankful to Adam Sabra's comments and encouragement to carry on my research. A great sociologist, Susan Carlson, and a great econometrician, Matthew Higgins, were extremely generous and provided me with many insights on how to do quantitative analysis. Finally, I am indebted to my mentor, Jim Butterfield, whose effort, patience, and wealth of knowledge contributed the most to the completion of this work. This book would not be what it is now without his guidance.

At Lynne Rienner Publishers, Marilyn Grobschmidt's dedication, professionalism, enthusiasm, and commitment to what she is doing were the driving force behind this book. I am greatly appreciative of all her efforts. Shena Redmond and Ruth Goring assumed the responsibility of reviewing and editing the final draft of the book. Their suggestions are highly appreciated.

Finally, I thank my wife, Ghada, and my children, Zina and Adham, for allowing me the time to travel and work freely to complete this project. Ghada deserves special thanks for her kind and generous support both emotionally and practically. I am most grateful to her for allowing me to make use of her statistical skills.

Last but not least, I am thankful to Allah for all the blessings He bestowed upon me, *al-Hamd li-Allah.*

—*Moataz A. Fattah*

1

Introduction

It is outrageous and amazing that the first free and general elections in the history of the Arab nation are to take place in Iraq, under the auspices of the American occupation, and in Palestine, under the auspices of the Israeli occupation.
— Salameh Nematt, in the Arabic daily *Al-Hayat,* March 27, 2005

Democratization in the Muslim world is in the interest of the U.S. . . . Bahrain, Qatar and—to a certain extent—Jordan [have] several reformist elements. We want to be supportive of them.
— Condoleezza Rice, US national security adviser,
in the *Financial Times,* September 23, 2002

We in the Arab and Muslim world know our way. We have our own will and we hold firm to our rights. Besides, we do not need anybody to give us lessons in how to run our countries.
— Ahmad Maher, Egyptian foreign minister, in response to
Rice's comments, in the Arabic daily *Al-Hayat,* September 25, 2002

There is no question that Muslim countries are disproportionately autocratic. In 1975, predominantly Muslim countries were the seats of around 25 percent of the world's nondemocratic regimes (Potter et al. 1997), and by 2005 this number had grown to 55 percent. Moreover, no one single Muslim country qualifies today as a consolidated democracy by a commonly accepted measure (Linz and Stephan 1996). One study shows that predominantly Muslim countries "are markedly more authoritarian than non-Muslim societies, even when one controls for other potentially influential factors" (Fish 2002: 37).

Another commentator put it this way: "Islamic democracy has no

1

track record, since it barely exists as yet" (Burma 2004). Even worse, "while the countries of Latin America, Africa, East Central Europe, and South and East Asia experienced significant gains for democracy and freedom over the last 20 years, the Islamic world experienced an equally significant increase in the number of repressive regimes" (Karatnycky 2002: 103). Using Robert Dahl's typology, we find that the great majority of Muslim polities are classified as nondemocratic. And while six are considered new democracies, none qualify as well-established democracies (Dahl 1998).

The predominance of authoritarian and semiauthoritarian regimes in the Muslim world, as well as the current nation-building projects in Afghanistan and Iraq, continue to make some wonder whether Islam is compatible with democratic governance. In other words, why do Muslims not cry out for democracy when the evidence suggests that they should? Or do they?

Surprisingly, despite the prevalence of this question in scholarly, journalistic, and policy circles, there have been very few attempts to systematically measure Muslim attitudes toward democracy or to assess whether there is a single Islamic mindset regarding democratization. Journalistic answers have always been somewhat cursory, anecdotal, and normative, and even the scholarly work has been largely historical and interpretive, failing to let Muslims speak for themselves. The present work presumes that popular values structure—and perhaps set limits on—both the pace of and the possibilities for social and political change. Thus, to gauge the potential for democratic reform in the Middle East, one has to understand the values of its citizens.

This book, then, explores the following questions: Do the values and attitudes of Muslims obstruct or decelerate the democratization process in Muslim countries? If yes, why? If no, who are the possible social agents of democracy in the Muslim world? These questions are examined, in turn, in the following three ways: by analyzing how opinion leaders understand and portray democracy to the masses, by exploring individual attitudes about democracy and the factors that shape them, and by discerning commonalities and differences among Muslim societies in their potential for democratization.

While this is not the first investigation of Muslim public opinion, it is distinctive in that the survey questions were designed exclusively for a Muslim audience, they are supplemented with responses to mostly open-ended questions from focus-group discussions, and these responses are situated in the larger landscape of Muslim political and religious thought. When appropriate, the findings of other surveys have been brought in to shed more light on a particular aspect of the Islam-democracy question. Though no single study can claim to be the final word on Muslim public opinion, the multiple methods and sources used here should give readers a fairly high degree of confidence in the reliability of the reported findings.

The survey itself covers 31,380 literate Muslims in thirty-two Muslim countries across the Middle East, North Africa, and Central and Southeast Asia, as well as minority Muslim communities in the United States, Europe, and India. Borrowing from previous analyses of democracy, this study seeks to capture two major components of democratic values. The first involves democratic norms, or the public's commitment to the political equality of all citizens and to the negotiated settlement of political disputes. Students of democracy have been particularly interested in whether citizens will tolerate political activity by their most hated opponents or the traditionally disenfranchised, because without tolerance, genuine democratic competition is impossible. To test Muslims' commitment to democratic norms, this project looks specifically at tolerance for the political involvement of women and of members of racial, ethnic, and religious minorities.

The second component of democratic values relates to support for political institutions such as elections and political parties. Most of the literature on democracy recognizes the importance of other features of democracy such as an independent judiciary, legal constraints on the state, the separation of powers, a viable civil society, and a free press. Nevertheless, this analysis focuses on the former set of institutions, since they are the most basic elements of democracy and the key requisites of democratic transitions. Probing for more than general beliefs about democracy, the study also gauges individual attitudes about incumbent rulers and the extent to which Muslims are willing to make sacrifices for their political rights.

What, generally, does this study tell us about Muslim attitudes toward democracy? Many of the findings do not lend themselves to pat summaries. As in other societies, there are often tensions in Muslims' thinking about democracy. Support for political institutions, for example, does not always translate into support for political tolerance, and general support for democracy does not mean that people are willing to make significant sacrifices to bring it about. Many of these tensions must be understood in the particular social and political contexts in which they arise.

Other findings, however, allow for clearer and more sweeping conclusions. What is particularly intriguing is the wide degree of variation in the potential for democratization based on the measurement of democratic values, something not captured by a simple examination of regime type in the Muslim world. The diversity of Muslim views demonstrates the need to refine our statements and debates about Islam and democracy. The issue is not whether the two are compatible but how to identify the contexts and manners in which the two can be reconciled. This book takes an important step forward in identifying the strongest correlates of democratic attitudes in the Muslim world.

Another striking conclusion is that, whether or not Muslims are supportive of democracy, personal experiences and perceived benefits of democratization play an important role in shaping Muslim attitudes toward democracy. We can conclude, then, that Muslims are not passionately and irrationally antidemocratic as the popular media and some scholars have often implied, but rather they are conditioned to view democracy with positive expectations or skepticism. This finding offers hope, then, that with the right mix of experiences and incentives, Muslims will be motivated to demand more from their leaders and to push for democratic reforms.

Muslims' values are shaped by personal experiences, including religious influences, so it is natural that democracy in Muslim countries would be influenced by religion. This study demonstrates that Islam is one of many environmental factors shaping attitudes about democracy and that its salience, while relatively strong, varies from society to society and individual to individual.

The analyses of Muslim public opinion found in the subsequent chapters will illuminate these conclusions in greater detail. Chapter 2 offers a brief overview of contemporary Muslim religious and political thought, based on interviews with opinion leaders and textual analysis of their debates. It identifies the major strains of debate about political reform and introduces the three predominant worldviews influencing religion and governance: traditionalist Islamists, modern Islamists, and secularists. These categories will reappear throughout the text to illuminate the ideological underpinnings of beliefs expressed in the survey and focus groups. The overview of opinion leaders also reveals that ordinary Muslims do not randomly choose their positions on political issues but rely on opinion leaders to make sense of the world they live in and to respond to the challenges they face.

Chapters 3 and 4 focus on the factors and actors that shape individual Muslims' attitudes toward democratic norms and institutions. In Chapter 3, the collected data are analyzed to discern the impact of demographic factors: income, education, age, and gender. The effects of personal religiosity and experience with democracy are also tested. Chapter 4 examines Muslim attitudes toward their respective incumbents, the West, and religious scholars to understand how each of these shape Muslims' political values. Detailed comments obtained from focus-group discussions supplement the statistical analysis in both chapters to allow for a richer understanding of why certain factors correlate with democracy and to offer insights into unexpected findings.

Chapter 5 aggregates the survey data to investigate how opinions differ across communities and countries and to illuminate the prospects for democracy in each society. The concluding chapter summarizes the most important findings and highlights their implications for democratization and the promotion of democracy in the Muslim world.

This book is meant to speak to a wide variety of readers, and thus every attempt has been made to meet the needs of specialists and nonspecialists alike. For those who lack detailed knowledge of the Muslim world, the first appendix offers a glossary of Arabic and Islamic terms. Also, to enhance the readability of the chapters and to focus on the larger implications behind the wealth of statistical findings, more technical statistical discussions have been placed in Appendixes 2 through 5. There readers will find extensive information about data collection, the survey instrument, and various methods of statistical analysis. Other technical issues will be addressed in the endnotes.

2

Elite Opinion and the Big Debates

Today we [Muslims] are the poorest, the most illiterate, the most backward, the most unhealthy, the most unenlightened, the most deprived, and the weakest of all the human race.
    —Pakistani president Pervez Musharraf, BBC, February 16, 2002

Some skeptics of democracy assert that the traditions of Islam are inhospitable to the representative government. This "cultural condescension," as Ronald Reagan termed it, has a long history. After the Japanese surrender in 1945, a so-called Japan expert asserted that democracy in that former empire would "never work."
    —US president George W. Bush, November 6, 2003

One of the most intriguing findings of the survey and focus-group discussions is that ordinary literate Muslims are highly influenced by opinion leaders who present ready-made intellectual meals for consumption. Without understanding these "meals," one would ignore a core aspect of the sources of Muslim political knowledge and attitudes. This chapter provides a road map to the schools of thought that shape Muslims' political attitudes and the relative weight of their adherents in each of the thirty-two Muslim societies studied (excluding Iraq).

The data collected suggest that these opinion leaders function as influential agents of political socialization. These opinion leaders, through public debates on the relationship between Islam and politics, shape the cultural repertoire that identifies a set of ideological positions between which ordinary literate Muslims place themselves. As a Syrian computer engineer put it: "Each software developer has to provide a tutorial for the end users. The same goes for politics. I need somebody to explain what politics is all about. That is why I read and listen to these intellectuals. I want to know. They help me know."

However, unlike software manuals, politics is always open to debates between these opinion leaders. Other studies show that these intellectual debates portray a set of visions that ordinary Muslims can hold regarding an issue such as democracy. These repertoires are "learned, shared and acted out through a relatively deliberate process of choice" (Tilly 1995:42).

Thus, Muslim attitudes toward democracy arise out of a learning process and deliberate choices that individuals make from among the options presented to them by contemporary opinion leaders. Hanan, a young Jordanian student in the United States, stands as a good example for the impact of these opinion leaders. In her words, "If all what I hear about democracy is coming from Hizb al-Tahrir, there is no way that I think positively of it." She actually stated that she had not understood what democracy truly was until she came to Canada and then the United States. Hanan is not an exception. My research finds that most Muslims adopt political positions based on the views of a rather homogenous group of opinion leaders whom they trust, and they dismiss the positions of opinion leaders who come from a different perspective.

If Muslims are not exposed to various accounts of democracy, most likely they will consume opinion leaders' preprepared political interpretations and attitudes without critically considering their contents. Instead of offering an exhaustive list of the opinion leaders as suggested by the respondents, this chapter will highlight the most emblematic figures in each group and the discourse they adopt regarding democracy.

Portrait of the Opinion Leaders' Debates

One of the questions on the survey asked for the names of three *ulama* (religious scholars), intellectuals, or politicians who had the most influence on the respondent's personal political knowledge and positions.[1] On the basis of the textual analysis and interviews with some of the opinion leaders mentioned by ordinary Muslims, it is clear that there is consistency between the opinion leaders' discourses and the positions adopted by the ordinary literate Muslims who read or listen to them. The literature of political socialization has always referred to the impact of opinion leaders on their followers. This project confirms this impact.

The focus-group discussions and the survey responses suggest three broad patterns of Muslim attitudes toward Islam and democracy: traditionalist Islamists, modernist Islamists, and secularists. These three patterns of thought diverge regarding which aspects of democracy are Islamic (ordained and accepted by Islamic teachings), non-Islamic (did not originate in Islam but are still acceptable in Islam), and un- or anti-Islamic (contrary to Islam and thus unacceptable).

The respondents categorized as traditionalist Islamists, hereafter referred to as traditionalists, searched for what they perceive as an *Islamic* government, which is contradictory to what most contemporary academicians and democracy students label democracy. Thus, they fully reject democracy on Islamic grounds. Modernist Islamist individuals, hereafter referred to as modernists, search for a modern (democratic) government that is *compatible with Islam*. They usually call it "Islamic democracy." Such a state would be different from the ancient state established by the Prophet and his companions in its format and procedures, yet identical to it with respect to goals and framework. Secularist respondents do not worry about how compatible their ideal system is with Islamic labels, since they consider that Islam, or any religion for that matter, can be used to justify any form of government.

Traditionalists are subject to another division based upon their attitude toward violence: they are either pacifists or advocates of political violence. The examination of the attitudes of Muslims and their opinion leaders suggests that both subgroups—pacifists and violent—take antagonistic attitudes toward democracy. One expresses its rejection of democracy violently, however, while the other does so without violence. In the same vein, secularists can be divided between autocratic statists and liberal pluralists, based on their position on political plurality. Both traditionalist Islamists and statist secularists reject democracy, the former for religious reasons and the latter on secular grounds.

Modernist Islamists and pluralistic secularists accept democracy but also for different reasons. The former perceive it to be a modern mechanism to apply the Islamic principle of *shura* (mutual consultation); the latter perceive it as a political necessity to achieve their liberal goals.

It is important to note that traditionalists and modernists are both Islamists and have similar assumptions and doctrines regarding the role of Islam in politics. For both schools of thought, Islam is both religion and state. When encountering the secular slogan "Political Islam," Islamists will respond by stating that Islam cannot be anything but political. A Tunisian Islamist interviewed in the United States is highly critical of secular Muslim governments' equation of "political Islam" with "fascist Islam." This complaint is raised by numerous Islamist activists and *ulama* (al-'Aawa 1989; al-Khalidi 1984; al-Qaradawi 2001a; No'amani 2002).

Secularists, who are not necessarily atheists or disbelievers, perceive Islam as a personal relationship between God and his servants. This is the point on which they utterly disagree with Islamists. In Iran, a group of young men and women dressed in Western style refused to call their government "the Islamic Republic of Iran." One of them shouted: "Show me where in the Quran or teachings of the Prophet Mohamed or Imam Ali that al-Khomeini has the right to speak in the name of Allah." The same rhetoric is heard in many other Muslim countries. A student of law in Cairo University refers to the Quran as a book with many interpretations. Its verses mean different things to different people. Some secularist writings reflect the same notion (al-Sa'eed 2001; Baghdadi 1999; Khalaf Allah 1984; Mernissi 1992). It is clear from the collected data that secularists are highly influenced by nonreligious education, obtained outside the Muslim world or from translated materials. These secularist tendencies defy the semiclosed religious stratum of *ulama* who for generations had monopolized learning and intellectual activity (Sharabi 1970). Not surprisingly, many of the interviewed traditionalists think that secularists are no longer Muslims, while most modernists perceive them to be misguided Muslims.

Traditionalist respondents identified some *ulama* and Islamist activists as their most influential sources of political knowledge and ideas. The most common and emblematic names that influenced the traditionalists include Imam Khomeini of Iran,[2] Sayyid Qutb of Egypt,[3] Abu Bakar Bashir of Indonesia,[4] Sayyid Abul Ala Maududi of Pakistan,[5] Shaikh Abdul Hamid Kishk of Egypt,[6] and Ibn Baaz of Saudi Arabia.[7] Traditionalists named these people as the most influential opinion leaders in shaping their attitudes toward politics.

Modernist Islamists, however, combine deduction from holy texts with inductive *ijtihad* (independent reasoning). They perceive democracy as a modern extension of the great Islamic principle of *shura*. Sunnis who responded to the survey and participated in the focus-group discussions identified Yusuf al-Qaradawi of Egypt and Qatar[8] as the most influential modernist Islamist opinion leader. Some of the other names that appeared on the list of opinion leaders who have been influential in shaping the attitudes of modernist Islamists are Mohamed al-Ghazali of Egypt,[9] Mohamed Iqbal of India,[10] Abdolkarim Soroush of Iran,[11] Rachid al-Ghannoushi of Tunisia,[12] Abdurrahman Wahid of Indonesia,[13] and President Moahmed Khatami of Iran.

Secular Muslims mentioned the names of some opinion leaders

whom they perceive as having influenced their political positions. Some of the most well-known names are Mahathir Mohamed of Malaysia,[14] Said al-Ashmawi of Egypt,[15] Ahmad Baghdadi of Kuwait,[16] Mohamed Arkoun of Algeria,[17] Muhammad Ali Jinnah of Pakistan,[18] and Yadollah Sahabi of Iran.[19] It is noteworthy that the previous names were not the only names mentioned by the studied respondents and participants, but they were the most commonly mentioned opinion leaders.

It is worth noting that Abo Al-A'laa Maududi of Pakistan and Imam Khomeini of Iran, more than any other names, were named by both modernists and traditionalists as their most influential opinion leaders. Mention by both modernists and traditionalists appears to be an inconsistency. This inconsistency should be understood in the framework of the writings of these *ulama*. Maududi has inconsistent positions that make him both a traditionalist and modernist in the same time. Based on his book *Concepts of Islam Regarding Religion and State* (Mawdudi 1977a), he can be easily classified as a modernist who respects the rights of minorities and democratic procedures, such as elections, voting, and representation. Yet in some of his other books that were written during the same period, such as *Islam and Modern Civilization* (Mawdudi 1977b) and *Islam Facing Modern Challenges* (Mawdudi 1980), there is a clear tendency to attack democratic principles and values and the same mechanisms that he praised elsewhere, such as elections and majority rule. Khomeini, similarly, can be used to illustrate both a very traditionalist theological pattern of thinking and a very modernist perspective—the latter because he argues for democratic procedures and respect for basic human rights. It depends on which quotes are used, because some of his comments support the modernists and others support the traditionalists. For instance, in 1977 he was quoted as stating that "the real threat to Islam does not come from the Shah. . . . The real threat comes from the idea of imposing on Muslim lands the Western system of democracy, which is a form of prostitution" (Taheri 2003). However, he was also quoted as urging Iranians to participate in the "heavy responsibility" of electing the presidents and the members of the Shura Council as part of their Islamic obligations (Esposito 1996:24).

Kuwaiti Islamists are not much different from Maududi and Khomeini; they adopt a quasi-traditionalist and quasi-modernist position too. Kuwaiti Islamists act as modernists when they participate in elections and form the majority of the Kuwaiti parliament, yet they always object to women's enfranchisement based on verbatim interpretations of Islamic teachings and local tribal rhetoric (al-Tabetba'i 2002). The

Kuwaiti parliament eventually enfranchised women, but only after strong opposition was expressed by Islamists.

Abdolkarim Soroush of Iran is another person whose quotes are often cited by both modernists and pluralist secularists. This discrepancy is not surprising in the case of Soroush, as he is a man of religious training and secular approach (Vakili 1996).

Understanding the Traditionalist Mentality

It is reasonable to infer from the discussions and interviews of traditionalist Islamists that they found their refusal of democracy on three arguments.

Democracy defies the Islamic creed. Traditionalists think of themselves as the keepers of the Islamic traditions. Obeying, assimilating, and making deductions from the Quran and Sunna (sayings and praxis of the Prophet Muhammad) as understood and interpreted by *al-salaf al-salih* (the pious predecessors) are what distinguish a Muslim from a non-Muslim, according to traditionalists. Based on this reasoning, they perceive democracy as a replacement of the will of Allah with the will of people; thus they deem it anti-Islamic. According to a traditionalist Sudanese imam, "Islam has no prefixes or suffixes. Islam is beautiful and complete. Attaching words such as *democracy, socialism*, or the like to it takes away from its beauty and makes it in need of human beings to beautify it. There is not such a thing in Islam."

The focus-group discussions reveal that the more Muslims set themselves free from the authority of the Quranic text and the appeal to traditions, the more they move from traditionalism into modernism and secularism. A typical traditionalist's self-ascribed image is that they are the most adherent to the verbatim and literalist interpretations of Islamic texts such as the Quran, the Sunna, the writings of his companions, and those of the *ulama*. Modernists contend that the interpretations of previous scholars are indicative and suggestive but not obligatory or binding, leaving some room for inductive learning from other civilizations. Thus, they think they are responsible for introducing the contemporary and modern reading of holy texts to the public. To the contrary, secularists argue for a more rationalist, relativistic, and inductionist reading without assuming any supremacy of past interpretations over those of the present.

Democracy implies the insufficiency of Islamic sharia. According to traditionalists, democracy, liberalism, capitalism, socialism, communism, fascism, nationalism, and so forth cannot be justified in Islam, either as a means or as a system of values, since it is forbidden for Muslims to imitate the disbelievers or non-Muslims (al-Gazza'eri 1984). One of the articulate traditionalist interviewees quoted two hadiths (sayings of the Prophet Muhammad) clearly warning Muslims against imitating nonbelievers. In the first one, the Prophet said: "'You will surely follow the ways, steps, or traditions of those who came before you, span by span and yard by yard [very closely]; even if they entered a lizard's hole you will enter it.' The companions asked, 'Oh Prophet, you mean the Jews and Christians?' So he answered, 'Who else!'" (reported by Imam Bukhari). The other hadith reads, "He is not one of us, he who imitates others. Do not imitate either the Jews or the Christians" (reported by Imams Termithy and Abu-Dawd).

These two hadiths, among others, have been taken by some traditionalists to be part of the creed of al-wala' wa al-bara'a (alliance with Muslims and disloyalty to non-Muslims), meaning Muslims should be allies of Muslims and keep themselves separate from non-Muslims' wrongdoings. Ayman al-Zawahri and his supporters base their jihad against non-Muslims on this creed (Al-Howaini 1998; al-Zawahri 2002).

According to many of the interviewed traditionalists, imitating non-Muslims (and adopting democracy is one way of doing that) has always been a part of a conspiracy to "destroy Islam and annihilate its people." One respondent advised me to read a book that calls democracy a way of making Muslims "roll toward Western civilization and away from Muhammad and his book." The book warns Muslims against following the path of Turkey, which adopted a "civil constitution instead of its sharia-based system of government" (al-'Alem 1975: 48-49). When ordinary Muslims are encouraged to legislate for themselves in a civil constitution, they are also seduced into challenging Islam's essence. "No God but Allah" means no legislator but Allah (al-Badry 1983: 150; Qutb 1989). As Allah said to his Prophet: "Judge thou between them by what Allah hath revealed, and follow not their vain desires, but beware of them lest they beguile thee from any of that [teaching] which Allah hath sent down to thee" (The Holy Quran 4:49). A traditionalist scholar infers from this verse that "it is not appropriate to use the term 'democratic Islam' or 'democracy in Islam'; Islam is self-sufficient and does not need the facades of others. . . . No democracy, communism, socialism, or nationalism in Islam. If there is something good in any of these principles, Islam preceded them and does not have the distortions that they have" (al-Sawaf 1979:38).

Thus, adopting un-Islamic political or socioeconomic systems is not good or right since it makes individuals compete for worldly benefits such as political power or social prestige; yet Islamic *bai'a* (allegiance) is based on belief for the sake of piety. As a result, "Islam ordains that its *al-ra'eeya* [subjects] not give the oath of allegiance to any except a pious man" (al-Sharawi 1980:18).

Democracy is sinful because of its association with non-Muslims. To traditionalists, democracy is un-Islamic not only in origin but by association as well. It comes from the Judeo-Christian West with all its covetousness, lack of respect for religion, and devotion to personal liberties. Muslims are highly encouraged to not even visit the West, let alone import its systems and values (al-Nadwi 1985). Ayman al-Zawahri perceives a label such as "Muslim democrat" to be self-contradictory. "Whoever labels himself as a Muslim democrat or a Muslim who calls for democracy is like saying he is a Jewish Muslim or a Christian Muslim" (al-Zawahri n.d.: 22). Al-Zawahri's censure is not limited to the label "democracy" but to its mechanisms and assumptions. The title of a response he wrote to a fatwa that would allow Muslims to join parliaments is self-explanatory: "Advice to the Ummah to avoid Ibn Baaz's Fatwa of Permissibility to Join Majlis al-Ummah [Parliament]."

Some of the respondents to the survey supported al-Zawahri's argument. One Pakistani respondent refused to answer the survey. Instead, he wrote a full page commenting on the use of the word *democracy* in it; he perceived the choice of this word and subject matter to be an act of heresy and of admitting to Muslims' inferiority to the West. He even accused the researchers who were administering the survey of being sinners and called on others not to respond. Some followed his advice, but others answered the questions. At the end of this chapter, I offer an educated guess about the relative weight of the traditionalists' influence on literate Muslims.

Types of Traditionalists: Violent and Pacifist Islamists

All violent (militant) Islamists are traditionalists, but not all traditionalists are violent; some of them, in fact, are pacifists. However, Muslims in general, regardless of their ideological preferences, may support violent resistance against Israel's occupation of Arab/Muslim lands or the US occupation of Iraq and Afghanistan (al-'Abeykan 2003). The difference between the violent and the pacifist traditionalists depends on which verses they choose to articulate their concept of jihad. Violent traditionalists disagree with pacifist traditionalists (such as Sufis) and modernists on the applicability of the so-called verse of the sword.

To understand the textual logic behind the use of violence by traditionalists such as those found in Al-Jama'a al-Islamiya, Al-Jihad, Al-Qaida, and Al-Salfiya al-Jihadiya in Pakistan, Egypt, Algeria, Malaysia, Morocco, Indonesia, Saudi Arabia, and the United States, it is important to know that there are three types of verses in the Quran and hadiths that pertain to the issue of violence. First, some verses ask Muslims to treat non-Muslims justly and kindly—for example: "Allah forbids you not, with regard to those who fight you not for [your] Faith nor drive you out of your homes, from dealing kindly and justly with them: for Allah loveth those who are just" (60:8). Second, there are verses that ask Muslims to lean toward peace if others do the same—for example, "But if the enemy inclines towards peace, do thou [also] incline towards peace" (Quran 6:61).

A third type of verse demands that Muslims fight infidels (non-Muslims). The "verse of the sword," for example, reads[20]:

> But when the forbidden months are past, then fight and slay the Pagans wherever ye find them, and seize them, beleaguer them, and lie in wait for them in every stratagem [of war]; but if they repent, and establish regular prayers and practice regular charity, then open the way for them: for Allah is Oft-Forgiving, Most Merciful. (Quran 9:5)

The interviewed violent traditionalists, and the *ulama* whom they quote, believe that this verse, among others, propels sincere believers to wage violent jihad against all infidels, by virtue of their infidel status. These infidels include any rulers who have replaced the sharia of Allah with Western laws and falsified *Hakemeyat* Allah (the sovereignty of Allah; Mawdudi 1977a; Qutb 1989). Pacifist traditionalists, along with modernist Islamists, think of this verse as an exception to general principles mentioned elsewhere in the Quran that equate jihad with self-defense and require justice and kindness as a path for coexistence (Quran 49:13; Ibn Baaz 1992). Further, pacifist traditionalists use very tough criteria to weigh the permissibility of violence against their rulers; these must have committed such acts as prohibiting prayers, denying the authenticity of a verse or hadith, or publicly renouncing Allah's verdicts and replacing them with others (Othaimeen 1998).

Modernists in particular refuse the radical concept of jihad adopted by violent traditionalists. If the conceptualization of jihad as advanced by violent traditionalists is true and authentic, they argue, then the Islamic state is a colonial state that aims at plundering the nations it occupies (al-Ghazali 1985). One modernist describes the violent traditionalist argument as "ignorance, stupidity, even madness" (al-Rikabi 2003). Another eminent Pakistani modernist called attention to the success of Islamists in general in guiding a considerable percentage of young men and women toward love of and respect for their origins. Yet he also noted that this success was coupled with a magnificent failure to develop civilizational and intellectual depth and modern understanding of Islam's peaceful and tolerant message (Rahman 1982).

In their defense, traditionalists like Sayyid Qutb of Egypt and his student al-Zawahri of Al-Qaida claim that the "verse(s) of the sword" are chronologically later and thus abrogate and amend earlier verses (al-Zawahri 2002; Azzam 1984; Qutb 1989). A Palestinian traditionalist interviewed in Egypt highlighted two verses in the same chapter: "O ye who believe! Fasting is prescribed to you as it was prescribed to those before you" (Quran 2:183), which assigns fasting to each capable Muslim, and "Fighting is prescribed upon you, and ye dislike it" (Quran 2:216). "How come Muslims comply unquestioningly with the prescription of fasting yet question and philosophize the prescription of fighting?" he asked.

Nonviolent traditionalists would be reluctant to accept the idea of abrogation without another clear text that states it (al-Buraiq 1993). Thus, they give higher priority to the verses that ask Muslims to seek peace than to those that call Muslims to wage war. Modernist Islamists, for their part, reject the idea of abrogation and instead think of various verses as directions that were given for different occasions (al-Ghazali 1985). Thus, modernist Islamists would not think that the above-mentioned verses from chapter 9 (Sura al-Tawba) had actually abrogated 120 other verses that were revealed earlier to show the way toward peaceful coexistence of Muslims with non-Muslims, let alone many verses and hadiths that prohibit Muslims from killing each other (Abo al-Magd 1988; al-Ghannouchi 1993; al-Qaradawi 2001; Anwar 1995; Howaidi 1999). This is why modernists think that "the [Muslim] rulers are not infidels even if they [do] not apply Sharia" (al-Din 2001: 85; al-Qaradawi 2001a).

The pacifist traditionalists' main field of jihad is *da'wa*, inviting Muslims and non-Muslims to a better understanding of Islam; they devote themselves to responding to questions, teaching the Quran, explaining its verses, issuing fatwas, and reviving old *ijtihad* to remind Muslims of the basics of their religion (Ma'moon 2003).

That said, modernists and secularists are very critical of traditionalists mainly because they exhibit noticeable hostility to intellectualism, pluralism, and any sectarian divisions within Islam. The indeterminacy of rational thinking and true *ijtihad,* they say, is not tolerated by traditionalists (Arabeyat 1998). Wahabism is considered, from the perspective of its critics, to be the worst example of traditionalism. A prominent scholar of Islamic law argues that typical Wahabists do not consider themselves as one "school of thought within Islam, but [as] Islam" (Abou El Fadl 2001).

Understanding the Modernist Mentality

Typical modernist Islamists, by definition, do not a priori extend the classification of "un-Islamic" to non-Islamic sources and civilizations. Rather, they say, Muslims can learn about anything they believe is good for themselves and society regardless of its origins (Fasi 1972). Thus modernist Islamists find no ethical or religious problem in adopting democratic mechanisms as long as they are within an Islamic context. Modernist Islamists ground their acceptance of democratic mechanisms on two foundations.

Early Muslims Adopted Non-Islamic Innovations

Yusuf al-Qaradawi is the most prominent name in the modernist school, as identified by the respondents. He preaches that Muslims currently need two types of *ijtihad*: selective, to choose the most fitting and useful religious verdict if there is a plurality of opinions, and reconstructive, to come up with new fatwas or religious verdicts that match current and contemporary circumstances as long as they do not contradict well-established authentic holy texts (al-Qaradawi 1984). Both types of *ijtihad* take into consideration the changing circumstances of the modern world and would lead to plural interpretations of the same texts. Modernists, as a result, tend to show a higher level of tolerance of non-Islamic ideas and innovations as long as they do not contradict the core teachings of Islam.

Typical modernists do not perceive the creed of *al-wala' wa al-bara'a* as part of sharia (Islamic legislation); rather, it is considered a part of *fiqh* (jurisprudence) that may not be valid for Muslims right now. Even if Muslims abide by this creed, it should not be an obstacle to learning from other civilizations (al-Qaradawi 2003). Modernists believe that whatever achieves justice and fairness among human beings, even if it is not explicitly mentioned in the main sources of sharia, is part of it and vice versa. That is because sharia in its origin and purpose is based upon the interest of people in this life and hereafter. Modernists usually quote a famous saying by a medieval scholar: "Everything that may divert people from justice to injustice, from mercy to its opposite, from what is good to what is evil, from wisdom to foolishness is not part of sharia even if [somebody has] associated it with sharia through [false] interpretation" (al-Jawziyah 1969: pt. 3, 1).

A high school teacher in Algeria cited the early praxis of the Prophet and his companions, who took up many worldly inventions from the Persians, Romans, and Egyptians, as long as they did not contradict clear-cut dos and don'ts of the holy texts. Many modernists quoted an unauthentic hadith that reads, "Wisdom is the wandering goal of the believer. Wherever he finds it, he will be the first to follow it." Thus, if Muslims refute Darwinism, Marxism, or the contributions of Sigmund Freud and Immanuel Kant, it is not because everything these thinkers said was wrong. Some of what they said may be useful and deserves to be studied. The following statement best reflects the modernists' position on cultural exchange: "I am Muslim. I may like to eat an Arab grilled fat sheep or a European simple boiled dish. No problem as [long] as I mention the name of Allah and eat from what is in front of me according to Islamic teachings" (al-Ghazali 1985).

Democracy Can Be Islamized

When I asked Mahfouz Nehnah, then head of the Algerian Islamist Peaceful Society Movement, how different Islamic democracy is from any other form of democracy, he responded, "Democracy should be Islamized. . . . Islamic democracy does not enjoin the evil and does not forbid the good." He argued that whatever is known to be *haram* (taboo) in Islam should be beyond the consent of the people. In other words, "the government cannot legislate for gay marriages, gambling, allowing alcoholic beverages, or the like. Legislation is only possible within the area of the permissible."

Mohamed al-Ghazali of Egypt, another modernist, refused the nominal Islamic constitution prepared by Taqi el-Din al-Nabhani, the traditionalist founder of Hezb al-Tahrir, because it does not have enough legal guarantees to ensure *shura*, political freedoms, and public interests. Al-Ghazali praised the 1923 Egyptian constitution that was mainly imported from the West as practically more Islamic than most of the so-called Islamic constitutions (al-Ghazali 1997: 156).

According to the thinking of modernists, a mature Muslim may read un-Islamic and non-Islamic philosophies and may pick and choose what is compatible with his or her ethics and creed (Shariati and Rajaee 1986). Muslims cannot refute the wisdom that may exist in the books of the "people of falsehood" (al-Qaradawi 2000: 45). Most of what Muslims have learned from others, modernists argue, is mainly what these others had previously learned from Muslims (al-Ghazali 1997; Rahman 1982). However, this learning must not violate or contradict the fundamentals of Islam. That is why they may accept Western technologies and institutions but not some principles as separation of mosque and state (Arabeyat 1998), which contradicts the oneness of religion and state in Islam and assumes conflict between them. A conflict can exist between two separate parties but cannot exist within the one (al-Ghannouchi 2003). Some modernists even give the right of *ijtihad* to all Muslims to choose among the *ijtihad* of *ulama* (al-Turabi 2003; Arabeyat 1998). Unlike secularists, modernists wish to advocate "modernization without encouraging servility to the West and discouraging confidence in one's own cultural resources" (Keddie 1972).

Understanding the Secularist Mentality

Secularists, unlike both traditionalists and modernists, typically start from two different but compatible assumptions. The first is that Islam does not offer a concrete guide for governance. Adel, a secular Pakistani government official, put it this way: "Holy texts do not tell Muslims much about how to run their societies. Holy texts are excellent sources of *aqeeda* [creed] and ethics but not politics and economics." A Sudanese student found it ironic that numerous, and sometimes contradictory, interpretations and inferences that have been made are based upon the same verses or sayings of the Prophet. In his mind, these contradictions indicated that most of these texts have "no one meaning until the human mind imposes its understanding on them."

Rif'at al-Said, the president of the secular Tajjmou' Party in Egypt, is a very influential source of secular arguments, according to many of the Arab respondents to the survey. Al-Said refuses the Islamists' argument that Islam has an answer to all questions. He argues that the Prophet "told Muslims that they are encouraged to brush their teeth before prayer. Yet he did not tell them how to select his political successor." The silence of sharia regarding many political issues is a sign that Allah wants the human intellect to function and flourish without textual constraints.

The other assumption is that Muslims need to follow the paths of the most successful societies in order to outdo them. This is exactly what the West did by learning from ancient Muslims and others. Soaat, a Turkish journalism student, said, "The Islamists' slogans about the peculiar and idiosyncratic nature of Muslims have been obstacles rather than catalysts for development and modernization." Secularists argue that interaction with and learning from other civilizations is a human necessity, yet it will never succeed until Muslims are emancipated from the hold of "holy" interpretations and traditions that are assumed to come as a package with the holy texts (Arkoun 1994). Actually, they lament, Muslims imprison themselves in the *turath* (old books of the past) whether they are useful or not-useful, while the world around them advances in all fields. Unlike traditionalists, who refuse to let foreign languages spread among the masses, secularists consider translating texts from other civilizations a very important sign of the perseverance of Muslims and their capacity to make up for what they missed. Yet, a secularist argues, the number of books that Arabs have translated into Arabic since the time of Caliph al-Ma'moun (1,000 years ago) is around 10,000, while in just one year Spaniards translate the same number into Spanish (Bagabeer 2003).

To some secularists, Karl Marx, Immanuel Kant, John Locke, Niccolò Machiavelli, Voltaire, James Madison, and Jean-Jacques Rousseau are more acceptable sources of knowledge and virtue than most of the ancient scholars of Islam because of the capacity of these Western thinkers to set the human mind free from the chains of the church. They think that a similar reform is needed in the Muslim mind too (Barakah 2002). Mohamed Arkoun's intellectual project collapses the artificial gaps that both Islamists and Orientalists create between Islamic and Western civilizations and intellectual heritages. Both civilizations are built upon religious beliefs and commitments. There will be no salvation for Muslims, he argues, if they do not acknowledge their influence on the West and internalize the West's influence on them (Arkoun 1994).

A secularist Algerian lawyer, Mohamed Bo Fadl, agreed with the above characterization. In his mind, Muslims' contemporary intellectual and political dilemmas are similar to those of the Western Middle Ages. "There is not much difference between the pope and his priests [during the Middle Ages] trying to defend their status and Islamists' attempts to jump to power." Karim, an Algerian friend of Mohamed, accused Islamists of imposing their custody over the minds of most Muslims and calling any criticism of their authority some type of "intellectual invasion" from the West. Both Mohamed and Karim described themselves as active members of the secular Algerian Party for Democracy and Socialism. A philosophy student in Cairo argued that Islamists promote nostalgia for a golden past and a rejection of the modern inventions and innovations, thus constraining development of Muslim societies. This student said that some of her university professors were her main source of ideas about Islam and politics. When one consults her professors' writings, the influence becomes very clear (al-Eraqi 2002).

Statist Secularists

Some secularists are more pluralistic than others. Statist secularists prefer a strong central government to protect the unity of the state, even if it is not democratic. According to Mahdi Bin Araffa, a Tunisian diplomat, "Most third world countries, including Arab and Muslim governments, adopted variations of the current Chinese model with strong central government accompanied by limited or deferred political liberalization." In the history of the Muslim world, almost all rulers were autocratic statists with very strong personal political domination but not necessarily unjust dictators. This distinction should be understood in light of Olivier Roy's observation that in the Muslim world the opposite of tyranny is not liberty but justice (Roy 1994). A just, benevolent autocrat was the basis of an ideal system of governance. Thus, in the history of the Muslim world, autocratic governance should not necessarily be equated with malicious dictatorship. Secularist statists are proponents of this tradition, but on nonreligious grounds. Their fear of democracy is based on two factors.

Fear of Islamists. Statist secularists oppose and fear Islamists (traditionalists and modernists) more than they respect democratic principles and procedures. Put differently, they argue that if real democracy were allowed in Muslim countries, the public could be easily mobilized by Islamists who might give lip service to democracy but would not really be committed to it. Thus, once allowed, free and fair elections would mean the end of democracy. The statists' best bet, then, is to guide and minimize liberalization. Zobaida, a member of the ruling party in Tunisia, equates all Islamists with long-bearded fascist fanatics who want to establish totalitarian theocracies once in power. According to her, "If there are differences among Islamists, then it is a difference in degree rather than in kind." This was the argument made by the Tunisian president Zein Abdin Ben Ali in favor of decimating the Islamic opposition (Renaissance or Nahda Party) after he won the elections of 1993 with 99.91 percent of the vote (King 2003). This argument was also made by President Anwar Sadat of Egypt, who said, "Jama'at, Jihad, Ikhwan . . . all are the same."

Similarly, the head of the Foreign Relations Committee in Egypt's parliament contended, "If you open the door for genuine democracy, you have the chance that fundamentalists will still come to power. What will the Americans do with them?" (Faki 2003). In the statists' mind, maintaining the status quo, though it is not democratic, is better than risking the theological dictatorship that would result from naive trust in Islamists' respect for democracy (Fouda 1993).

Secular statist discourse is associated with many intellectuals who earn their living through glorifying and defending the rulers in Muslim countries (Abu Odeh 2003; Sharabi 1988). Most of these regimes have learned how to play the game of statist tactical liberalization through the measures of "state-monitored political openness to promote reforms that appear pluralistic but function to preserve autocracy" (Ottaway et al. 2002). These regimes are highly skillful at controlling "elections, manipulating divide-and-rule tactics, [regulating] civil society organizations, and [obstructing] meaningful political party systems. . . . They have created deeply entrenched systems that are surprisingly effective at resisting democratic change" (Ottaway et al. 2002).

Most statists face a dilemma of credibility as they use democratic rhetoric yet systematically exclude or marginalize their most important rivals, the Islamists, whose discourse resonates with an important segment of the public. To skirt this dilemma, many governments, such as those in Algeria, Kuwait, Indonesia, Niger, Pakistan, Jordan, Egypt, Lebanon, Yemen, Malaysia, and Morocco, allow a few Islamists into the political system, but not enough to pose a viable challenge (Esposito 1996; Etienne 1987). An immediate democratization process may make democracy a more remote possibility because it would "too quickly tip the balance in favor of the groups that are best organized and enjoy grassroots support, Islamist organizations in most cases" (Ottaway et al. 2002).

The danger of premature democracy. According to statist secularists, Muslims are not ready for democracy; illiteracy, tribalism, apathy, emotionalism, and nostalgia combine to keep conditions unfavorable for it. It is argued that most of these problems are not outcomes of policies adopted by the statist rulers themselves (Mahathir and Hashim 2000); instead, they were inherited from the distorting experience of colonialism, which led to urbanization without industrialization, education without productive training, secularization without scientific inquiry, and capitalist greed without capitalist discipline (Mazrui 1990:35).

According to statists, democracy requires time, and it is not necessarily the immediate task of the moment. A former Jordanian prime minister argues: "Democracy is an evolving being; [it is] born and grows up. It is never created all at once. Whoever asks for something prematurely will be punished by not getting it. The baby that is born bigger than its natural size will die, or the mother will die, or both will die" (al-Rawabda 2001).

The statist discourse is unique in its defense of the status quo. To the question, is the ruler autocratic because of the people, or are the people not democratic because of the ruler? autocratic discourse would definitely refer to the masses who are not ready for liberty (Zartman 1982) as the reason that democratization must come slowly. Hosni Mubarak of Egypt has been quoted as saying, "We are providing doses of democracy in proportion to our ability to absorb them" (Kassem 1999: 54).

Some cases may support the statist argument. The Lebanese democratic experiment ended with a severe civil war (Fisk 2002). The democratic political opening in Egypt in the 1980s encouraged the growth of massive and violent fundamentalism (Mubarak 1992). The rebellion against Siyad Berri in Somalia ended up with a chaotic state breakdown (Schofield 1996). Free elections in Algeria led the country into a civil war with tens of thousands of deaths and casualties (Martinez 2000). Hafez al-Assad's statist policies managed to break the vicious cycle of coups d'etat through the systematic removal of his opponents for "the interest of Syrians and all the Arab ummah" (Assad and Talas 1990). Democratic attempts in Nigeria, Pakistan, Algeria, Côte d'Ivoire, and the Sudan, among others, ultimately succumbed to military intervention. Interestingly, statist discourses commonly put forth the argument that each government should maintain the highest possible level of freedom given the risks of instability (Berberoglu 1999; Musharraf 1999; Soekarno 1959). Still, they typically prioritize other tasks, such as defending national integrity and security, over democracy (Hussein 1988). Adopting this position, Emran, a Pakistani supporter of President Pervez Musharaf, said, "Pakistanis do not need democracy. They need jobs, services and education. Look at Bangladesh: they have elections but very weak government. We need a dictator with noble goals. Believe me, brother, democracy will not work in Pakistan."

Statists emphasize the divisions in Muslim countries and the apathy and irrationality of the masses; that is why the autocrat has to create and shape the majority around his persona. Muslim statist rulers attempt to hold their countries together by mobilizing symbols, pictures, and slogans and by annihilating possible opponents (Diamond, Plattner, and Brumberg 2003).

Pluralist Securalists

Pluralist secularists disagree. They argue that no limitations on anyone's right to be a part of the political competition should be allowed. That is why their main target of criticism and opposition is not Islamists; rather their main battle is with statist rulers, whether they be Islamists or secularists.

> For decades after independence, most populist autocrats had suspended democracy until national liberation; until Palestine had been liberated; until we have economic development; until we have true social justice, and so on. As it turns out now, after fifty years of depriving ourselves of democracy, we find ourselves with none of these things! And we are no closer to democracy. . . . We must not continue to allow ourselves to be manipulated by these false messiahs. . . . Now we know better than to fall for the despots' delaying tactics. (Ibrahim 2003)

Pluralist secularists are the Muslims who are politically closest to the Western concept of liberal democracy. They think that all citizens, Muslims and non-Muslims alike, should enjoy all basic human and political rights, including Islamists insofar as they abide by democratic principles (Abul Khair 2003). They base their defense of immediate democratization on two grounds.

Modernist Islamists should be included in the democratic process. Pluralist secularists perceive nondemocratic regimes as being a more dangerous and immediate challenge than Islamists are (Abdelrazeq 2001). From their perspective, the widespread appeal of Islamists stems from the fact that in most societies they have not had the chance to rule and fail (Hariq 2001). The more they reach for power and fail to convert their demagogic slogans into practical solutions, the more Muslims will refrain from electing them. Pluralist secularists argue that the failures of Islamists in Sudan, Iran, and Indonesia, among other places, will prove that politics is not about slogans and symbols but about running trains, building bridges, delivering public services, fighting diseases, and eliminating illiteracy (Ibrahim 1984). With those kinds of problems, how many times Islamists pray each day will not be the main factor in determining their reelection. Pluralists do not buy the autocrats' argument that fundamentalists would annihilate all available freedoms once they were in power.

Counsel Said al-Gamal, an active member of the secular liberal Egyptian party of al-Wafd, criticized the official lack of tolerance toward opposition parties, even if they are moderate. He pointed to the example of al-Wassat Party (the middle way). It is Islamist and liberal. However, "the government perceives it to be a threat. Thus, it refuses to give it the permission to become legal." This party "advocates political pluralism and human rights [and] . . . has a woman and a Christian on its central committee, setting it apart from other Islamic groups" (Rouleau 2001). Akram, a lawyer and active member of a research center in Egypt, commented, "The Egyptian government does not (or does not want to) see the difference between the al-Wassat Party and other Islamists." Whether out of conviction or out of opportunism, many Islamists have learned how to shape their political discourse and propaganda, repudiating "all forms of violence, whatever their sources" (al-Nahda, quoted in Rouleau 2001), to underscore the statist tendencies of the rulers. They are asking for a real opportunity to prove their adherence to democratic principles. Statists, however, are convinced that this is a risky and irreversible path (Saad Eddin Ibrahim 2002).

Postponing democratization weakens pluralist secularists. Pluralists contend that statist rulers' argument that their countries are not ready for democracy is self-serving and self-fulfilling. An Indonesian political science student commented online, "So long as people believe their culture is not ready for democracy, they will be less likely to press for democratization or support those who do, which has placed tremendous inertia on the prospects for democratization."

A Pakistani pluralist secularist thinks that liberal parties have fewer supporters than Islamists because they do not have access to people: "Islamists have mosques and madrassas, and the government has the media. Liberals have fewer windows of opportunity to recruit new members." The present study confirms other studies in suggesting that in most Muslim countries, pluralist secularists have the weakest voice and are the fewest in number too (Salamah 1994). They do not have the baksheesh (tips and free services) that statist rulers have (Korany 1994). They do not have the legacy of the past and claims of Islamic *assala* (authenticity) that Islamists have. No wonder that their program of democratization has failed so far. "How can you have democratic institutions if you have few democrats?" (Gerges 2001).

Table 2.1 sums up this discussion of elite debates. As the table

Table 2.1   Three Main Schools of Thought on Islam and Democracy

	Traditionalist Islamists	Modernist Islamists	Secularist Muslims
For something to be Islamic, it should	be consensually accepted by sharia and *ulama*	not contradict the sharia	be in the interest of society regardless of holy texts
Silence of sharia is	impossible	opportunity for *ijtihad*	a sign of the indeterminacy of sharia
Zones immune to skepticism are	sharia and *fiqh*	sharia	no immune zones
Violation of consensus among *ulama* is	destroying the unity and uniqueness of the *ummah*	dangerous but possible	necessary to eliminate traditional consensus
Cultural exchange with non-Muslims is	human innovation and imitation of nonbelievers	a search for wisdom	better than blind imitation of ancestors
Sects are	violent, pacifist	Islamist democrats	pluralists, statists
Democracy is	anti/un-Islamic	Islamic/Islamizable	necessary (for pluralists); impractical (for statists)

shows, the three schools face common challenges and concerns but respond to them differently.

Traditionalist Islamists limit what is acceptable under Islam to what has long been accepted under sharia and consensually condoned by *al-salaf al-salih* (the pious predecessors). To them sharia can never be silent, even if they need to resort to *qiyas* (analogical reasoning) to apply its principles. Preserving the identity of this *ummah*, or Muslim nation, requires traditionalists to keep both sharia and traditional *fiqh* protected from skeptics who would corrupt the ideal legacy of the past. That is why they would argue against any *bid'a* (human innovation) or violation of the consensus among *ulama*. The greatest threat to this pure Islamic tradition of *al-salaf al-salih* comes from external sources of values, norms, and ideas, most notably the West. Traditionalists differ, however, in their strategies to make their ideals a reality. Some are violent; others are pacifists. Whether violent or pacifist, they think ill of democracy, because they see it as an alien or anti-Islamic system of government that replaces the will of Allah with the will of the masses.

Modernists respond to the previous questions differently. They accept new ideas, mechanisms, and values insofar as they do not contradict authentic and well-established sharia. They would accept that Allah deliberately left Muslims with some legislative vacuums for the human mind to fill through *ijtihad* within the boundaries offset by sharia.

Well-established and clear-cut verses of the Quran and hadiths are the only material that is not subject to skeptical scrutiny; yet the interpretations of these verses and hadiths are subject to *ijtihad*. The scholars of the past and *al-salaf al-salih* carried out *ijtihad* to respond to the new challenges that they faced. Now it is time for contemporary Muslims to take their turn at *ijtihad*. Modernists think that their *ijtihad* rarely violates consensually agreed-upon fatwas (religious verdicts) of the past. If there is such a violation, a direct and clear reference to authentic sources of Islam must be made to justify the violation of the previous *ijma'* (consensus). Modernists find nothing in the Islamic authentic sources that hinders them from communicating with and learning from non-Muslims as long as the thinking of these outsiders does not violate authentic Islamic principles. To modernists, most aspects of democracy are compatible with Islam.

Secularists, meanwhile, do not think that Islam has anything to do with modern politics. Secularists believe that all texts and issues are subject to human scrutiny with no immunity zones. Through such scrutiny, Muslims can replace their obsolete, impractical perceptions of the world with more contemporary science-based ideologies. Cultural exchange with other civilizations is a must in this regard. Some secularists are pluralists, while others are statists. Pluralists tend to think of democracy as good and possible; statists think that democracy is not possible in their country, for it would afford Islamists a golden opportunity to establish a theological state.

The Impact of Opinion Leaders

It is not enough to divide the survey respondents and the focus-group discussants among these categories. This book uses the pooled data to produce an educated estimate of the weight of each school in the examined countries. To gauge the relative weight of traditionalist Islamists in the survey, I have identified them as those who consistently refuse the norms and institutions of democracy on the basis of their being un-Islamic. The best example of this mentality is Ali Belhaj, a leader of Algeria's Islamic Salvation Front, which almost won the 1988 elections:

"When we are in power, there will be no more elections because God will be ruling." Hadi Hawang of Partai Islam Sel-Malaysia (PAS) echoed the same mentality: "I am not interested in democracy. Islam is not democracy, Islam is Islam" (quoted in Pipes 1995).

Traditionalists have been identified by their take on (1) Islam as a state and religion (a slogan taken up by Islamic groups throughout the Muslim world), (2) their negative definition of democracy (an open-ended question), and (3) their belief that Islam and a publicly elected and accountable government are incompatible. Modernist Islamists, unlike traditionalists, have been identified as those who consistently accept both the norms and the institutions of democracy (since they are Islamic or Islamizable—that is, condoned by Islam) in both their definition of democracy and their response to the survey questions. Modernist Islamists in general argue that democracy is a priority over sharia—not a priority of supremacy but rather a priority of order. Analogously, the street is prior to the mosque, since you need to move along the street in order to get to the mosque. Statists consistently and strongly disagree with the linkage between Islam as a religion and Islam as a political institution. They also oppose democracy as not suitable or not the top priority of Muslim countries. Pluralists are the subgroup of secularists who consistently accept democratic norms and institutions in their responses to these two critical questions.

It is significant that around 4.5 percent of the respondents did not respond to two or more of the questions mentioned in Table 2.2. Based on tabulations of the 21,143 respondents who consistently fall into one of the four categories, Table 2.3 shows the relative percentage of each of these groups by country.

Table 2.2   Classification of Respondents' Attitudes Toward Democracy

	Islam as a source of political doctrine (Q. 26)	Are Islam and elected polity compatible? (Q. 28)	Associating democracy with negatives? (Q. 25)	Definition of democracy (open-ended) (Q. 47)
Traditionalist Islamists	(strongly) agree	(strongly) disagree	(strongly) agree	(very) negative
Statist secularists	(strongly) disagree	not applicable	(strongly) agree	(very) negative
Modernist Islamists	(strongly) agree	(strongly) agree	(strongly) disagree	(very) positive
Pluralist secularists	(strongly) disagree	not applicable	(strongly) disagree	(very) positive

Table 2.3   Percentages of the Four Cultural Categories in Thirty-two Muslim Societies

	1 Traditionalists	2 Statists	3 Modernists	4 Pluralists	1+3 Islamists	3+4 Democrats	Democratization Potential
Turkey	1	5	31	63	32	94	High
Senegal	9	0	68	23	77	91	High
Morocco	9	0	72	19	80	91	High
Albania	5	6	33	57	38	90	High
Egypt	3	7	63	27	66	89	High
Tunisia	6	8	37	50	42	87	High
Iran	2	12	79	7	81	86	High
USA	10	8	33	50	53	83	High
Mali	2	15	50	33	43	83	High
Gambia	3	15	54	29	56	82	High
Turkmenistan	11	9	31	49	42	81	High
Malaysia	14	6	62	18	76	80	High
EU	15	5	47	33	62	80	High
India	10	16	50	23	61	73	Medium
Kuwait	17	11	41	32	58	73	Medium
Bangladesh	20	8	48	24	68	72	Medium
Jordan	20	9	48	23	68	71	Medium
Qatar	23	8	45	24	68	69	Medium
Bahrain	23	10	58	10	81	67	Medium
Syria	26	7	40	27	66	67	Medium
UAE	30	3	60	7	90	67	Medium
Lebanon	20	14	31	35	51	67	Medium
Algeria	25	10	33	33	58	66	Medium
Indonesia	28	7	40	25	68	65	Medium
Oman	31	5	46	18	77	64	Low
Libya	27	9	59	5	86	64	Low
Yemen	35	1	46	17	81	63	Low
Sudan	26	12	55	7	80	62	Low
Pakistan	24	15	42	19	66	61	Low
Nigeria	31	14	38	17	69	55	Low
Tajikistan	11	36	35	19	45	54	Low
Saudi Arabia	46	2	48	4	95	52	Low
Average	17.59	9.16	47.59	25.84	65.13	73.41	Medium

Source: E-mail and written survey 2002.

Table 2.3 is very informative in a variety of ways. First, it suggests that literate Muslims are predominantly Islamists (either traditionalists or modernists). This finding in itself confirms Islamists' argument that they control important streets and mosques, while secularists control palaces and media. Only in Tajikistan (55 percent), Turkmenistan (58 percent), Mali (57 percent), Tunisia (58 percent), Albania (62 percent), and Turkey (68 percent) were secularists in the majority.

Second, there is a common factor that characterizes all the countries with a secularist majority. In each of these countries, Muslims were forced through governmental policies to be secular, through a secular system of education, secular mass media, and governmental control over Islamic institutions, either by Communist regimes (e.g., Albania, Tajikistan, and Turkmenistan) or by Muslim rulers who decided to Westernize their country through nondemocratic means (e.g., Turkey, Mali, and Tunisia). Apparently, rulers of these countries were not particularly successful in legitimizing their regimes. In five of the previous six cases, the majority of the examined respondents were more liberal than their autocratic rulers, Tajikistan being the exception.

Third, by measuring the modernist Islamists and the pluralist secularists in each society, we can gauge the likelihood of democratization. The addition of these two groups is shown in the seventh column, titled "3+4." These data suggest that Muslims of Turkey, Senegal, Morocco, Albania, Egypt, Tunisia, Iran, the United States, Mali, Gambia, Turkmenistan, Malaysia, and the European Union are the most amenable to democracy.

Finally, Table 2.3 suggests that the average Muslim is not necessarily prodemocracy but is receptive to many democratic norms. As shown, 73 percent of Muslims overall (irrespective of the country) are either modernist Islamists or pluralist secularists.

Concluding Remarks

This chapter's analysis shows that Muslims are more heterogeneous than portrayals offered in some academic and media circles in the West would suggest. Muslim intellectuals and scholars advance different and even contradictory readings of Islam and democracy.

Indeed, the debate among Muslims on issues such as modernization and democracy dates back at least to the early twentieth century, when Muslims discovered the huge gap between their holy texts, which describe the *umma* as a superior nation, and the reality that defies this assertion. In response to this gap, Muslims have forced a debate on good governance. The result has been the emergence of three broad schools of opinion: traditionalists, modernists, and secularists. Each Muslim society has its share of members of each group. The relative weights of each group in Muslim societies vary, which raises the question of what causes people from the same society to have different perceptions and understandings of democracy.

The fact that Muslims are heterogeneous does not tell us much about ordinary Muslims' attitudes toward democratic norms and institutions. In the following chapter, I will use the current survey, along with others, to explore correlations between the demographic and personal characteristics of Muslims and their attitudes toward democratic norms and institutions.

Notes

1. Question 37 in the survey. See Appendix 2.
2. Imam Khomeini (1900–1989) was the political and spiritual leader of the 1979 revolution in Iran. His vision of Islamic rule upended more than a thousand years of classical Shiite tradition, which had prohibited clergy from ruling the state.
3. Sayyid Qutb (1906–1966) was an Egyptian Islamist whose critique of modern civilization provides the theoretical underpinnings for many contemporary Islamic militants.
4. Abu Bakar Bashir (1938–) is the leader of the Indonesian Islamic Jama'a.
5. Sayyid Abul Ala Maududi is better known as Maulana Maududi (1903–1979); he was one of the most influential Muslim theologians of the twentieth century and the founder of Jamaat-e-Islami, an Islamist political party in Pakistan.
6. Shaikh Abdul Hamid Kishk (1933–1996) was one of the most influential *ulama* in Egypt and the Middle East. He was highly critical of all Muslim governments because he considered them non-Islamic.
7. Ibn Baaz (1909–1999) held the position of grand muftee of Saudi Arabia, the presidency of many Islamic committees and councils; the prominent among these positions was head of the Senior Scholars Committee of the kingdom.
8. Yusuf al-Qaradawi (1926–) is a very influential scholar who tackles highly controversial questions. Al-Qaradawi is very popular: his tapes and videos are available as far away as Indonesia and Malaysia. His fatwas are heeded around the world.
9. Mohamed al-Ghazali (1917–1996) was an eminent Egyptian scholar.
10. Mohamed Iqbal (1877–1938) was an important Indian Muslim poet from the colonial era, a philosopher and thinker of Kashmiri origin. He is considered one of the preeminent founding fathers of Pakistan.
11. Abdolkarim Soroush (1945–) is a thinker who gained his reputation through his *ijtihad*. In the survey data, Soroush is mentioned equally by Shiite pluralist secularists and modernist Islamists as the opinion leader who most influenced their political views.
12. Rachid al-Ghannoushi (1941–) is the exiled leader of the Tunisian Islamic an-Nahda (Renaissance) Movement.
13. Abdurrahman Wahid (1940–) was a widely respected populist Muslim cleric and leader of the Nahdatul Ulama before being elected president by the Indonesian parliament. Later, however, he was impeached.

14. Mahathir Mohamed (1925–) was Malaysia's fourth prime minister until he relinquished his post in 2003.

15. Said al-Ashmawi is a contemporary former superior judge on Egypt's High Court.

16. Ahmad Baghdadi is a contemporary professor of social sciences in Kuwait.

17. Mohamed Arkoun is a contemporary French-Algerian philosopher.

18. Muhammad Ali Jinnah (1876–1948) was the founder of Pakistan.

19. Yadollah Sahabi (1906–2002) was a leading Iranian reformist who was jailed for his opinions under the shah and later the Islamic republic.

20. There is disagreement about which verse is actually the verse of the sword. Most likely it is the quoted verse or the following one, which is usually quoted with it, from the same chapter of Surat al-Tawba: "Fight those who believe not in Allah nor the Last Day, nor hold that forbidden which hath been forbidden by Allah and His Messenger, nor acknowledge the Religion of Truth, from among the People of the Book, until they pay the Jizya with willing submission, and feel themselves subdued" (Quran 9:29).

3

Muslim Public Opinion and Democracy

Many societies in the region struggle with poverty and illiteracy, many rulers in the region have longstanding habits of control; many people in the region have deeply ingrained habits of fear. The chances of democratic progress in the broader Middle East have seemed frozen in place for decades. Yet at last, and suddenly, the thaw has begun.
—US president George W. Bush, March 11, 2005

Because one cannot explain a variable with a constant, or unchanging attribute, it would be logically flawed to ascribe Muslims' widely varying beliefs about democracy to Islam. This chapter provides some insights into the possible variables that cause Muslims to adopt different readings of democracy even though they share the same religion. One can think of two major sets of possible causes behind why some Muslims favor democratic norms and institutions while others do not. The first group of possible causes focuses on *personal factors*, such as demographic characteristics, personal experiences, and religious affiliation and commitment. The other causes centered on the attitudes of Muslims toward the *political actors* who may be responsible for a lack of democracy. The distinction between personal factors and attitudes toward political actors corresponds to a shift in the literature on democratization from a focus on the prerequisites and structural determinants of democratization to a focus on the processes and the strategic choices made by the actors.

In this chapter I examine the possible causes that militate both for and against literate Muslims' support for democratic norms and institutions. To measure attitudes toward democracy, I developed two scales using factor analysis techniques, as described in Appendix 4. Suffice it to say here that support for democratic institutions is a composite variable combining support for voting, elections, and democratic institutions generally, and support for democratic norms entails support for the political inclusion of various repressed and minority groups, such as Christians, Jews, Muslim women, and various Muslim subgroups.

The relationship between various individual-level factors and support for democratic norms and institutions is summarized in Table 3.1. This table displays the statistical relationships that will be discussed in

Table 3.1   Explaining Attitudes Toward Democracy: Factors and Actors

	1. R. Income		2. Education		3. Age		4. Female		5. Vote		6. Reside in Dem.	
	Norms	Inst	Norms	Inst	Norms	Inst	Norms	Inst	Norms	Inst	Norms	Inst
Pos/Neg	+	−	+	−	+	−	+	−	+	−	+	−
Albania	*		*	**			**	***	*	***	***	***
Algeria			***	**			***				***	***
Bahrain		*	***	***		*	***	*			***	***
Bangladesh			***	***			***	***	*	***	***	***
Egypt			***	***			***	**	*		***	***
Europe	***	*	**	**			***	*	***	**		
Gambia	*	*				*	**	*			***	***
India	*	***	***	***	***	***	***	**	**	***		
Indonesia	**		***	***		*	***	***			***	***
Iran			***	*		**	***	***	**	***	***	**
Jordan	**		***	***	***		**				***	***
Kuwait	*	*	***		***	**	***		**		***	
Lebanon				*	**		**	***				***
Libya			**	**			**	***			*	***
Malaysia		**	*	*			***	***	**		***	***
Mali			***	***	***		***	***	*		**	***
Morocco		***	***	***			***	***	**	***		**
Nigeria	**			***	***		***			*	***	***
Oman				***				***			**	***
Pakistan			***	***	**		***	**			***	***
Qatar			***	***	***		***	**			***	***
Saudi Arabia			***	***	***		*	*			***	***
Senegal			***	***			***	***	***	***	***	***
Sudan			***	***			***				***	***
Syria			***	***			***				***	***
Tajikistan				***	***		***	**			*	***
Tunisia			***	***	**	*	**	***			***	***
Turkey	*	*	***	***	***	***	***		***	***	***	***
Turkmenistan			***				**				***	
UAE		**	***		***		*	*			***	***
USA		**	***	**	*		**	***	**	***		
Yemen			***				***				*	**

(continues)

this chapter. Horizontally, the table lists the variables hypothesized to influence Muslims' attitudes toward democratic norms and institutions. The effect of each variable is reported in two columns: one for the impact on democratic norms and the other for the impact on democratic institutions (Inst.). The impact may be positive (increasing one's support for democratic norms or institutions) and thus given the sign (+) or negative (decreasing support for democratic norms and institutions) and thus given the sign (–). The cells either are empty (indicating a lack

Table 3.1   (continued)

	7. Religiosity		8. Shura/Dem.		9. Pol. Islam		10. Incumbents		11. West		12. Ulama	
	Norms	Inst.	Norms	Inst.	Norms	Inst.	Norms	Inst.	Norms	Inst.	Norms	Inst.
Pos/Neg	+	–	+	–	+	–	+	–	+	–	+	–
Albania			*	**			***	*	*	*	*	
Algeria		***	*	**	*						*	
Bahrain	***		**	**			***	*			*	***
Bangladesh	***		***	**			***	***			***	***
Egypt	***		***	***	***		***	**			*	
Europe	**	***	***	**			***	***			**	***
Gambia	*		***	***			***				**	***
India	***		***	***	**						***	*
Indonesia	***	***		**	***		**				***	***
Iran	***		***	*			***	***			*	***
Jordan	***		*	***			***	*			***	*
Kuwait	***		*	***			**	***			**	***
Lebanon		**		***	***		***	*			*	**
Libya				**			***				*	*
Malaysia		***	*	**				*			**	**
Mali	**		**	**	***		***	*	*			
Morocco		*	***	***			***	**			**	
Nigeria	***			***	**		***	**			***	**
Oman	***	**	***	***			***	**			***	
Pakistan	***		***	***	**		***	***			***	***
Qatar	***	***	**	***			***	*			***	**
Saudi Arabia	***	***	**	**	***						***	***
Senegal		*	*	**			***	**			***	***
Sudan		*	**	***	**		*	**			**	
Syria			***	***			***	**			*	
Tajikistan				*				**				
Tunisia			*	***	***		**	*				
Turkey		***	**	**	***		**	*				
Turkmenistan	*			**			***					
UAE	***	**	**	*			***	*				**
USA			**	**			***	***	*	***	**	
Yemen	***	***	**	**	**		**	**			***	**

Notes: "Norms" stands for democratic norms and "Inst." stands for democratic institutions.
***: the related variable has a statistical significance at 0.01 level; ** at 0.05; and * at 0.1.

of statistical significance) or have stars (indicating the existence of a statistically significant relationship). These stars reflect the seemingly unrelated regression (SUR) and multiple logistic regression models' tests of significance. Three asterisks (***) in the body of the table mean that the related variable has a statistical significance at 0.01 level, (**) at 0.05, and (*) at 0.1. In short, the more asterisks are shown, the more certainty there is that a true relationship exists between the variables.

This table can be read horizontally to demonstrate the capacity of the suggested variables to explain why certain Muslims are for or against democracy in each society. For instance, in Albania democratic norms are mostly supported by female Muslims who are relatively rich, are well educated, tend to vote in public elections, have had direct experience with democracy (measured by residence in a democracy for a year or longer), believe in the compatibility between *shura* and democracy, trust incumbents, believe that the West is sincere about supporting democratization in the Muslim world, and tend not to trust the *ulama* as genuine agents of democratization.

The table can be read vertically as well to show the (in)consistency of certain variables across cases. For instance, the variable of income has a contradictory impact on Muslims' attitudes toward democratic institutions across Muslim societies. Relatively affluent Bahrainis tend to be less supportive of democratic institutions than relatively disadvantaged Bahrainis. Conversely, Indian Muslims become more supportive of democratic institutions the higher their income is.

A quick vertical look at the table suggests that some variables have more explanatory power than others. For instance, the effects of gender, residency in a democracy, and the perceived compatibility of *shura* and democracy explain positive attitudes of literate Muslims toward democracy. Trust in the West as a genuine "democratizer" does not seem to have great impact on how Muslims perceive democracy. What follows is a detailed discussion of the impact of the main factors.

Demographics

Demographic characteristics such as income, education, gender, and age are among the most standard yet debatable variables that may affect one's attitude toward many issues, including democracy. Some scholarship attributes Muslims' antagonism to the West to demographic aspects such as poverty, poor health conditions, a growing number of youth as a percentage of the general population, failure of development, and lack of education (Abootalebi 2000; Sachs 2001; Stern 1999; Stern 2003). In the Western experience, it is said that more educated and better-off individuals of the middle class will generally adhere to values conducive to democracy (Bermeo 1997; Kaufman and Haggard 1997).

However, an in-depth examination in 1980 of jailed Egyptian radical Islamists revealed that the typical member is young (early twenties), of a rural or small-town background, from the middle or lower middle class, with high achievement and motivation, upwardly mobile, with science or engineering education, and from a normally cohesive family. In other words, they are "significantly above the average in their generation" while being among the most extreme (Ibrahim 1980).

With such conflicting accounts, the data here can help determine whether demographic characteristics influence Muslims differently across societies. To aid in this analysis, the most important demographic characteristics suggested by the literature—income, education, age, and gender—are laid out in Table 3.1.

Effect of Income

A nine-point scale was developed to gauge the income of respondents. It is a measure designed to capture the effect that socioeconomic status may have on individual attitudes toward democracy. There are competing explanations about how income affects support for democracy. As was mentioned, many democratic theorists contend that middle classes are most supportive of democracy and are crucial to the democratization process. Dahl suggests, however, that this support may be fleeting if democracies fail to meet basic needs, as was the case for the pre–World War II regimes of Italy, Germany, and Spain (Dahl 1971).

Middle classes may also be less supportive of democracy if their comfort and wealth are derived from government benefits and an absence of government taxation. By providing material benefits, autocratic governments may be able to buy legitimacy (Luciani 1995). Or, as Bernard Lewis puts it, "With no need for taxation, there is no pressure for representation" (Lewis 1993: 54–55). Many believe that this classic rentier-state argument applies perfectly to the wealthier oil-exporting Arab countries, which make up a significant number of the world's Muslim countries (Sherman 1998). Beyond the rentier-state argument, however, Martin Sherman asserts that there is generally no correlation between wealth and democracy among Muslim countries and identifies them as the great exception to the general rule that wealth promotes democracy. Relatedly, Daniel Pipes does not find any link between wealth and Muslims' attitudes toward modernity (Pipes 2002).

The following sections employ the project's survey to test these assertions. Instead of evaluating general support for democracy, however, I break down support for democracy into two components: support for democratic norms, or political tolerance, and support for democratic institutions—elections and voting specifically. The disaggregation of democracy in this fashion allows for a more nuanced understanding of the various ways in which income affects beliefs about democracy.

The impact on democratic norms. As Table 3.1 demonstrates, relatively high income is correlated with more support for democratic norms in Albania, Europe, Gambia, India, Indonesia, Jordan, and Turkey. In other words, richer people tend to be more tolerant toward women and minorities. When controlling for the effect of education, one finds that income loses its significance in the cases of Indonesia and Jordan. In other words, education functions as an intervening variable between income and support for democratic norms in these two cases.

However, high income has the opposite effect in two other countries: Kuwait and Nigeria. Differently put, the affluent Muslims who responded to the survey tended to be less supportive of democratic norms in these two countries. Controlling for the effect of income did not change the significance of other coefficients, which suggests that the negative effect of income on democratic norms in Kuwait and Nigeria is not due to any interaction with other variables. Ahmad, a Kuwaiti engineer, was surprised by this finding, but he could imagine that a number of rich people in his own family supported the status quo, since "change is scary."

Determining the mechanisms of causality between income and negative support for democratic norms will require more scrutiny with more empirical data. At this point it can be noted, however, that there is no statistically significant relationship between relative affluence and democratic norms in the other twenty-three cases, even after one controls for the effect of other variables. In other words, in most cases, Muslims' relative economic status does not help explain their political attitudes toward minorities and women.

The impact on democratic institutions. The impact of income is more significant in explaining Muslims' attitudes toward democratic institutions than in explaining their attitudes toward democratic norms. Relatively high income produces more support for democratic institutions in Europe, Gambia, India, Kuwait, Malaysia, Morocco, Turkey, and the United States. These countries share very few common economic, cultural, or political characteristics. In the most capitalist and affluent countries of the world (United States and Europe) and in a number of the poorest economies in the world (Gambia and India), there could be different mechanisms that lead relatively affluent Muslims in these countries to support democratic procedures and mechanisms. As Bahgat Korany of Montréal University pointed out in an interview in Cairo, the rich may be appreciative of the connection between democracy and their economic status, while the poor in certain societies are hopeful of achieving the same kind of connection.

However, high income produces less support for democratic institutions in the cases of Jordan, Oman, Saudi Arabia, the United Arab Emirates, and Bahrain. This result suggests that, with the exception of Kuwait, Arab (semi-)rentier states produce relatively undemocratic affluent individuals. The Arab Gulf states in general are clear examples of rentier states that function as "baksheesh or stipend petrocracies" (Korany 1994) whose citizens are direct or indirect recipients of state stipends. The wealth of citizens is derived primarily not from their own productive activities but rather from the state's controlled oil fields. In other words, almost all citizens work for the government. The citizens rarely make demands for representation since they are not asked to pay any taxes. This study reveals that often the most affluent in these societies are enthusiastic opponents of democracy, fearing that it might lead to redistributive policies that would reduce their stipends. This finding adds more evidence to the argument that oil wealth impedes democracy (Ross 2001).

If this is the case, however, why were Kuwait's relatively rich citizens more supportive of democratic institutions while less supportive of democratic norms? Despite their relative acceptance of democratic institutions, socially conservative attitudes prevail when it comes to tolerance for women and minorities. Around 58 percent of Kuwaiti respondents were Islamist. In the words of one respondent, Kuwaiti men tend to believe that "Kuwaiti women are not suitable for outdoor challenges." Regarding democratic institutions, the history of representative politics in Kuwait since the adoption of the 1962 constitution may shed light on the issue: some democratic elements have existed without necessarily bringing abrupt shifts that would have jeopardized the privileged status of Kuwait's most affluent citizens (Byman and Green 1999).

In other Muslim societies surveyed, being rich or poor did not show much correlation with Muslims' attitudes toward democratic institutions.

Effect of Education

Education has always been thought to be a very important factor in shaping an individual's political attitudes. It is suggested that for highly educated people, the cost associated with acquiring information about how democracy works in other countries is low, and as a result, they exhibit more support for democracy. Educated people also tend to have a higher sense of efficacy and thus seek control over their lives; they are likely to view democracy as empowering. Conversely, the least educated may pose a threat to democracy in the face of any socioeconomic dislocation (Lipset 1983). Education is also hypothesized to instill and reinforce liberal and democratic norms such as equality, sociopolitical tolerance, individual liberty, and democratic institutions, as suggested by theory and evidence from other cultures (Semali 1995). In the Muslim context, it is argued, relatively lower levels of education explain the weakness of civil society and democratic praxis (Diamond, Plattner, and Brumberg 2003).

I use a five-point scale to measure the level of education. As indicated in Table 3.1, this study finds that education has a significant effect on attitudes regarding democratic norms and/or institutions in all Muslim societies other than Gambia and Oman. The following discussion will explore the effects of education on democratic norms, emphasizing the Muslim countries where education has a significant impact.

The impact on democratic norms. Education has a negative effect in regard for democratic norms in the cases of Saudi Arabia and the United Arab Emirates. In the case of Saudi Arabia, this is not surprising given the content of its curriculum. "The domination of higher education by the *ulama* has led to a general rise in complaints by Saudi students about the curriculum's lack of relevance to their everyday practical needs" (Yamani 2000). The Saudi intellectuals whom I interviewed were critical of the priority given to rote learning at the expense of critical thinking. Though the Saudi *ulama* deny this link between education and intolerance (al-Buraiq 1994; Ibn Baaz 2002), a Shiite Saudi contends: "The religious curriculum in Saudi Arabia teaches you that people are basically two sides: Salafis, who are the winners, the chosen ones, who will go to heaven, and the rest. The rest are [Shiite] Muslims and Christians and Jews and others" (al-Ahmed 2002).[1] A liberal Saudi professor who was saved from prison by a special decree from the crown prince accused the local education system of producing most of the Saudi extremists (Mazyanni 2005).

The negative effect of education regarding democratic norms in the case of the United Arab Emirates comes as a real surprise given that 72 percent of registered UAE students in higher education are females. However, a plausible explanation for this negative impact can be found in the role of age. By controlling for the effect of age, one finds that education loses its negative impact. This clarifies it is not education that is the primary factor in determining a lack of democratic norms, but rather the age of the person. Older people, regardless of their education level, tend to be less supportive of democratic norms. Moreover, though UAE women occupy more school and college places than men (the ratio in high schools in 2002 was 2.7 to 1), most education experts find that UAE society still does not encourage women to work outside the fields of education and some governmental positions (AbdelGalil 2003).

Another interesting finding is that graduates of the Pakistani educational system did not appear in this survey to be especially intolerant, despite Pakistan's 8,000 religious schools or madrassas, which are considered by many to be incubators for Islamic militants (Iqbal 2003). This might be explained by the fact that, unlike educated Saudis, most educated Pakistanis do not send their children to madrassas, as it is extremely difficult for students who attend them to be admitted to college later on. In fact, these schools tend to function as a parallel education system that is not under the supervision or control of the central government.

The impact on democratic institutions. As in the case with democratic norms, according to this study's data, more education leads to more support for democratic institutions, except for the cases of Saudi Arabia and the United Arab Emirates. This finding supports claims made by some scholars that Muslims' lack of support of democracy is not a peculiar function of Islam's influence on Muslims' political culture but rather a common problem that Muslim societies share with other developing countries (Abootalebi 2000). It also lends support to the argument that mass literacy, economic modernization, urbanization, and the flow of information associated with the communications revolution all lead to the rise of the middle class, which is usually supportive of democratic procedures and mechanisms (Sivan 1997). Based on a similar analysis, a prominent researcher projected that mass education, along with independent mass media, would have the same impact on Muslims as the printing press had on sixteenth-century Europe (Eickelman 1999).

The policy recommendation suggested by these findings is that if Muslim governments intend to advance genuine democratic reforms, they need to review their curriculums to make sure that they do not advance antidemocratic norms instead. For instance, Saudi education is in need of revision to accommodate Muslims from all sects and women as politically equal. Other Muslim countries need not only fight illiteracy but also to expand a post–high school education that fosters and sustains democracy.

Effect of Age

While the young tend to be enthusiastic about change (Inglehart 1997), this may not necessarily extend to democratization. Some reports suggest that there is a tendency among young Muslims, who dominate the populations of most Muslim countries, to be increasingly devout. This tendency has become a concern for the West since those religious young men resent Western values (al-'Affifi 2002). This study finds that the five-point scale of age is not significantly related to democratic institutions or norms in fourteen cases but does show a correlation in the rest.

The impact on democratic norms.   Other things being equal, age has a positive effect on enhancing democratic norms in India, Kuwait, Lebanon, Pakistan, Saudi Arabia, Tajikistan, Tunisia, and the United Arab Emirates. In these cases, older people surveyed were more tolerant toward non-Muslims, Muslims from other sects, and women than were younger people. This result offers cause for alarm. If this trend holds in the future, these societies may end up having relatively less tolerant cultures. Some scholars have noted the relative erosion of tolerance in India with the ascendancy of the Hindu party called Bharatiya Janata, compared to the older generation that tended to support the secular Conference Party (Jayal 2001). In Lebanon, older people who remember the fifteen-year civil war are more tolerant of minorities and women than are younger people. Samir Salmani, a Lebanese sociologist, points out that while older Lebanese people do not want to repeat the cultural environment of the civil war, the younger generation has been socialized with a sense of defeat that makes them feel that they are not fairly treated economically and politically.

Only among Muslims of the United States do older people support democratic norms less than younger people. Fortunately, around 73 percent of the respondents from the United States were under the age of thirty, and their responses provide a good indication that they are assimilating the relatively tolerant democratic culture of the United States. In the remaining cases, the age of respondents had no impact on their level of tolerance toward minorities and women, even when the effects of other variables were controlled for.

The impact on democratic institutions.   In two-thirds of the societies studied, there was no correlation between age and attitudes toward democratic institutions. Still, older Muslims in Gambia, Indonesia, Kuwait, Mali, Nigeria, and Tunisia tended to be more supportive of democratic institutions than younger Muslims in these countries, while older Muslims in Iran, Saudi Arabia, Turkey, Turkmenistan, and the United Arab Emirates were less supportive of democratic institutions than were members of the younger generation. The difference between these two groups of countries is not easily attributable to differences in experience with democracy, given that the great majority of Muslims are born and have lived in autocracies. Even the attempts of nationalist governments to launch ambitious programs of mass education have failed to serve the purpose of political development, mainly because of the logic of mass mobilization and indoctrination, which has not allowed a focus on basic freedoms and civil rights (Eickelman 1992).

Researchers have generally found it easier to explain why older people are resistant to democratic procedures by referring to historical experiences that leave older people less satisfied and less comfortable with modernity. New generations, by contrast, have greater access to electronic communications and media that can educate them about democratic standards. The inconsistent link between age and support for democratic institutions found by this study, however, points to the need for further refinement of these theories.

Effect of Gender

Islam was described in a 1920 article as "a religion that ignores the personal existence of an entire sex . . . [thus it] can hardly hope to survive outside the dark places of the earth" (Kinross 1920). More recently, Adrian Karatnycky has argued that any "interpretation of Islam that relegates women to second-class status" has a detrimental impact on democratization in the Muslim world (Karatnycky 2002). While M. Steven Fish confirms this impact (2002), it is not clear to what extent women have been socialized or forced to acquiesce in their own disenfranchisment. Put differently, do Muslim women perceive their political roles in the same way Muslim men do? My analysis categorically suggests that literate Muslim women in all countries are more supportive of democratic norms and institutions than are Muslim men.

We should keep in mind that the survey captures the attitudes only of literate women and that international sources put illiteracy rates for Muslim women at up to 55 percent (World Bank 2001b). Many scholars, relying on ethnographic research and deep knowledge of specific societies (Ahmed 1992; Ahmed 2001; Barakah and Nasif 2001; Bayes and Tohidi 2001; Engineer 2001; Rosen 2002; Shahidian 2002), argue that average Muslim women are not aware of their lack of efficacy. Other scholarship suggests that men may be more supportive of democracy than women in Egypt and Morocco (Tessler 2002a).

Still, my focus-group discussions revealed a general trend: even the most modernist and pluralist men talked as if they were traditionalists when the discussion took up the status of women. Almost 78 percent of the men who participated in the focus-group discussions advanced various arguments in favor of women's home-based duties such as taking care of children and bringing up good families. At the same time, the present data show that there is an overall awareness among literate Muslim women of their plight. I did not find support for the claim made by some researchers that women are responsible for their own plight in that they socialize their daughters to believe that their role in life is secondary to men's (Farjani 2002b; Hijab 1988; Mernissi 2003). Though this may be applicable to illiterate women, it simply does not apply to the literate women surveyed for this study.

The focus group discussions illustrated women's thinking about their place in society. In all groups, women portrayed themselves as being treated unfairly socioeconomically by men but not by Islam. They accused society of depriving them of the rights given to them by sharia. Making a distinction between Islam as a creed and the cultures of individual countries, interviewed women agreed that male-centered cultural norms do not give women a fair share even by Islamic standards. Defending her religion, a young Saudi university graduate with a degree in marketing stated, "Allah's rules are respected and will be respected in Saudi Arabia. We [women] do not want to dress inappropriately in streets or intermingle impolitely with men in offices. . . . Women should keep wearing the *abayas* [black cloaks] because Allah dictates chastity on us, not because men decided so." Fatema Nour of Iran sought to refute Western criticisms of Islam's treatment of women. "I can wear bikini, listen to music, and sing . . . but not in front of men.

. . . Some [Muslim] men do not understand Islam or abide by its rules. They harm Islam's image, and there are always people who are ready to blame everything which goes wrong on our religion."

Even among the most secular of women, there is a clear rejection of any attempt to link Muslim women's plight to sharia. Instead, they focus on male-centered schools of *fiqh* that degrade women. They are asking for an Islamic version of equal but separate rights and facilities. Another intriguing finding is that most of the interviewed women, even secular ones, are critical of the Western model of the man-woman relationship. As a Turkish female sociologist commented, "American movies scare Muslim conservatives. They are worried that if they give women their rights, Muslim societies will be like Western societies." As a supporter of the Islamist governing party in Turkey, she believed that her mission was to educate the masses that a Muslim woman can be free in an Islamic way without following the path of either Western women or the veiled women of Afghanistan. Most of the interviewees asserted that Islamic principles give them certain negative freedoms that any woman may aspire to: freedom from sexual harassment, freedom from pornography, and freedom from selling their bodies as market commodities. The real challenge they face is gaining the positive freedoms that Islam promises them but Muslim men have kept from them. Foremost among these freedoms would be equal opportunity with men in the workplace and in public office. As the feminist Iqbal Barka of Egypt put it, women deserve "the opportunity to fix what men messed up."

A significant minority of female discussants was uncomfortable about women's participation in politics. Once the issue of women taking office was introduced, roughly 20 percent of the interviewees began to quote fatwas that forbid women from having superiority over men in political affairs. That said, most literate Muslim women who participated in the survey were modernists (60 percent) or pluralist (15 percent) and argued for a more active role for women in politics. The models these women looked to, however, differed depending on their ideological orientation. Unlike pluralist women, modernist women barely made any references to Western examples; instead they cited examples of Muslim women who govern(ed) important Muslim countries as efficiently as men.

Are there ways to empower Muslim women amid a male-dominated culture? The focus-group discussions revealed that literate women are contemplating possible solutions. Empowering women through a quota system in political positions was suggested by a secular Algerian female lawyer and human rights activist, an idea that was supported by the modernist and pluralist female participants in the focus-group discussions in almost all the countries where these were held. Her logic assumes that Muslim rulers have to empower women until they are capable of proving their merits and potential; otherwise, women's subordination to men will continue even as increasing numbers of Muslim women become educated. A Sudanese female student of medicine concurred. She believed that most women are not aware of their potential and do not know how to defend their political rights. It is the responsibility of governments in Muslim societies, she said, to allocate resources and positions to women. From her perspective, if governments decide to do that, they will succeed.

A contrast between Morocco's and Iran's experiences is telling in this regard. Though Iranian women are active in almost all socioeconomic and political arenas, they are still vastly underrepresented in the legislature—women occupy only 4 percent of Iran's parliamentary seats. Applying the quota system in Morocco raised the number of women in the Moroccan parliament from two to thirty-five, and five women won seats that were open to both sexes (11 percent of the seats).

Some recent developments have shown us that although cultural practices and beliefs matter, they are not insurmountable if the political elite decides to empower women. Qatar offers a striking example. In a clear contrast to the highly conservative traditions of the Arabian peninsula, the Qatari Constitution not only mentions equality between the sexes (article 34) but also emphasizes the government's responsibility to empower women (article 19). The Qatari government has been working hard in recent years to bridge the gap between women and men in education, employment opportunity, and political positions (al-Ansari 2003). A Qatari woman has become a minister of education, and another was appointed dean of the School of Sharia, where hundreds of male *ulama* work and study. From an Islamic point of view, if a woman can run the affairs of a school of shaikhs and *ulama* and the male gatekeepers of Islamic traditions present no objections, then she is also entitled to do many other things.

Surprisingly, there is not much difference between the culture of Qatar and the culture of Saudi Arabia, where women are not allowed to drive cars and, until December 2001, did not have personal identification cards because their faces were not to be exposed to strangers. All the members of the appointed Shura Council of Saudi Arabia are males, and elective posts on trade chambers are restricted to men. There is a clear difference between the political elites in the two countries. A Saudi citizen showed me a free booklet (with no author or publisher) in which the following quote was attributed to the famous Islamic scholar Abu Hamid al-Ghazali (twelfth century): "Women should stay at home and not see men, and men should not see them. A woman must only go outdoors in extremely awful clothes."

That said, the Saudi government may be learning from Qatar's experiences. It recently allowed women to participate in the national dialogue on reforms in the country, through video conferencing from separate rooms, a step that demonstrates a growing respect for their role in society. Increasingly there are discussions among the Saudi politicians and *ulama* on how to find an "Islamic way" to allow women to participate in politics in case the political decision is made.

A famous example that has been used to underscore the role of culture and tribalism in degrading women's political status in Muslim countries is Kuwait, where the supreme court and the parliament refused to give Kuwaiti women the right to participate in politics. These decisions invalidated a decree issued by the prince in 1999 to enfranchise women. However, one of my Kuwaiti interviewees argued that the prince was not fully serious about enfranchising women. "Had he been fully supportive of it, he would have got it." Is this a matter peculiar to the Kuwaiti culture? If it were a matter of culture, how could we explain the fact that literate Kuwaiti women have top positions as bureaucrats, academicians, journalists, and diplomats, but they are not allowed to vote in public elections? More generally, the Gulf States differ significantly in their treatment of women, despite their common culture.

Additional evidence that the political actors' commitments are more decisive than cultural/religious factors can be found in the role of women as judges. There are more than 1,000 Arab female judges. Approximately 50 percent of Morocco's judges and 67 percent of Sudanese judges are women (Somaya Ibrahim 2002). Female judges have been in Morocco since 1959, the Sudan since 1962, Lebanon since 1966, Tunisia since 1975, Yemen since 1990, and Jordan since 1995. Egypt appointed its first female judge only in 2003.

According to Togan al-Faisal, the first woman to be elected into the Jordanian parliament, opposition to women's public role is not based on religion or culture but on a "political agenda." Her evidence is twofold. First, King Hussein of Jordan appointed two women to the Jordanian parliament after she was elected in 1993, contrary to the conservative and tribal culture that emphasized honoring women by having them stay at home. Second, though members of the Muslim Brotherhood of Jordan were very critical of women's participation in politics based on religious and cultural reasoning during the 1989 elections, they retreated after al-Faisal won her parliamentary seat. Contrary to its previous discourse, the Jordanian Muslim Brotherhood then appointed a woman to its Shura Council—a first in the whole Arab region—and later nominated a woman for parliament (al-Faisal 2003). Had there been an actual religious and cultural mandate prohibiting women's participation in politics, al-Faisal argues, the king and the Islamic groups would not have shifted directions that quickly.

While worldwide Sweden has the highest percentage of women's representation in parliament (54 percent) and US women have reached 41 percent, Senegal and Morocco (19 and 11 percent respectively) are the highest among Muslim countries, mainly because of the political support women get from the governing elites. Notably, the attempts to empower women in these countries have been coupled with progressive interpretations of certain verses of the Quran and Sunna (sayings and praxis of the Prophet Muhammad), which allowed for rapid shifts in the treatment of women.

Experience with Democracy

Previous Political Participation

Following a proceduralist reading of voting in meaningful elections as the main form of political participation (Dahl 1989; Downs 1956; Sartori 1962; Schumpeter 1976), this project measured political participation in the countries that carry out public elections through voting (question 7, Appendix 2). While detractors of this approach may cite data from the 1970s to show that countries like North Korea, Romania, and Bulgaria, among others, had very high levels of voter turnout (Bollen 1980), in the countries studied in this project, only Turkey had compulsory voting. The variable of voting has not been used in the cases of Saudi Arabia, United Arab Emirates, Oman, Qatar, Bahrain, and Libya because elections had not been held there prior to the data collection process.

The impact on democratic norms. Intuitively, one would anticipate that individuals who participate in politics through voting would tend to be open-minded regarding the right of minorities and women to run for office and participate in the democratic process. However, in this study this assumption held true only among Muslims of Albania, Bangladesh, Europe, India, Iran, Malaysia, Morocco, Turkey, and the United States.

These countries have two important characteristics in common. First, they all have a relatively long tradition of elections, with clear opportunities given to minorities and women. Moreover, these countries have the most compatible aggregate attitudes toward democratic norms and institutions, as will be discussed in greater detail in Chapter 5.

This finding also suggests that people who vote are more likely to be pluralists and modernists than traditionalists. The traditionalist position contradicts the democratic ideal of voting for the best candidate regardless of faith. Typical traditionalists refuse Muslims' participation in elections since voting is *bid'a*, but some unconventional traditionalists accept participating in elections under extreme conditions. Some suggest that male Muslims should always vote for Muslims even if a non-Muslim seems to be a better candidate, in accordance with some verses of the Quran, such as 2:221.[2]

These results support the dialectical relationship between democratic mechanisms and institutions and cultural values. Democratic institutions may be capable of creating the cultural environment conducive to democracy's sustainability. People who value democratic institutions and participate in their dynamics tend to support the civic spirit that favors individuals' rights to participate in politics on equal footing. In addition, people who are tolerant and trustful of minorities and women tend to esteem democratic mechanisms as fair outlets for minorities and women to express their interests.

The impact on democratic institutions. Unsurprisingly, the more people vote in public elections, the more supportive they are of democratic institutions in Albania, Bangladesh, India, Mali, Morocco, Nigeria, the United States, Turkey, Senegal, Iran, and Europe. What is perhaps more interesting is why this relationship is limited to Muslims of only eleven societies. Why would some individuals' participation in elections have no effect on their support for democratic institutions? The answer comes from many observers who noted that meaningless or entirely uncontested elections are increasing in the Muslim world. "Most of these elections barely change anything," as Ahmad Mufta of Nigeria commented.

Of the fifty-three countries with Muslim majorities, around fifty officially hold some sort of elections and referenda. Most of these practices, however, could be described as "nothing more than the people's periodic renunciation of their sovereignty" (Sartori 1962: 24). The countries that sponsor these elections are electoral authoritarian regimes that "neither practice democracy nor resort regularly to naked oppression"

(Schedler 2002: 36), a reminder that elections on their own are necessary but not sufficient for a polity to become a democracy.

If one strictly applies Adam Przeworski's criterion that "no country in which a party wins 60 percent of the vote twice is a democracy" (Przeworski 1992: 126), one will conclude that elections matter in only seven Muslim countries: Albania, Iran, Senegal, Bangladesh, Mali, Turkey, and Indonesia. As one might expect, this list closely resembles the list of Muslim countries above, in which participation in public elections reinforces support for democratic institutions.

In Iran, even if elections produce a relatively weak president and parliament while the actual authority remains in the hands of the supreme leader, the regression results show a significantly positive relationship between voting and support for democratic institutions. While most moderate interviewees expressed concern that liberal Iranians may give up voting if real reform does not come soon, another study suggests that most Iranians still have hope that voting will eventually advance reforms through the election of pluralists and moderates to the presidency and parliament (Jahanbegloo 2003).

In Bangladesh, elections are largely an opportunity for an exchange of seats between Shaikha Hesseina (daughter of Muguid al-Rahman, the founder of Bangladesh) and Khaldha Dheya (the widow of Dheya'a al-Rahman, president of Bangladesh in the 1970s). One Bangladeshi respondent described the Bangladeshi elections as "ceremonial" in their impact but said that Bangladeshi people "still think that elections tell whoever is in power that we can change you."

Voting by Muslims of Pakistan did not have an impact on their support for democratic institutions, though elections were periodic occasions for changing the prime minister's post to be switched between Nawaz Sharif and Benazir Bhutto. "Most Pakistanis welcomed [Musharraf's] coup in hopes that the military would institute long-awaited structural reforms" after eleven years of misgovernance under what most Pakistan experts considered democratic rule until 1999 (Shah 2002: 72).

There is no democracy without elections, but in most Muslim countries there are elections without democracy, elections that breed dictatorship. An Iranian journalist firmly refused to describe his country's polity as a democracy, though he has participated in all the elections that have taken place in the Islamic Republic of Iran. As a journalist, he measured democracy by freedom of expression and of the press. He referred me to the international reports on freedom of the press. According to the Reporters Without Borders' first worldwide press freedom index, even the Muslim countries that hold regular elections rate very poorly. Indonesia is number 57, Turkey is number 99, Bangladesh is number 118, Pakistan is number 119, and Iran is 122. These indices clearly indicate that elections have not been translated into substantive respect for freedoms and rights.[3]

Public cynicism also stems from the fact that many elected bodies in the more democratic Muslim countries are not vested with much, if any, political power. A female Algerian lawyer argued that the real challenge facing Muslim countries is not providing women the right to vote and participate; rather, it is the efficacy and relevance of the elected councils, regardless of whether they are dominated by men. When I asked, "Why do people vote then?" she cited many examples of people who vote for money, to take a vacation from work on the day of elections, or because of an appeal to ethnic and religious commitments, but "not because of any trust in the politicians" they elect. In searching for a good illustration of Fareed Zakaria's illiberal democracies (1997), one would only need to look to the electoral authoritarian regimes of the Muslim world.

Though highly controlled elections may promote a high degree of cynicism among the public, they may be one step above the informal consultation practiced in Libya, Saudi Arabia, the United Arab Emirates, and, until recently, Qatar, Bahrain, and Oman. Though this consultation may allow for some feedback and lend an air of legitimacy to the ruling regime (Byman and Green 1999), in most cases, according to focus-group participants, informal consultation gives elites considerable latitude in defending their interests, opens the gates to nepotism, and weakens the role of institutions, further promoting an accountability-free culture. They are, in sum, much easier to manipulate than are elections.

Residence in a Democracy

The variable "residence in a democracy" is measured dichotomously (question 14, Appendix 2), coded 1 for Muslims who had lived for a year or more in a democratic country (North America, Europe, Japan, or India). It was dropped from surveys in democratic countries such as the United States, India, and the European countries because all Muslims who have citizenship in one of these countries have already lived there for a year or more.

There is some controversy concerning whether and how living in a democratic country influences Muslims' political and social attitudes. Some studies suggest that living in the West by itself does not have any effect on Muslims' attitudes toward modernity. For example, the perpetrators of the September 11 attacks lived in the West enough to experience democracy but were not influenced by it (Pipes 2002). One can cite as well the example of Sayyid Qutb, who became more radical after visiting the United States (al-Khaledi 1987). Other Muslim intellectuals who lived in the West as students or visitors, however, have been highly impressed by socioeconomic and political modernization and have assimilated the Western experience in building their intellectual program. Some researchers refer to the triumph of the United States in the Cold War as another factor that ensured "the growing impact of the U.S. democracy and of American popular culture in the Islamic lands. . . . This kind of relationship is further encouraged by westward migration" (Lewis 1993b).

The pooled data helps to test the effect of residing in a democracy for a year or longer on attitudes toward democracy. As Table 3.1 demonstrates, when other variables are held constant, in almost all cases Muslims who lived in a democratic country for a year or more were more supportive of both democratic institutions and democratic norms than were Muslims who had never enjoyed this experience. This result indicates that travel and living in a democracy are among the most, if not the most, influential agents of democratic socialization.

Some focus group discussions conducted in the United States and others conducted with Muslims who lived in a democracy for a year helped to explain the impact of living in a democracy on Muslims coming from nondemocratic countries. Most Muslims who were interviewed were impressed by the peaceful rotation of power. A Palestinian student who had been in the United States for three years commented that democracy means that "people can choose their ruler and not to wait until he dies"; a Pakistani student who had spent four years in Canada and Britain liked the freedom of religion in Canada: "I pray without fearing being arrested for letting my beard grow." A Saudi student in the United States for five years suggested that the "rulers of Muslim countries should come and stay in the U.S. for two years to learn how to govern." A Lebanese administrator who had lived for three years in the United States opined that the democratic system is an Islamic system. "If there were a modern Caliphate, it would be like the U.S." He had in mind two aspects, federalism and democracy, but with one caveat. He did not approve of using the word *democracy*: "It will contaminate the Muslim mind." Instead he wanted to call it "*shura* system."

An Egyptian engineer had worked in Egypt, Iraq, Saudi Arabia, Germany, and the United States (with four years in the United States and

Germany). He believed that the United States has the fairest and most just system. "There is no discrimination in the U.S. If I am more qualified than a U.S.-born American, I will get the job and be the boss of other Americans. This cannot happen in Iraq or Saudi Arabia. . . . [The] American system is more Islamic than all Arab nominally Muslim countries." An Emirati student (eighteen months in the United States) had many reservations about what he called "excessive freedoms" but was still very impressed by elections, Congress, and most of all the idea of a supreme court. He enjoyed his class on the American political system, which described for him what Muslims need to do in their countries. Another student, a Sudanese (fourteen months in the United States), commented on the capacity of US society to accommodate different religions, ethnic groups, and languages.

Although Muslims who had lived in the United States were not fond of US foreign policy, as will be discussed later, most of them maintained that democracy works very well for Americans and can work for Muslims with necessary modifications to accommodate Islamic sharia, such as safeguards to ensure that certain basic Islamic teachings cannot be violated.

A small number of interviewees were critical of the democratic ideal itself. Their main criticisms focused on defects in the mechanisms, such as the effect of money on the campaigning and electoral process, the perceived control of a Jewish lobby over the American political agenda, and "the freedom of wrongdoing," as a Nigerian female put it.

In sum, living in a democracy for a year or more had a clear positive impact on Muslims' support for both democratic institutions and democratic norms. Definitely, Muslims' experience in the United States is not identical to the experience of Muslims in Europe or India. Nevertheless, the comments of these Muslims reveal that democratic principles are contagious and that Muslims are quick learners. Once they are exposed to real democracy, most likely they will assimilate it.

The Effect of Islam

How much influence does Islam have on individual Muslims' attitudes? The main task of this section is to understand how Muslims' attitudes toward democracy are affected by their religiosity, understanding of the relationship between *shura* and democracy, and their perception of Islam as a source of political ideology or as *deen wa dawla* (religion and state).

It has been argued that Islam itself has no impact on the political attitudes of Muslims. "The roots of Islamic radicalism must be looked for outside the religion, in the real world of cultural despair, economic decline, political oppression and spiritual turmoil in which most Muslims find themselves today" (Amirahmadi 2002). This result was confirmed by World Value Survey data from four Arab countries (Tessler 2002a). Here I will assess the impact of Islam by breaking down its impact into three dimensions and by highlighting cross-cultural differences among literate Muslims' attitudes toward democracy.

An eminent scholar of Islam starts his book with a striking statement: "My own experience of Islam began with a surprised and uncomfortable recognition that things are not what they seem" (Gilsenan 1982:9). Later on he warns, "So we should be especially wary of assuming that it is Islam that is the most important area on which to focus" (Gilsenan 1982:20).

Conversely, Islam's impact on Muslims' attitudes and behavior has been a core aspect of the new Orientalists' analysis of the undemocratic tendencies among Muslims. "Such familiar pairs of words as lay and ecclesiastical, sacred and profane, spiritual and temporal, and the like have no equivalent in classical Arabic or in other Islamic languages" (Lewis 1999:28). "Islam remains a religion of the Dark Ages. The 7th-century Koran is still taught as the immutable word of God, any teaching of which is literally true. In other words, mainstream Islam is essentially akin to the most extreme form of Biblical fundamentalism" (Johnson 2001). It has been reported as well that Nobel laureate and poet Octavio Paz once fumed, "Islam today is the most obstinate form of monotheism in a world that otherwise accepts plural truths" (Gardels 2003). Politicians have doubted the capacity of religious and orthodox Muslims to have "an Islamic path toward modernity and to a society that is established on human rights, individual freedom and equality among men and women" (Fischer 2002).

Muslims, on average, are said to be more influenced by their religion than are other monotheists (Hassan 2002). For instance, 17 percent of books issued in the Arab world are religious, while this percentage is merely 5 percent in other parts of the world (Farjani 2002a). A Gallup survey of nine Muslim countries indicated that "religion dominates daily life in the Islamic world" (Gallup 2002). Other surveys found similar results (Hassan 2002). According to Shibley Telhami's 2004 survey, pluralities in Jordan and Morocco and majorities in Saudi Arabia and the United Arab Emirates identified themselves primarily as "Muslim," as opposed to a citizen of their country, an "Arab," or a "citizen of the

world." This marked a significant rise in Islamic consciousness compared to previous surveys, according to Telhami, who suggested that it
may be evidence of a "backlash" against US foreign policy, which is
seen as increasingly directed against "Muslims" (OneWorld 2004). A
Pew 2003 survey showed that 86 percent of Pakistanis, 82 percent of
Indonesians, 73 percent of Jordanians, and 41 percent of Turks thought
that "Islam should play a major role in [their] nation's political life. This
view was supported by only one-third of the people in countries with
more secular traditions, such as Senegal and Mali" (Allen 2005).

Religiosity

Religiosity in this project is measured as the combined factor of two
indicators: refraining from alcoholic beverages and observing daily
prayers (alpha = 0.926, as discussed in Appendix 3).[4]

The impact on democratic norms. The more Muslims in the study
observed Islamic rituals, the less supportive they were of democratic
norms in the cases of Bahrain, Bangladesh, Europe, Gambia, India,
Indonesia, Jordan, Kuwait, Nigeria, Oman, Pakistan, Qatar, Saudi
Arabia, Turkmenistan, the United Arab Emirates, and Yemen. This is a
very intriguing result, especially since it is uniform across a sizable
number of countries that are quite dissimilar in terms of their respective
history, economic status, and political experiences. This finding would
make sense if committed Muslims were predominantly traditionalists.
However, traditionalists in all these countries combined were around 16
percent of the respondents, while religious people (those who observed
at least 80 percent of the rituals) constituted approximately 27 percent of
the respondents.

Use of focus-group discussions was a must to reveal why a committed Muslim would be less tolerant toward women and minorities than a
less committed Muslim. There was a consensus among the interviewees
that committed Muslims tend to hear sermons and Islamic audiotapes
that subject them to a certain type of Islamic rhetoric. Muslims' intolerance, then, is a function of the discourses disseminated by *ulama*
through sermons and audiotapes—an issue that will be discussed in the
next section.

Why has this type of effect not appeared in countries such as Egypt
and Iran, especially since they are known for having extremely vocal
and efficient *ulama*, both official and unofficial? I took this question to
Salim al-Awa, a renowned Islamic thinker and researcher from Egypt

who has very solid ties with *ulama* and Islamic thinkers throughout the Muslim world. Given his knowledge of most of the countries studied here, he manifested no astonishment regarding these results. He noted that the Saudi and Gulf states' religious discourse has not been traditionally pluralist. This discourse is currently changing, but it will take time for these changes to have an effect on people's thinking. In Egypt and Iran, by contrast, the majority of committed Muslims are not absolutists because of their exposure to pluralist religious discourses of the *salafi* (traditionalist and conservative) and progressive *ulama*. They are part of the mainstream, moderate live-and-let-live reading of Islam.

The impact on democratic institutions. The more Muslims observe Islamic rituals in Europe, Indonesia, Lebanon, Malaysia, Morocco, Oman, Qatar, Senegal, Sudan, and Turkey, the more supportive they are of democratic institutions. Conversely, in Saudi Arabia, the United Arab Emirates, Yemen, and Algeria, the more religious that Muslims are, the less supportive of democratic institutions they are. In the remaining countries, there is no statistically significant relationship between religiosity and support for democratic mechanisms and procedures. This result calls into question the sweeping assertion that Muslims refuse freedom because it sanctions "disposable marriages, sexual license and abortion on demand as much as it does self-government and the rule of law" (Pipes 2003).

Perception of Islam as Religion and State

This section discusses the effect of Islam not as a religion but as a political ideology. Thus, the more strongly one agrees with the slogan "Islam as a religion and a state," the more Islamist one is (question 26, Appendix 2). The less one believes in it, the more secularist one is. Some commentators have made democracy in the Middle East contingent upon secularism (Binder 1988; Gellner 1991, Gellner 1992; Sharabi 1988; Tibi 1998). Most researchers in the West and secularists in the Muslim world think that Islamists with political power would seriously set back the cause of democratization in the Muslim world. Two reasons are usually advanced. First, Islamists are the clearest embodiment of Islam's antidemocratic nature. Islam is inherently antidemocratic, and Islamists are the most antidemocratic Muslims. Second, certain Islamists who have attained power have proved to be less democratic than they had claimed while in opposition, specifically the mullahs of Iran and Hassan al-Turabi in the Sudan. And though the Islamic

Salvation Front's electoral victory was nullified in Algeria, it had sent a clear message of antidemocratic rule through its lack of commitment to future free and fair elections.

Some commentators predict a gloomy future for democracy in the Muslim world because of the widespread politicizing of Islam, especially among young men and women. Muslim secularists judge that the support of political Islam, which is unequivocally antidemocratic in their minds, is rooted in the failure of all secular programs of political and economic development, concomitant with military defeats in major wars since independence in the 1950s and 1960s. Consider the words of an Egyptian secular intellectual interviewed by the *New York Times* in Cairo: "'It's easy for the average Egyptian to say, we tried modernity but it didn't take us anywhere and we didn't become Europe,' said Tarek Heggy, a wealthy Cairo businessman and political analyst. 'It's easy for him to say, we tried pan-Arabism and it didn't work. And, if he's a simple-minded person, he might say they didn't work because God wasn't with us'" (Sachs 2001a). Others concur: Muslims are less influenced by "scriptural principles than by immediate political, social and economic needs" (Abrahamian 1993).

Some secularists also argue that *ulama*, shaikhs, and imams of mosques have poisoned the well of secularism in the Muslim world by "quoting certain verses that lead Muslims to believe that secularism is equal to disbelief and infidelity," as an Iranian housewife explained. Ironically, George Holyoke coined the term *secularism* in 1854 to convey the value of the non-religious arena and to distinguish it from such terms as "infidel, skeptic and atheist" (Holyoke 1860). Holyoke's success in the West is as magnificent as his failure in the Muslim world, where the term has been rejected by the masses as a loanword or neologism whose meaning is popularly perceived as antithetical to Islam itself.

The impact on democratic norms. Results of the Seemingly Unrelated Regressions (SUR) and logistic regression models, as summarized in Table 3.1, indicate that the association between political Islam and the lack of tolerance for women and minorities has a certain validity in some countries but not in others. The more people support a political role for Islam in Egypt, India, Tunisia, and Turkey, the more they also support democratic norms. Islamists of Algeria, Indonesia, Lebanon, Mali, Nigeria, Pakistan, Saudi Arabia, the Sudan, the United Arab Emirates, and Yemen, by contrast, are less tolerant toward women and minorities than are secularists of the same societies. This discrepancy is understandable in light of the recent histories of the two sets of countries. Many modernist Islamists—who have a greater presence in the first set of countries—simply argue that tolerance is the essence of Islam. Tariq al-Bishri of Egypt explains that Islam "has a long history of justice, pluralism, coexistence, and perseverance of rights of non-Muslims."

It is also notable, however, that many of the more tolerant societies have been subjected to a kind of top-down secularization. And within these secularist societies, most modernist Islamists have learned to denounce any acts of terrorism in their home country, congratulate non-Muslims on their religious feasts, nominate a woman for public office, publicly declare their respect for democracy and commitment to abide by it if in power, and adopt the most liberal interpretation of debatable verses and hadiths. Whether modernists will be committed democrats or not when in power is an issue beyond our capacity to predict, but they are definitely changing their discourse to neutralize secular attacks on them.

There is a bit of irony in the observation that secularization must be imposed from the top to promote democratic norms, particularly because most Muslims view Islam as an integral component of any democratic system they would support. As Hamed Ramadan of the Sudan put it: "When you read the Quran you find many verses discuss governance issues such as *hudud* [penal codes], *shura*, and responsibility of Muslims to apply Allah's *hokm* [rule]. What shall we do with them? Ignore them or rewrite the Quran to please the secularists?" A prominent Muslim intellectual echoes this sentiment, arguing, "Secularism is necessarily atheistic" (Rahman 1982: 15). And a 2003 survey in Iraq demonstrated that while 90 percent of Iraqis wanted democracy over other forms of government, two-thirds believed that Islam should play a major role in governance, and 61 percent "agreed that the government should be made up mainly of religious leaders" (ORI 2003). Furthermore, top-down secularization has more often than not meant the suppression of basic political and civil rights and a slide into autocracy. "In Turkey, Ataturk closed all madrassas, forced the Sufis underground and forced men and women to wear Western dress. In Iran, Shah Reza Pahlavi gave orders to shoot at hundreds of demonstrators protesting compulsory Western dress. In that environment, you can see how secularization is experienced as an assault" (Armstrong 2002). "Many Muslims recognize the conundrum: when a government tries to impose a new version of religious correctness, it is a political act, and no one has yet figured out how to remove religion from politics without paying a price" (Sachs 2001b).

Finally, it is questionable how sustainable secular regimes are in the Muslim world considering the fall of the Pahlavi regime in Iran and the electoral success of Islamic parties in Turkey and Algeria (though the results were nullified in the latter case). Indeed, Islamists are the main opposition group in almost all officially secular Muslim-majority states, from Indonesia to Mauritania.

How do we explain the clear lack of tolerance among Islamists in the latter group of countries? With the exception of the United Arab Emirates, in the past thirty years all these countries have been through violent tension for which Islam has been either a cause or justification. This tension seems to exert a negative effect on the level of tolerance and support for minorities' political rights.

It may be, then, that the best way to promote tolerance among Islamists is to focus on the cause of hostilities among them and to create structures that minimize conflict, short of forced secularization—admittedly no small task.

The impact on democratic institutions.   Unlike the diverse impact of support for political Islam on democratic norms, this project finds no statistically significant differences between Islamist and non-Islamist individuals' attitudes toward democratic institutions in any of the cases. This result confirms the logic of differentiating between democratic norms, which seem to be more problematic, and democratic institutions.

Compatibility of Shura and Democracy

Most Muslims tend to think of an ideal Islamic political system as one based on *shura*. In fact, some thinkers have propagated the concept of "shuracracy" to refer to the Islamic political system (Nehnah 1999). My survey therefore explicitly asked respondents to relate *shura* to democracy (question 21, Appendix 2). The logic behind this question is best made clear by the following statement: "The existence of democracies depends, other things being equal, on the popularization of the idea of democracy, in the sense that a clear understanding of what democracy is about is a major condition (although not the only one) for behaving democratically. For wrong ideas about democracy make a democracy go wrong" (Sartori 1962: 5).

Arguably, the more Muslims perceive democracy as a modern application of Islamic *shura*, the more supportive they will be of its norms and institutions. It was hoped that empirical examination of the pooled data would reveal the truth or falsity of this assumption.

In one of the most consistent results in this study, one finds that people who believe in the compatibility of *shura* and democracy are more supportive of democratic institutions and norms. This effect is present in almost all cases but is noticeably stronger and more frequent with respect to democratic institutions than in regard to democratic norms (see Table 3.1). Muslims in countries such as Indonesia, Lebanon, Libya, Nigeria, Tajikistan, Turkmenistan, and the United Arab Emirates were more supportive of democratic institutions the more they believed in the compatibility of *shura* and publicly elected and accountable institutions. However, in these same countries a belief in the compatibility of *shura* and democracy did not have any impact on regard for democratic norms.

A possible explanation stems from the fact that the process of Islamic *shura* was usually limited to pious Muslims rather than extended to non-Muslims or ordinary men. Though the Prophet Muhammad himself was known to consult everybody, including women and non-Muslims, many Muslim *ulama*, fearing the plots and conspiracies of hypocrites and non-Muslims, limited the candidates for *shura* to the most pious of the *ummah* (nation). Muslims of the societies that support democratic institutions and mechanisms as modern applications of *shura* thus do not extend *shura* to mean trust of and tolerance toward non-Muslims and women.

The finding cited above confirms the oft-made claim that Islam pervades the collective Muslim consciousness, but it also lends credence to the modernist Islamist reading of the compatibility between Islam and democracy.

Focus-group discussions were an indispensable source of information regarding the underlying reasons for the survey result. To learn how Muslims relate *shura* to democracy, I sought the participants' opinions on why the system of *shura* did not hold throughout Muslim history and was employed only at the discretion of the leader. Most responded that the system of *shura* assumes a certain level of *iman* (piety) on the part of the ruler and the ruled. However, there was almost complete consensus on blaming the rulers and their corrupt henchmen, including some *ulama al-sultan* (religious scholars of authority), for corrupting the inherently noble principle.

Most interviewed Muslims did not think of the rightly guided caliphs (the first four caliphs after the death of prophet Mohamed) as rulers in the literal sense of the word. These caliphs are *governors* who do not make up rules. They just govern according to the Allah-given rules, and when there are different interpretations of Allah's rules, they choose, upon consultation, the one that best fits. Thus under Islamic sharia, there is no place for arbitrary authority without infringing upon key Islamic principles. The system of *shura* collapsed, however, when the caliphs became rulers.

Responses such as this took the discussions to the issue of democracy and its capacity to drop the assumption of *iman* on the part of the rulers and the ruled. The interviewees were asked, "Can democracy be introduced as a replacement of *shura*?" Participants' answers were divided among several options:

1. *Shura* is superior to democracy, but democracy is still good (36 percent of the interviewees agreed).
2. *Shura* is equal to democracy. *Democracy* and *shuracracy* are synonyms. Democracy is just a modern representation of *shura* (33 percent of the interviewees agreed).
3. Democracy is evil or even apostasy. *Shura* is not only superior to democracy but is its antithesis (12 percent of the interviewees agreed).
4. Democracy is inherently superior to *shura* (11 percent of the interviewees agreed).

The first two groups of interviewees, clearly forming the majority, thought that democracy is genuinely compatible with the Islamic principle of *shura*, but not necessarily from an Islamist point of view. That is, some secularists believe that Islam's principle of *shura*, which was actually practiced by Arabs before Islam, makes Islam inherently pluralistic. Modernists argue, meanwhile, that some aspects of democracy are Islamizable as a means to the common end of fighting dictatorship.

The *first group* (36 percent of the interviewees) believes that *shura* is superior to democracy for two reasons. First, *shura* is a religious, social, and economic principle. Democracy, from their point of view, is a political system only. A participant in Libya stated that "Muslims are required to consult on everything they are doing. Even a man is required to consult his wife on their daughter's future husband." The obligation of a husband to consult his wife is truly an Islamic principle. Ironically, however, most of the interviewees did not acknowledge the absence of legal and political mechanisms to apply the principle of *shura* to these other arenas.

Second, some of the interviewees referred to the different roots of the two systems. In a democracy, humankind is the master of the world. What one's mind surmises to be true becomes "true" even without reference to or adherence to any moral or ethical code. In democracies, the fallible human mind is sovereign. The people are the source of the law, and the law is meant to ensure the will of the majority, even if they defy all ethical and divine principles. A Syrian physician who was interviewed in Saudi Arabia cited the cases of colonialism, slavery, and racism throughout Europe and North Africa as examples of how the rule of the majority may lead to unethical results. *Shura*, in contrast, is limited to the arenas for which Allah "has not revealed His just commands. . . . Only in these areas, Muslims can consult and make decisions on one condition, which is not to violate Allah's rules."

Despite their belief that *shura* is superior to democracy, the first group favored democratic institutions and mechanisms as acceptable tools to implement the great principle of *shura*. An Algerian female graduate student used the example of the car in comparison to the horses that early Muslims used for transportation. In her own words: "Prophet Muhammad and his companions used camels and horses. Had they known cars and trains, they would have used them. . . . Likewise, had they known elections and parliaments, they would have adopted them."

The *second group* of Muslims (33 percent of the interviewees), who believed in the absolute compatibility of *shura* and democracy, emphasized the similar essence of the two. Limiting rulers' arbitrary rule and establishing the consequent rule of law are common purposes of both *shura* and democracy. Thus they are on an equal moral footing.

To this group of interviewees, "had the Prophet lived in the twentieth century, he would have prescribed a democratic system of government . . . excluding the taboos," as an Algerian Islamist put it. An Iranian student and activist pointed out: "During the Prophet's time, sharia functioned as a complete code of ethics that stipulates for every contingency. Muslims deliberate and eventually the Prophet judges. There is no Prophet anymore." Such logic leads some Iranians to think highly of democracy without assuming the superiority of Western values. The best exemplification of this attitude is Shaikh Mahfoud Nahna's concept of shuracracy as a "Catholic marriage between *shura* and democracy" (Kutty 1998).

The *third group* of interviewees (12 percent) would consider it a compromise of God's supremacy (represented in sharia) to transfer decisionmaking to human actors through democracy. The interviewees who considered *shura* far superior to democracy postulated that the outcome of *shura* is not binding by any quantitative measurement (majority rule, for instance). The only criterion is to fulfill Allah's pleasure. None of the interviewees could come up with an empirically verifiable way to judge if one's opinion fulfills Allah's pleasure without assuming that (some) humans have perfect access to God's will and intentions. If they did, why would they need consultation at all? An Algerian interviewee in a somewhat loud voice accused me of "repeating by rote the Westerners' logic of thinking."[5]

The *fourth group* (11 percent) found democracy, with its separation of powers and institutionalized checks and balances, superior to *shura* and considered it an inherently Arab practice that had existed before Islam and fit well with the tribal nature of pre-Islamic Arabia. This position does not mean that Islam is incompatible with democracy. These respondents echoed the traditional secularist position that Islam as a religion has been used to justify different political and economic systems based on one's choice of holy texts and interpretations.

Three observations can sum up the effect of Islam on Muslims' perception of democracy at the individual level. First, all the interviewees, even secularists, perceived Islam in absolute terms. In the mind of most Muslims, Islam is equivalent to Truth, Goodness, and Beauty. If democracy is good, then it is Islamic. If it is bad, it is not Islamic. This assertion is related to almost every other issue. To most of my interlocutors, a good Muslim cannot do such a horrible thing as carry out the September 11 attacks. If the attacks were committed by Muslims, then they were not good Muslims. A Gallup survey supported this finding: 61 percent of the 1,000 Muslims polled said they did not believe Muslim groups carried out the September 11 terrorist attacks, and around 21 percent said they were not sure (Gallup 2002).

Second, Islam is a very important vehicle for Muslims to differentiate between what is acceptable and what is not acceptable. According to Muqatder Khan, "Islam is common sense. But to convince some Muslims of certain conclusions, one has to color his argument with an Islamic discourse."[6] Any position with an Islamic logic and rhetoric acquires more legitimacy and appeal among most Muslims. I found this thinking very common among the overwhelming majority of the interviewees, and it allowed many to support the practice of democracy.

Third, the influence of Islam on Muslims' perceptions of democracy is not a spontaneous phenomenon. Rather, it is the outcome of the effort of *ulama*, shaikhs, and imams who function as cultural entrepreneurs and agents of political socialization. The overwhelming majority of Muslims who read the Quran hardly relate it to everyday issues. They usually need the *ulama* to interpret the verses for them. If a Muslim is taught that democracy is antithetical to Islam's principle of *shura*, the chance that he or she will refuse democracy is very high, and vice versa (Maddy-Weitzman 1997).

Concluding Remarks

The analysis provided here suggests two larger conclusions. First, the typical profile of a prodemocratic Muslim is a female who is affluent and better educated. Prodemocracy Muslims also are likely to have experienced democracy through previous voting and/or living in a democratic country for a year or longer, to believe that democracy is an extension or application of the Islamic principle of *shura*, and to have a negative attitude toward undemocratically elected Muslim rulers.

That said, Muslims who hold similar political values often do so for heterogeneous reasons. Factors such as income, age, and religiosity, which are correlated with prodemocratic views in one Muslim society, can be associated with negative views of democracy in another. Thus it is wise to avoid any facile, one-size-fits-all interpretation of Muslim political values.

The next chapter will focus on the political actors who are perceived as responsible for the perpetuation of autocracy or to be credible agents of democratization. Three actors in particular will be discussed: incumbent rulers, the West, and *ulama*.

Notes

1. The Saudi government has started a program of "revising school curriculums, condemning Islamic extremism and easing restrictions on the press" and working hard on "promoting a tolerant and pluralist vision of Islam" in the Saudi education system; these reforms may result in a different type of graduate (Kristof 2002a). These revisions have been adopted as part of the war on terrorism as well as some anticipated political reforms.

2. www.Islamweb.net/fatwas, Fatwa 5141.

3. Available online: www.rsf.fr/article.php3?id_article=4116.

4. Around 8 percent of the interviewees did not hold consistent or clear attitudes.

5. Concern for my physical safety guided me to change the topic and accept his answer as the final word.

6. Here I am quoting from memory.

4

Muslim Public Opinion and Dictatorship

By now it should be clear that decades of excusing and accommodating tyranny [in the Middle East] in the pursuit of stability have only led to injustice and instability and tragedy.
—US president George W. Bush, March 8, 2005

Who, in the mind of Muslims, are the actors responsible for the dearth of democracy in the Muslim world? And can they function as credible agents of democratization? The two questions are closely related. This chapter explores literate Muslims' reading of the main three actors who have, through their action or lack of action, steered Muslim countries to autocratic rule. These three actors, as determined by the respondents, are incumbent rulers, the West, and the *ulama*. Literate Muslims not only pinpoint the actors but give some useful insights into the mechanisms used by these actors to perpetuate dictatorship in the Muslim world.

The Incumbent Elites

To understand Muslims' views about incumbent elites, respondents were asked to choose between incumbents and democratic rulers (question 43, Appendix 2). As shown in Table 4.1, it is clear that almost all Muslim polities face a legitimacy crisis. Only 14 percent of Muslims are proincumbent, according to the survey, and these amounted to 10 percent of focus-group participants. Educated Muslims least supportive of incumbents were Kuwaitis, Egyptians, Syrians, Moroccans, Sudanese, Malians, and Gambians.

Table 4.1   Prodemocratic or Proincumbent (percentage)

Country	Proincumbent	Not Sure	Pro–Democratic Rulers
UAE	93	3	4
Oman	65	17	18
Turkey	37	6	57
Albania	35	7	58
India	34	11	55
Qatar	34	18	48
Senegal	34	14	52
Mali	32	11	57
Jordan	16	28	56
Libya	15	30	55
Pakistan	15	35	50
Tajikistan	14	31	55
Algeria	13	35	52
Indonesia	13	38	49
Lebanon	13	18	69
Saudi Arabia	12	51	31
Bahrain	12	29	59
Bangladesh	12	27	61
Malaysia	12	48	40
Iran	11	36	53
Nigeria	11	36	53
Tunisia	11	34	55
Turkmenistan	10	21	69
Yemen	10	43	47
Gambia	6	24	70
Morocco	6	31	63
Sudan	6	26	68
Syria	6	23	71
Egypt	5	20	75
Kuwait	4	8	88
Average	20	25	55

Source: E-mail and written survey 2002.

Only the United Arab Emirates can be considered to have a system of government with clear mass support among its literate citizens, with 93 percent of respondents asserting that the status quo is better than a democratically elected ruler. Among most of its citizens, there was clear support for the regime headed by Shaikh Zayid al-Nahyan, who founded the United Arab Emirates. Based on the interviews with Emirati citizens, it was clear that democracy was not on the agenda of the public and that the political status quo was highly desired. As one interviewee indicated, "Westerners . . . do not understand our system. We do not need to vote to check the government and solve problems. Voting is going to upset the social balance in society."

Although the United Arab Emirates is the only Arab Gulf state that does not have any kind of electoral political representation, it enjoys a high degree of political stability. This is most certainly due to the country's affluence: with gross national product (GNP) per capita at roughly $22,800, the United Arab Emirates is the richest of the thirty-two Muslim countries surveyed. Stability might also be attributable to the extensive social freedoms that UAE citizens enjoy compared to citizens of neighboring countries. Further, the equal disenfranchisement of Emiratis may be a secret blessing if it serves to tamp down tensions resulting from the heterogeneity of the UAE population. Seventy-two percent of those living in the United Arab Emirates are noncitizens, and there is a divide between the majority Sunnis and minority Shiites, who amount to 7 percent of the population.

After the United Arab Emirates, Oman came in second, with 65 percent of the population preferring the unelected incumbents over publicly elected rulers. Sultan Qabus Bin Said's appealing personality and his modernization efforts have generated substantial support among Omani citizens. Some political reforms, including the elected *shura* council with limited powers and the enfranchisement of women, have led the country one step on the path of tactical liberalization. Like the United Arab Emirates, Oman's relative affluence with $8,200 gross domestic product (GDP) per capita helps to offset the potentially destabilizing effect of religious plurality among different sects of Islam (Barnett 2003).

Malaysians, Yemenis, and Saudis, though not pro-incumbent, seemed to be dubious about what democracy could bring that might improve on the status quo. Forty-eight, 43, and 51 percent of the respondents, respectively, were not sure about democracy. Yet given the restrictiveness of Saudi society, it might be surprising that 31 percent of Saudis were in favor of democratically elected rulers. Trying to interpret these numbers, a Saudi university professor commented, "Most Saudis want change, but not necessarily democracy. If democracy leads to change, they may reluctantly accept both."

Though proincumbents are clearly in the minority in most Muslim countries, it is helpful to understand why some people would support nondemocratic incumbents. The focus-group discussions shed light on this phenomenon. One interesting finding is that most of these proincumbents adopted the logic of "dictators but . . ." That is to say, there is always a tendency among proincumbent Muslims to justify the autocratic practices of their rulers on grounds such as fighting foreign enemies or preserving national unity (Sudanese interviewees), achieving domestic stability (Egyptian interviewees), redistributing resources more equitably (Libyan and Emirati interviewees), achieving independence (Algerian interviewees), or applying sharia (Saudi and Iranian interviewees).

Muslims who adopt the logic of "dictator but . . ." do not accept the principle of "sinner but . . ." That is to say, when the interviewees who supported incumbents were asked whether they would support a non-pious ruler (I consistently named former US president Bill Clinton as an example) who pursued the ends listed above, they responded with a resounding no. Modernists rejected what they perceived as a false dichotomy between "sinner but" and "dictator but." They preferred a third scenario: a devout Muslim who acts according to *shura* and respects the public will. Secularists, meanwhile, gave no heed to the issue of personal piety. A democratic liberal ruler is preferred to the "shaikh of Islam if the shaikh of Islam is not publicly elected and keeps his understanding of Islam to himself," an American of Lebanese origin commented.

Interestingly, support for incumbents has inconsistent influence on Muslims' support for democratic institutions and norms.

The Impact on Democratic Norms

Table 3.1 suggests that except for the cases of India, Malaysia, Saudi Arabia, and Tajikistan, where there was no statistically significant relationship between opinions about rulers' legitimacy and regard for democratic norms, Muslims who support tolerance of minority and oppressed groups tend to prefer publicly elected rulers. It is not clear, however, whether individuals' support for democratic norms and institutions affects their lack of support for the incumbents or vice versa. It may be that they are mutually reinforcing and that other factors promote both attitudes.

The Impact on Democratic Institutions

There was no relationship between participants' views on incumbents' legitimacy and their preference for democratic institutions in the cases of India, Indonesia, Libya, Saudi Arabia, and Turkmenistan. In the United Arab Emirates and Oman, Muslims who were supportive of the incumbents tended to be less supportive of democratic institutions. In the remaining cases, however, when other variables are held constant, Muslim people tended to be more supportive of democratic institutions the more they supported having publicly elected rulers instead of the incumbents.

The focus-group discussions revealed three trends among Muslims' attitudes toward their rulers. First, secular critics of autocratic Muslim societies always referred to the negative impact of politicizing religion for political gains. They argued that Muslims are passive and parochial subjects because Islam habituates them to obedience and indoctrinates Muslims in fear. One critic of this sort argues that

> Muhammad ruled in accordance with the will of Allah as revealed to him and translated into his own will. Nothing could have been more irrelevant to his rule than the consent of the governed. There was no room for "we the people" or for legislation by elected representatives of the people because the whole body of laws as laid down in the Sharia was valid and binding for all times. That is the reason why parliaments in Muslim countries even today are rubber-stamp bodies. Neither citizens' right to criticize nor to dissent from their rulers are recognized. Islam admonishes Muslims to obey Allah, his Prophet and those in power, as it admonishes women to obey men, because "men are a degree above them." (Ali 2000)

Moreover, Mirza Agha Kermani was once reported to have said, "The rise of the Western powers as masters of the world, and the decline of Muslim nations into abject servitude, are due to one fact only. In Europe, governments fear the people. In Islam people fear the government" (quoted in Taheri 2003)—and for good reason. "From South Asia to North Africa, an entire generation of Muslim intellectuals is at this moment under threat: Many have been killed, silenced, or forced into exile" (Ahmad and Rosen 2002).

Passivity toward government, however, may also result from a sense of religious duty (al-'Azm 1969; Lewis 1988). Most Sunni jurists have argued that "a ruler is not removable from power unless he commits a clear, visible, and major infraction against God" (Abou El Fadl 2003), something on the level of preventing Muslims from praying.

As much as Sunnis may respect this teaching, rulers have manipulated it for their own preservation, and these cynical tactics are not lost on the Muslim public. Indeed, most of the Muslims interviewed for this study—men and women, young and old—had a clear sense of dissatisfaction with their rulers. They believed, however, that they had few options for effecting change.

Hassan Hanafi of Cairo University argues against the notion that all or most Muslims are passive out of obedience and fear. He differentiates among four types of rebellious responses that have existed in Muslim history since the eighth century and still prevail in Muslim societies.

First, there is the militant opposition, for example the *kharijite* (dissidents). Second, there is the manifest opposition according to the famous Islamic principle of enjoining the good and forbidding the evil that was institutionalized into the ancient institution of *hisba* (observing moral codes in markets). Contemporary Muslims still enjoin the good and forbid the evil through modern opposition parties and independent intellectualism. Third, there are secret movements that wait for the opportunity to take over power, like the Shiites under the Sunni caliphate. Fourth, others resort to patience and a waiting obedience, such as ancient schools of Sufism and mysticism.

Hanafi's analysis is borne out by the views expressed by focus-group participants. Of the 188 Muslims who participated in focus groups, only one advanced submission to the ruler as a religious duty. Focus-group discussions also revealed that some Muslims oppose incumbents and support democratically elected politicians as a means to be rid of their rulers. A Tunisian professor interviewed in the United States argued that democracy is equally as good as any other means to get rid of an incumbent. While this bodes well for democracy on the one hand, it is troubling that democracy is appreciated more as a means to an end than as an end in itself. Though we do not know how prevalent this thinking is, a Sudanese student expressed the feeling that democracy would be judged by the outcome of elections. Referring to his own community, he said, "Democracy that brings al-Mirghani [an opposition figure] into power will not be accepted by [a certain] tribe."

The overwhelming majority of the interviewed Muslims did not trust that incumbents would give up power voluntarily. "The rulers do not give up power unless forced," according to an Algerian secondary school teacher. A Saudi computer engineer echoed the same argument: "Swearing by Allah, [the rulers] consider themselves above questioning or accountability. . . . The only way to reform the system is by threatening their thrones. Then they will pay attention to the public's demands."

Take Saudi Arabia as a test case for this argument. In Saudi Arabia, the rebellion of 1979 in Mecca propelled the government to suggest establishing the powerless Shura Council. The unrest calmed down. Some commentators link the reemergence of the Shura Council fourteen years later to the liberation of Kuwait and the crisis of legitimacy that swept over the whole region. After the bombings in Riyadh (May 12, 2003), more reforms were debated and advanced (al-Khazen 2003). There were partial local elections in early 2005 and promises for more partial elections in colleges and athletic and social clubs.

A Shiite Syrian professor of journalism who was exiled in Germany for eleven years was interviewed in the United States. He blames the dearth of democracy on autocratic statist rulers. "Within four months after ousting Saddam Hussein, Iraqis issued 190 newspapers representing all possible Islamic [Sunni and Shiite], Marxist, liberal, nationalist, pan-Arabist, anti-pan-Arabism, Kurdish, and independent trends and streams," he argued. His conclusion: statist rulers are the ultimate factor behind the dearth of freedoms in Muslim countries. A liberal female poet and intellectual from Pakistan concurred that Muslim rulers are responsible for Muslims' plights. "Arab and Muslim rulers are fond of Napoleon, Bismarck, and Machiavellian politics rather than being students of Washington, Locke, or Mill."

Is the West a Credible Agent of Democratization?

For several years, the United States has mounted strong rhetorical, diplomatic, and military campaigns for the democratization of Muslim countries. Bush proudly declared in 2003 that "after defeating enemies, we did not leave behind occupying armies, we left constitutions and parliaments." The United States assumes that a democratic Middle East will be safer and eventually less hostile toward the West, following the famous Kantian axiom that "democracies do not fight each other." The current campaign raises two questions: First, is the West trusted by Muslims to act as a credible agent of democratization? Second, is it true that a more democratic Muslim world will be less hostile toward the West?

These questions were explored using the survey data, focus-group discussions, and elite interviews. First, respondents in the survey were asked to (strongly) agree or (strongly) disagree to the following five-point statement: "The West (the US and its allies such as Britain) does not want Muslims to freely elect their rulers" (question 29, Appendix 2). While this survey was completed before the US invasion of Iraq, the results should still offer some indication of how Muslims perceive the West's attempts to establish democratic constitutions and parliaments in the Muslim world. The survey reveals that, across the board, Muslims are highly skeptical that the West is really sincere in boosting prodemocratic changes in the Muslim world.

Only 8 percent of Muslims surveyed either trusted or strongly trusted that the United States really supports free and fair elections in the Muslim world; 17 percent of US Muslims trusted their country's interest in a democratic Muslim world. This distrust of the Western commitment to democracy reached its highest level in four Arab countries, none of them a surprise: Syria, the Sudan, Libya, and Yemen. Between 72 and 73 percent of literate Muslims in these four countries (strongly) agreed that the West (the United States and its allies) do not want Muslims to freely elect their rulers.

These results confirm the findings of a 2002 Gallup survey: "The people of Islamic nations also believe that Western nations do not respect Arab or Islamic values, do not support Arab causes, and do not exhibit fairness towards Arabs, Muslims, or in particular, the situation in Palestine."

If anything, these feelings are likely to have intensified since President Bush's public and diplomatic campaigns to democratize the Middle East and Muslim world. Indeed, for months, newspapers throughout the Arab world unleashed a barrage of angry articles that denounced the Bush administration's stance on democracy, calling into question its sincerity and attacking it as a smoke screen designed to distract attention from Bush's real agenda: to grab Iraq's oil and give Israeli Prime Minister Ariel Sharon a free hand in dealing with the Palestinians (Ottaway 2003).

A postwar commentary based on the Pew Global Attitudes Project supports this assessment: "There is no evidence, however, that support for democracy will necessarily do much to diminish the extensive anti-Americanism throughout the Muslim World. In Pakistan, those who strongly support democratic values . . . are just as hostile to the United States as those who place little or no importance on such values" (Allen 2005).

Even the Bush administration has acknowledged the United States' long history of opportunistic policies in the Muslim world. Secretary of State Condoleezza Rice referred to the argument made by many Arab and Muslim scholars that the United Sates has actively promoted autocracy in the Middle East. She said, speaking first in the voice of these scholars, "You [US government] talk about democracy in Latin America, you talk about democracy in Europe, you talk about democracy in Asia and Africa but you never talk about democracy in the Middle East. [In her own voice:] And, of course, they were right because this was the decision that stability trumped everything, and what we were getting was neither stability nor democracy" (Rice 2005).

A group of modernist Muslims watched Senator John McCain on videotape, inquiring why the United States does not force Saudis to do something revolutionary like allowing women to sit in the driver's seat of the car (McCain 2002). Though critical of the subordination of women in Muslim countries, the Muslim viewers highly resented the senator's comment, since it reflected a great deal of disrespect for their traditions.

Even where intense distrust of Western institutions was evidenced among Muslims, these feelings did not translate into distrust of democracy. The seemingly unrelated regression and multiple logistic regressions models portrayed in Table 3.1 show that the distrust variable does not explain much. This is not surprising when one considers that distrust of the United States among Muslims is almost a constant or universal, while support for democracy is much more variable.

Fearing that this result might be the artifact of this specific question, I used another three-point-scale question that was meant to measure, among other things, the relationship between the West (among other factors) and autocracy in the Muslim world (question 42, Appendix 2). The question read: "Which one of the following reasons can best explain why dictatorship prevails in the Muslim world? (Check all that apply.)" One of the possible options is "The West (by supporting authoritarian rulers)." A three-point scale was developed to quantify the respondents' choice among "a very important reason," "a somewhat important reason," and "not a reason at all."

When the three-point scale was used instead of the previous five-point scale in the regression models, differences emerged for three groups. The Malaysians and Senegalese were more supportive of democratic institutions the more they blamed the West for supporting authoritarian rulers. Also, the significant relationship between trusting the West and support for democratic norms among the Albanians disappeared. That said, the descriptive statistics of the three-point scale question show a highly consistent tendency among Muslims to blame the West for supporting Muslim authoritarian rulers.

How would Muslims defend their argument that the West is behind their political plight? It is enough to sit down with a Muslim to get a litany of offenses—the Crusades colonialism, the imposition of arbitrary political borders that have fomented civil unrest, the nurturing of repressive rulers, and support for Israel, among many others. An Indonesian cited what he saw as the West's double standard in supporting independence for East Timor but not for Palestine and Chechnya.

Four broad lessons can be learned from Muslims' open discussions of the role the West plays in their political lives and the West's capacity to work as an agent of democratization. First, Western support of Muslim rulers is not perceived positively by most Muslims even if it takes the form of economic and military aid. On several occasions my interlocutors talked about the West as the Muslim rulers' real constituency. Judged by the focus-group discussions, most Muslims perceive the negative role of the West as the "in, out, and on" game: for the West to remain *in* the Muslim world, it needs to keep anti-Western rulers *out* of power and the West's henchmen *on* top of power. Thus, the West works very hard to make sure that elections will never bring its enemies into power. With the exception of the United Arab Emirates, there was a clear sense of resentment and lack of trust among most Muslim interviewees regarding the role the West plays in their countries. "Why would the West support both Iran and Iraq fighting each other? Why would the West turn a cold shoulder to the army's intervention in Algeria? Why would the West support the mujahidin and then destroy them? Why would the West encourage Saddam to invade Kuwait and then push him out? They know what they want. Tell them that we know what they want too," Shaikh H. al-Hamid of Saudi Arabia argued in an interview. "The West has an agenda to be superior over the Muslim world. They will achieve it as far as [our] rulers work for them," an Egyptian science teacher said. A Syrian male working in the field of information systems in the United States said, "They [the West] want their own tailored version of democracy that serves their own interests." In his mind, if the West encourages democracy, it is the kind of democracy that excludes Arab nationalists or Islamists.

Second, this lack of trust is highly related to a sense of humiliation among most educated Muslims. According to a Lebanese female schoolteacher: "Muslims are not Muslims any more. Our food is Western, our cars are Japanese, our shirts are Chinese, our [political] borders were not decided by us. . . . I think this is the worst period in Muslims' history." Holy Scripture tells Muslims that they are the best nation to come to humanity because of their capacity to enjoin the good and forbid the evil. Yet "instead of being one of the leaders of world civilization, Muslims found themselves quickly and permanently reduced to a dependent bloc by the European and later the American military, economic, political and cultural dominance" (Armstrong 2000: 21).

Many Muslims attribute this situation to Western oppression. Indeed, when Muslims talk about a clash of civilizations between the West and the Muslim world, they see it as the West's war on Islam rather than the war of Islam on the West. A Libyan professor of business administration who lived for eleven years in five European and North American countries said, "Muslims have been the target of the West since the eighth century. The West knows that there is a religion behind us that teaches us not to be like them in their worship of the dollar." He wanted to teach me the following lesson: "The West is not Christian. It has no God. The only God they have is the dollar and franc. Their place of worship is the stock market." This professor, like other Muslims I interviewed, was very articulate in portraying the Arab and Muslim leaders as defenders of Western interests in the Muslim world. One could debate the truth of this claim, but what is inescapable is how pervasive this thinking is.

A group of highly educated Tunisian Muslims complained that in their country they have to shave their beards and to limit their attendance at mosques for fear that they will be suspected of being Islamists. Ben Ali eliminated all Islamist opposition through police action, nationalized all the mosques, locked their doors except for prayers, and is strictly monitoring the sermons of its government-employed prayer leaders, who are often heard making supplication to the president as part of their prayer rituals. My Tunisian interlocutors, who are by no means fanatics or extremists, attributed this perplexing situation to the elites' attempts to Westernize the country by force. This feeling that Muslims are just following a Western model without having a real say in their affairs exacerbates the sense of humiliation among Muslims. "Is it his father's farm to run it as he pleases? Why does not he have real elections and let everybody express his solution?" one of the interviewees lamented, referring to the ruler of his country.

It is paradoxical that most Muslims who are in favor of Western democratic values and systems find the West responsible for preserving autocratic regimes. An Algerian taxi driver who lived in France for six years lamented, "Democracy is like a success recipe. Whoever owns it has the key to success. The West does not want us to have it and blames us as being unfit to have it." A law professor from Bahrain, asked whether he believed that the United States would support democracy in oil-producing countries if that meant an increase in oil prices, firmly answered no. Even Graham Fuller, former vice-chair of the National Intelligence Council at the Central Intelligence Agency, recognizes that "many Muslims are very angry since they prefer to adopt Western values of democracy, human rights, and pluralism but they cannot" (Fuller 2001).

Antagonism against the West is not limited to violent traditionalists. Yet violent traditionalists put the West, rulers of Muslim countries, and whoever is silent about their wrongdoing in the same basket. A famous statement by al-Zawahri is highly striking: "We have chosen to blow up the Egyptian embassy in Pakistan instead of the US embassy due to shortage in resources" (al-Zawahri 2001). All the interviewed made it clear that killing Westerners is not their first choice; they would do it only if forced. If there is a clash of civilizations, they argued that it will be because the West wants it.

Third, Muslims in general think of the West as conspirators against Islam and Muslims. As two Iranian secular researchers living in the United States put it: "To Muslim minds, the West and its ways have become a powerful myth—evil, impenetrable, and incomprehensible. . . . But sadly, the great and brilliant works of the West's 'Orientalists' have found no echo in a Muslim school of 'Occidentalism'" (Boroumand and Boroumand 2002: 15–16). When Al-Qaida was blamed for the attacks of September 11, it was reported that "many people in Cairo reacted with anger and disbelief. 'Every time it has to be Muslims to blame, every time!' shouted Amaal Abdel Rabboh, a housewife of 42, outside a mosque on Friday. 'Our blood is cheap, eh? No, our blood is precious and the American blood is water. Bin Laden is just an excuse to occupy Afghanistan'" (Sachs 2001a).

Many Muslims do not think that the description of the war against terrorism as a crusade was a slip of a tongue; rather, it was an accurate depiction. "For a couple of thousands of people dying in New York, tens of thousands of Muslims die in Afghanistan. What about those who died in Palestine, Iraq, Somalia, the Sudan, and Kashmir?" Mustapha from Algeria exclaimed. A March 2004 Pew Survey found that "70% of Jordanians [and] 66% of Moroccans believe that the suicide bombings of Americans and other Westerners in Iraq are justifiable" (Allen 2005).

Muslims who believe in a Zionist-Western conspiracy against them usually start by thinking that any goal chosen by the United States and its allies will be in Israel's interest and thus is against Muslims' benefit. A Jordanian housewife in the United Arab Emirates used the example of the Jordanian government's campaign on birth control to show that the US government puts pressure on and provides medical aid to the Jordanian government to lower the number of Muslim births as a service to the Zionist project in the region.

The conspiracy theory employed by most Muslims has some basis in fact, according to Abdullah Al-Nefessi, a political science professor from Kuwait, who refers to a five-stage Western plan to distort the evolution of the Muslim world and uproot it from its origin. The stages are as follows: the violence against Muslims during military occupation; the partitioning of the Muslim world into heterogeneous states and countries; the solidifying of these divisions through the creation of capitals, flags, and diplomatic recognition; the enforcing of linguistic

Westernization by making the use of Arabic illegal; the creation of economic dependency on the West; and the creation and support of Israel to preserve the gains of the preceding four stages (Al-Nefessi 2002).

Fourth, there is a specific antagonism against the United States. Most of the respondents equate the West with its leader, the United States. For instance, a Gallup survey that was conducted before the US invasions of Afghanistan and Iraq found that overall views of the United States among Muslims were not positive: 53 percent of the Muslims questioned had unfavorable opinions of the United States, while 22 percent had favorable opinions (Gallup 2002). A student at Assut University in Upper Egypt cited the famous Egyptian play *My Mother America*, in which the United States is portrayed as the evil mother of poor Arabs. In the play the United States sponsors a project for the rights of donkeys while clearly violating the rights of Arab human beings by stealing their wealth, supporting their enemies, and propagating an image of them as terrorists.

The Islamic thinker Mohamed Omara of Egypt clarifies that Muslims are not against American science, values, technology, or individuals. They are against the US project to control and reshape Muslims' minds. As a modernist Islamist himself, he thinks that his mission is to derail this project by uncovering the elements of strength in Islam and developing an authentic Islamic alternative.

However, evidence from other sources suggests that this anti-Americanism is not limited to Muslims. "Even in close allies like South Korea, there has long been a deep strain of anger among ordinary people at supposed American arrogance, bullying and high-handedness" (Kristof 2002b). A US ambassador to South Korea, Thomas C. Hubbard, has argued that the United States may be well served allowing such resentment to be expressed: "When Koreans were able to express their anger in the late 1980's and early 1990's, they let off steam and the frustration dissipated. In short, we may be best off if radical clerics in Saudi Arabia and Pakistan remain free to denounce us" (quoted in Kristof 2002b).

Due to my ignorance of Korean culture, I cannot draw any lessons from the Korean situation. However, I can safely state that America is largely seen throughout the Muslim world as the rulers' ally and the people's enemy. Even if one focuses only on the US record as an agent of democratization and a harbinger of human rights in the region, the United States has very little credibility among Muslims.

When Paul Wolfowitz, former US deputy secretary of defense and president of the World Bank, offered Turkey as a role model of democ-

racy to the Muslim world (Wolfowitz 2002), the appearance of US backing may actually have undercut Turkey's ability to influence other
Muslim countries. Indeed, before Wolfowitz held up Turkey as a model,
an Egyptian writer complained, "The US wants all Muslim countries to
be like Turkey, [which] bombards its people with . . . pornographic
movies and television programs" (Mahmoud 2001).

Another commentator, citing recent US actions, argued that the
American position toward democracy is purely opportunistic. When the
Emirati Zayid Center for Research questioned US policies in the Middle
East and invited researchers who doubted the role of Al-Qaida in the
attacks of September 11, the United States pressured the Emirati government to close down the center. The Emirati government complied.
Meanwhile the United States pressured the Egyptian government to set
free Egyptian-American sociologist Sa'ad el-Din Ibrahim, whose positions are in tandem with US interests in the region (Howaidi 2003b).

One can never exaggerate the negative effect of US diplomatic, economic, and military support to Israel on its image among Muslims.
Given this notorious reputation, can a more democratic Muslim world
decrease the level of anti-Americanism? Theoretically, there are good
reasons to argue both yes and no. Anti-Americanism could increase with
more anti-American forces in power. However, it may decrease if the
United States is no longer perceived as the ally of autocratic governments. There is enough empirical evidence to support the first argument.
The second one is largely speculation.

Ulama as Agents of Democratization?

There is a debate among Islam's researchers about the roles that
mosques and *ulama*, *khateebs* (preachers), and shaikhs or imams play in
shaping Muslims' attitudes.[1] Some accounts state without qualification,
"Muslims are addicted to religion. Thus any attempt to reform Muslims'
affairs will fail unless it starts from Islam" (Omara 2002).

Indeed the notion that Islam must be the foundation of any legitimate government is continually instilled in Muslims by all religious
figures (al-Buraiq 1994; al-Gazza'eri 1984; al-Qaradawi 1980). Thus,
many believe that mosques will always be among the most important
agents of moral and political socialization in the Muslim world
(Neusner 1996; Sharot 2001; Zaman 2002), except, perhaps, some
within Tunisia (Ismail 2003; Tamimi 2001). Historically, the *ulama*
"were the purveyors of Islam, the guardians of its tradition, the deposi-

tory of ancestral wisdom, and the moral tutors of the population" (Marsot 1972: 149).

The political role of the *ulama* shifted dramatically after the abolition of their *waqf* (endowments) and their transition to salaried state technocrats (Mohamed 1989; Nettler, Mahmoud, and Cooper 2000; No'man 2003). Traditionally their role was to channel the demands of the masses to the rulers and to advise the rulers to enjoin the good and forbid the evil. Since most Muslim *ulama* have become salaried officials in mostly failed states (secular or Islamist), most Muslims have lost trust in them, perceiving them as attempting to legitimize illegitimate rulers and regimes. Islamists in opposition are now filling this vacuum of trust (Anderson 1997; Esposito 1992; Shariati and Rajaee 1986). Thus when one is evaluating public opinion about *ulama*, it is necessary to make the distinction between official *ulama* (*al-Islam al-rasmi*), who are limited to government-imposed agendas and positions, and independent *ulama* (*al-Islam al-sha'bi*).

This section evaluates the extent to which *ulama* have lost their influence over Muslim attitudes or are still a credible source of socialization in the Muslim world. If they still have a role, how does this role affect Muslims' support for democratic institutions and norms? Two questions were used to gauge the influence of *ulama*, shaikhs, and imams as credible agents of socialization. The first question intentionally avoids the issue of democracy: "Regarding the Arab-Israeli conflict, whose opinions do you trust most?" (question 33, Appendix 2). The respondents were given five options and the opportunity to write down "other." The five options were the government, official *ulama*, independent *ulama*, independent intellectuals, and none. Table 4.2 summarizes the responses, which support the above observations.

With regard to the issue of the Palestinian conflict, Muslim respondents from all countries except Albania, Turkmenistan, India, and Mali trusted *ulama* more than other sources (government officials and independent intellectuals). However, and more interesting, Muslims trust independent *ulama* who represent *al-Islam al-sha'bi* more than those who represent official Islam, or *al-Islam al-rasmi*, without any exception. This result might have been expected in countries that have not adopted Islam as their official ideology. Yet it was also found to be true in Iran and the Sudan, both of which base their legitimacy on Islamic ideology and both of which have very rigid anti-Israeli and pro-Palestinian stances.

Fearing that the question about the Arab-Israeli conflict might have its own biases, another question (question 42, Appendix 2) was devel-

Table 4.2   "Regarding the Arab-Israeli conflict, whose opinion do you trust most?"

Country	Government	Independent Intellectuals	Official *Ulama*	Independent *Ulama*	Total *Ulama*
Qatar	9	30	30	31	61
Senegal	19	18	26	37	63
Tajikistan	23	26	24	27	51
Iran	31	11	24	34	58
Saudi Arabia	17	16	24	43	67
UAE	31	18	23	28	51
Gambia	21	25	23	31	54
Nigeria	17	20	22	41	63
Bangladesh	11	34	21	34	55
Morocco	19	19	21	41	62
Albania	21	32	20	27	47
Turkmenistan	13	39	19	29	48
Malaysia	13	33	19	35	54
Tunisia	13	29	19	39	58
Jordan	11	26	19	44	63
Algeria	19	24	18	39	57
Pakistan	14	26	18	42	60
Kuwait	16	18	18	48	66
Egypt	13	22	17	48	65
Turkey	3	37	17	43	60
Mali	13	40	16	31	47
Libya	11	36	15	38	53
Yemen	18	27	14	41	55
Lebanon	19	25	14	42	56
Syria	20	22	13	45	58
Sudan	13	18	12	57	69
Indonesia	18	30	11	41	52
EU	1	42	8	49	57
USA	0.42	47	4	49	53
India	4	53	2	41	43

Source: E-mail and written survey 2002.

oped to focus on the issue of democracy. The respondents were asked to choose who might be responsible for the spread and continuation of dictatorships in Muslim polities. For each option—the West, individuals, rulers, the conflict between Islam and democracy, and scholars—the respondents could weight the significance of each with three further choices: "a very important reason," "somewhat important reason," or "not a reason at all."

The responses to this question had a normal distribution in almost all cases, with a clear majority (between 57 percent in Turkey and 83 percent in India) choosing "somewhat important reason." A young shaikh from Algeria argued that this was a "fair answer . . . because the *ulama* carry the *amana* [covenant of Allah] to lead Muslims to His way, and most of them could not deliver." He thought that their failure to deliver may be attributable to their current limited role, which is why they are "somewhat responsible for all the difficulties, not only the dictatorship issue."

A Turkish imam of a fairly large mosque in Istanbul added another dimension: the mosque is the first place where young Muslims learn about "the Prophet and his companions and most importantly where they get their moral frame of reference." This moral frame of reference is an absolutely important concept for understanding the *ulama*'s influence. Muslim *ulama* discuss things and issues in terms of what is *halal* (acceptable) and *haram* (forbidden) by Allah, rather than in terms of legal and constitutional versus illegal and unconstitutional.

Not everything considered *halal* by the *ulama*, however, is considered legal by the state. For instance, wearing *hijab* in government buildings is religiously *fardh* (obligatory) according to the overwhelming majority of *ulama*, yet in Tunisia and Turkey it is illegal. Drinking alcoholic beverages, allowing interests on loans and bank deposits, and showing inappropriate movies and music on national television are politically legal and religiously *haram*, which is absolutely inimical to the traditional understanding of Islam as both religion and state. *Ulama* have a term for all these discrepancies: *secularism*.

Secular outlets and agents of socialization such as government schools and state-controlled TV stations and newspapers in most Muslim countries are strongly condemned by *ulama* as the source of all evils. Most Muslims get exposed to this antisecular discourse at a very young age, well before any encounter with secular intellectuals and politicians.

Many *ulama* state forcefully that authentic Islam, not the one taught at government schools and preached by official *ulama*, is incompatible with secularism, because in a secular state there is no place for divine laws (which are the core of Islam), and secular laws are against Islam. Thanks to these *ulama*, democracy has been characterized in the Muslim world as an alien Western secular panacea.

Mohsan Al-'Awaggi, an independent modernist scholar from Saudi Arabia, criticized the official *ulama* for being state driven and not Allah driven in their *khotbas* (sermons). "They were very harsh in criticizing those who committed the September 11 [attacks] without being as frank in condemning what is happening in Palestine, Kashmir, Afghanistan, or elsewhere because the Saudi government prevents them from doing that."

I met Shaikh K. of Tunisia in the United States. He is an imam of a mosque and a *hafez*, which means that he has memorized the entire Holy Quran. He was very critical of the Tunisian government because it established a French education system in Tunisia. According to him, "The government has overhauled all education curricula from kindergarten to the universities to emphasize equality among all religions, as if Islam were just one option available to Muslims." He continued, "All the verses that emphasize chastity, women as mothers and housewives, and polygamy were expunged from all textbooks as if Bin Ali [the president] corrects Allah." When I asked whether he preached these objections in his country, he said of course not; he was trying to do his best as a good Muslim within the government-imposed boundaries.

To minimize dissent among the *ulama*, most secular governments nationalized Islamic outlets such as mosques, Islamic houses of publications, and the Islamic *waqf*. Muslim governments managed to make unofficial *ulama* go into hiding but could not completely silence them. Their tapes and books are available and are widely and passionately heard and read by young Muslims.

This duality in Islamic discourse is not new. It has always existed in the history of Muslims. Early *ulama* had to fight the rulers' transgressions. Through the first thirteen centuries of Islam, independent *ulama* counteracted the ambitions of the rulers, fended off the hypocritical stances of the official *ulama*, and supported grievances that arose from the injustices of the rulers.

Assuming that the *ulama* impact is still significant on most educated Muslims, does this impact help or hinder the cause of democracy? Column 12 of Table 3.1 shows the statistical significance of the effect of *ulama* on democratic norms and institutions in Muslim societies. To gauge the relevance of the *ulama* as credible agents of political socialization, a dummy variable was generated where 1 indicates trust in *ulama* (official and independent) and 0 represents other.[2]

The more Muslims trust *ulama* as agents of socialization, the less supportive they are of democratic institutions and/or norms in all cases except Tajikistan, Tunisia, Turkey, Turkmenistan (where there is no statistically significant effect), Gambia, Mali, Qatar, and Senegal (where trust in *ulama* drives up support for democratic norms and/or institutions). All these polities are formally secular except for Qatar, which, in any case, allows independent *ulama* the freedom to express views contrary to official government positions.

I asked some of the imams who were interviewed whether it was possible for them to discuss issues such as democracy, elections, and political equality with non-Muslims in their *khotbas*. The answer in almost all cases was no. A shaikh from Saudi Arabia said he could not and indeed no *khateeb* could do that, since "this is the *minbar* [stand] of the Prophet of Allah and we cannot dare say what he did not say."

A shaikh of a well-known mosque in Cairo thought that he could not use the word *democracy* in a Friday sermon. He did give a sermon on *shura* and how it was practiced by the Prophet and his companions. He is convinced that democracy is not like *shura*. Democracy may lead Muslims astray, but *shura* is bound by Allah's imperatives. In a clear example of the influence of this shaikh on his followers, my attempt to show that democracy has positive aspects that Muslims should consider was resisted. The three attendees I spoke to showed firm support for the shaikh's argument and started quoting verses, mostly out of context, to condemn the effect of the West on Westernized Muslims like me. This interaction was reminiscent of a pronouncement by Ahmad Nawafal, a member of the Muslim Brotherhood in Jordan: "If we have a choice between democracy and dictatorship, we choose democracy. But if it's between Islam and democracy, we choose Islam" (quoted in Pipes 1995).

Some of the interviewed Muslims tended to defend the role of *ulama* as politically bound by statist rulers. Many of the interviewees quoted several names of *ulama* and shaikhs who have been jailed for criticizing the rulers or galvanizing the masses around themselves. This persecution of *ulama* and shaikhs has hindered their service as reformists and increased their tendency to remain conservative. Thus for some interviewees, to hold *ulama* responsible for the continuation of autocracy is like blaming the victim, for they are not powerful enough to defend themselves.

According to the overall findings of this study, then, most Muslim countries' *ulama* and their followers are not very supportive of democratic norms and institutions. There are, however, more liberal voices as mass education and mass media erode, to some extent, the monopoly over ideas that *ulama* have had for centuries (Eickelman 1999).

A physician from India residing in the United States, whose father is an imam of a mosque in Ahmadabad, feels sympathetic with the *ulama* who excel at memorizing the Quran, books of hadiths, and many ancient interpretations without learning enough geography, sciences, philosophy, and mathematics. Given their lack of preparation, they do not look toward the future. Democracy for these *ulama* is "alien and improper."

The ulama "longingly keep repeating the virtues of the thirty-year reign of the al-Khulafa al-Rashidoon [the rightly guided caliphs] since they were the golden era of Islam." This comment is similar to an observation by Karen Armstrong that Muslim societies are "divided and split between an elite intelligentsia who have a Western education and understand what's going on and the vast rank and file who are essentially left to rot in a pre-modern ethos" (Armstrong 2002).

An engineer from Indonesia, who does not seem to be a Muslim anymore, decided to give up attending Friday *khotbas*. In his mind, the *khateeb* is shallow and does not address the serious challenges of Muslims. "Why do we still discuss the issue of *hijab*, application of *hudud* [Islamic penal code], or how to clean oneself for prayer while [there are] no jobs, no money and no hope?" He thinks that such *khateebs* are not only irrelevant but harmful, since they keep people preoccupied with useless matters.

A US citizen of Pakistani origin thinks that Islam has become the opium of Muslims: "*Khateebs* preach that we should obey the rulers as long as they do not prevent us from prayers. How come? They are corrupt, traitors, and ignorant. How can I listen to a [government] employee who teaches me nothing?"

An Iranian female liberal thinker agrees that rulers use *ulama* as tools legitimating their authority. Being Shiite, she explains that the *ulama* preach that the infallible Twelfth Imam went into concealment. The Shiite have been suffering under the political oppression of the unjust and await the return of this concealed imam as savior. "This is stupidity," she said. "I questioned this belief and challenged a female scholar, but she has no logic. She believes blindly and does not allow for multiple interpretations."

This comment on the lack of plurality sounds familiar to people who have studied all religions. Michael Gilsenan has similar words about religious fundamentalism: "The text is made esoteric and becomes the special preserve of scholars, who are self-defined as the only ones who can really understand it. The text becomes an instrument of authority and a way of excluding others or regulating their access to it. It can be used to show that others are wrong and we are right; what is more, we have the right to be right and they do not! We know" (Gilsenan 1982: 31).

Muslim *ulama* have been depicted as either catalysts for autocracy or its victims. However, they can be part of the solution as well. Take Iran as a test case. Obeying unjust rulers while awaiting the concealed imam has been a tradition in Shiite faith for over twelve centuries.

However, this creed was turned upside down when Imam Khomeini practiced *ijtihad* and coined the concept of *vilayat-i faqih*. This *ijtihad* was spelled out in full in article 5 in the constitution of the Islamic Republic of Iran:

> During the Occultation of the Wali al-Asr [the Twelfth Imam] (may God hasten his reappearance), the *wilayah* and leadership of the *Ummah* devolve upon the just [*'adil*] and pious [*muttaqi*] faqih, who is fully aware of the circumstances of his age; courageous, resourceful, and possessed of administrative ability, he will assume the responsibilities of this office.

This effort on the part of the Iranian *ulama* showed that even well-entrenched concepts and principles can be questioned and eventually altered. The prodemocratic role played by clerics in Iran is reminiscent of twentieth-century developments in Catholic societies. The map of the world after World War II did not include a single democratic polity among societies with a Catholic majority. Yet by the 1960s, "the attitudes of Catholic clergy and those victimized by oligarchies and tyrannies" had helped diminish the legitimacy of these autocratic regimes (Karatnycky 2002: 105).

One might argue that unless fighting dictatorship becomes prioritized in the public agenda through the efforts of *ulama* and others, the future of democracy in the Muslim world will be highly contingent on the free will of rulers.

Concluding Remarks

Overall, this chapter demonstrates that Muslims have a high degree of dissatisfaction with ruling elites. In twenty-four out of the thirty two countries where Muslims live, respondents desired a prodemocratic ruler rather than the ruling incumbent. Of respondents from the remaining eight countries, only those from two were clearly proincumbent, and those from the remaining five were unsure.

That said, the comments of respondents indicated that they do not see the West, or even Western-style democracy, as the answer to their dissatisfaction. First, they tend to blame the West for supporting autocratic rulers in their countries and view its prodemocracy rhetoric as mere lip service. As a consequence, they are wary of any kind of Western influence in their countries and distrustful of Western models of governance. Second, many Muslims believe that Western-style democracy would directly conflict with Islamic practices. If Muslim countries move toward a more democratic style of government, it is likely to be tailored to Islamic imperatives.

The importance of religion in Muslims' daily lives is evidenced by the weight they attach to the teachings of the *ulama*. Respondents in twenty-six countries surveyed pay more heed to *ulama* than to either public intellectuals or government officials. To the extent that state-sponsored *ulama* are essentially government officials, there is distrust, but in this case Muslims actively seek out independent *ulama* for their opinions on major social and political issues.

Having looked at the views of individual Muslims from a variety of angles, I will aggregate these views in the next chapter to discern how various Muslim societies differ in their support for democratic norms and institutions and to assess the likelihood of democratization in these societies.

Notes

1. These terms will be used interchangeably in this section.
2. There was not enough variation on the variable of the responsibility of *ulama* for dictatorship, so it was not used.

5

Prospects for Reform Across Muslim Societies

Unless a substantial majority of citizens prefer democracy and its political institutions to any nondemocratic alternative and support political leaders who uphold democratic practices, democracy is unlikely to survive its inevitable crises.

—Robert Dahl, 1998

Most literature on democratization suggests that the image of democracy has never been more favorable. It has been stated that democracy has become virtually the only model with global appeal (Inglehart 2000). Democracy, however, needs a political culture that would allow it not only to emerge but also to withstand the tests of time, political conflict, and crises. A democracy without a democratic political culture is extremely fragile. Even "a large minority of militant and violent antidemocrats would probably be sufficient to destroy a country's capacity for maintaining its democratic institutions" (Dahl 1998:158).

The history of democratization in the past 100 years reveals five major patterns by which countries have been democratized. These patterns are democracy through occupation (e.g., India, Japan, and Germany), elite-led transitions (e.g., Spain and Hungary), mass-led transitions (e.g., Romania, Peru, Georgia, and Ukraine), negotiated transitions (e.g., Chile, South Africa, and Taiwan), and naive liberalization that leads to the unintended breakdown of an authoritarian regime (e.g., the Soviet Union and Brazil).

Regardless of who initiates the process of democratization, democratic norms and institutions have to be appreciated by the majority of ordinary people; otherwise one authoritarian regime will be replaced by another. That is why serious accounts of the prospects for democracy in the Muslim world require an examination of three issues: First, how do Muslims aggregately perceive democratic institutions and norms? Second, how do Muslims identify their preferences if they are given a choice among governments that apply sharia without democracy, governments that have democracy without sharia, and others that may combine both? Third, if mass-initiated demands (petitions, riots, and demonstrations) are the only way for Muslims to achieve democracy, how ready are they to sacrifice for it? In other words, how elastic is their demand for their political rights?

The Aggregate Perceptions of Democracy

Though all Muslims by definition belong to the same religion, it should be clear that their heterogeneity (in their interpretation of Islam, among other factors) means that it would be fruitless to construct any grand, overarching theory of Islam. Figure 5.1, a map of the attitudes of mostly urban, educated, and nonpoor Muslims in thirty-three societies of the world (including Iraqis residing in Arab countries), further reinforces this awareness. On the horizontal axis, attitudes of Muslims toward democratic institutions and procedures (democratic institutions) are laid out on a 100-point scale. On the vertical axis, a 100-point scale of sociopolitical tolerance (democratic norms) is presented.[1] The pooled sample indicates a significant diversity of aggregate attitudes.

From Muslims of Turkey, Morocco, and Egypt on the upper right corner to those in Saudi Arabia, Yemen, and Libya, the idea that Muslims have one shared vision of democracy is not supported. The first observation regarding the map is that if one judges by the crude number of sampled societies that scored 50 points or more in terms of support for democratic institutions and norms (countries above the horizontal line and to the right of the vertical dotted line), one can infer that citizens in the socioeconomic bracket of survey respondents in most Muslim societies do not prefer autocracy over democracy. This finding, in general, is consistent with Pippa Norris and Ronald Inglehart's findings (Norris and Inglehart 2002). To avoid overgeneralizations, one can use the cultural map as a useful tool to categorize Muslim societies among four broad sets:

1. Societies that score high on support for democratic norms and low on support for democratic institutions.
2. Societies that score low on both scales.

Figure 5.1 Muslims' Attitudes Toward Democratic Institutions and Norms

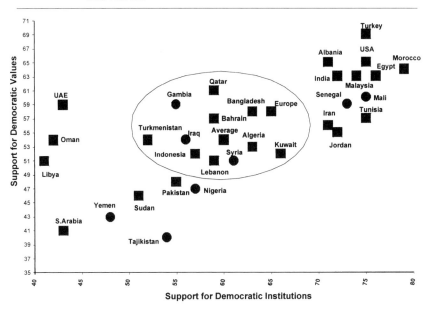

Source: E-mail and written survey 2002.
Notes: Black squares indicate Muslim respondents from both written and e-mail surveys. Black circles indicate Muslim respondents from e-mail surveys only. The oval indicates countries with average support for democratic institutions and norms.

3. Societies that score moderately on both scales.
4. Societies that score high on both scales.

Each one of these categories will be discussed in more detail.

High Support for Democratic Norms and Low Support for Democratic Institutions

This first category of Muslim culture is best exemplified by the United Arab Emirates, Oman, and Libya. In terms of sociopolitical tolerance, Libya, Oman, and the United Arab Emirates have moderate scores of 51, 54, and 59 points respectively, but they have significantly lower scores for democratic institutions, around 41–43 points.

In Libya, as one of the most homogeneous societies of the Muslim world, focus-group discussions reveal that the discriminatory attitudes of Libyans are focused primarily on non-Libyans, such as the half-million black Africans (around 10 percent of the population) who live and work there. Among Libyans, the dominant form of discrimination is male against female. Tribal traditions pervade men's thinking, even that of literate men, about women (Bianci 2003). Libyan men's relatively negative esteem for Libyan women is best illustrated by the fact that only 48 percent of Libyan male respondents believed that women should participate in politics according to this study's survey. Another survey showed that only 29 percent of men would accept women's holding jobs involving authority over men (Obeidi 2001).

What clearly boosts Libyan tolerance scores are the attitudes of literate Libyan females, who are far less parochial than their male counterparts. Today they enjoy a higher level of self-esteem and sense of political efficacy compared to a decade ago (Obeidi 2001). Around 64 percent of literate Libyan women think that women should be equally enfranchised and that they have the capacity to assume top executive positions. This result is almost identical to another survey conducted in Libya, in which 63 percent of Libyan women thought that they could hold positions that might involve authority over men (Obeidi 2001).

Educated Emirati women showed even more self-confidence in this study's survey, with around 73 percent of them defending their rights as political actors and 25 percent accepting that women should hold top executive positions. Unlike Libyan men, the majority of literate Emirati men (around 60 percent) accepted that women should participate in politics as legislative representatives, although only 7 percent would grant them the right to hold top executive positions.

Women in Oman are both self-perceived and perceived by men to enjoy a higher status than their peers in Libya and the United Arab Emirates. In the pooled sample, around 33 percent of Omani respondents (men and women) would agree to give women top legislative and executive positions; this percentage was only 26 percent in the case of Libya and 10 percent in the case of the United Arab Emirates. Though Muslims' values are not necessarily good predictors of Muslim regimes' official policies, it is worth noting that in 1994 Sultan Qabus of Oman, for the first time in all the Arab Gulf states, granted women the right to vote and participate in elections; in March 2003 he appointed the first female minister in the history of the region.[2]

Despite its comparatively pro–women's rights culture, however, Oman ranks significantly lower than the United Arab Emirates in terms of regard for democratic institutions. This lower status can be attributed mainly to the negative impact of cleavages between religious sects and tribal affiliations (Beasant 2002). However, growth in the government-administered sector is positively correlated with the level of trust and sense of equality compared to the late 1960s under the Dhofar Rebellion, which ended in 1975 (Economist 1998).

Why don't relatively high levels of political tolerance in these three countries translate into greater support for democratic institutions? As was discussed earlier, these countries could be classified as model rentier states, where "no taxation, no representation" seems perfectly acceptable to the majority of the public (Beblawi and Luciani 1987; Kechichian and Grunebaum 2001). It might also have something to do with government messages and political socialization.

Libya serves as an interesting example of an autocrat's legitimation of his regime (Tahir and Qaddafi 1996; Zartman 1982). The Libyan system claims full participation by all Libyans but with no political competition or clear contending platforms or political parties. Actually, according to an anonymous Libyan intellectual, "most [of the Libyan] people do not even know on what basis they are asked their opinions and what difference it makes to air them." No transparency, no opposition, and no partisanship, yet it is still a government by the people according to the Green Book that enshrines Muammar Qaddafi's theory of politics.

This is not to suggest that Libyans are being duped. In the survey conducted in the course of this research, when Libyans were asked how satisfied they are with the performance of the system, only 20 percent expressed a notable level of satisfaction. The rest were either unsatisfied or not sure. Even with noticeable resentment among almost half of the twenty-six Libyan focus-group participants, the solution from their perspective was not so radical as a totally new system of government but for officials to be "fair and conscious as Allah orders them to be."

Muslims of the United Arab Emirates and Oman were stronger advocates of their incumbents in both the written survey (in the case of the United Arab Emirates) and the e-mail surveys. Around 80 percent of Emiratis showed satisfaction with their political system, while around 52 percent of Omanis had the same attitudes. These two scores are among the highest in the whole sample. Among the ten participants in the focus-group discussions in the United Arab Emirates, there was not one supporter of the idea of copying Western democratic institutions. According to Sa'eed, one of the interviewees in the United Arab Emirates, who had lived in Britain for two years, "democracy is a good system of government that we do not need in UAE."

The classification of responses from persons of the remaining countries into three categories reveals more symmetry between support for democratic institutions and support for democratic norms.

Low Support for Democratic Institutions and Norms

Saudi Arabia, Yemen, Tajikistan, Sudan, and possibly Pakistan and Nigeria form what can be labeled the least democratizable cultures, given the attitudes of their citizens toward democratic institutions of participation and competition and sociopolitical tolerance and trust. These countries occupy the lower left corner of Figure 5.1, which puts them in the same category albeit for different reasons.

Saudi respondents' feeble support for democratic institutions can be understood in light of the legacy of the kingdom, never having experienced a publicly elected government of any sort since its modern inception in the 1930s (or even possibly since the early years of Islam 1,400 years ago). The fact that Saudi officials rarely, if ever, use or misuse the word *democracy* or any of its forms in any public speeches, or allow it to sneak into public school curricula, might also help to explain the kingdom's relative political stability. Saudi Arabia has kept a tight lid on dissent in other ways as well: political parties are prohibited on the grounds that they lead to *fitnah* (internal division; Fandy 1999), and most opposition is equated with treason. There is evidence to suggest that the government has been effective in selling the message of unity.

Though I was unable to conduct well-organized focus-group discussions in Saudi Arabia, I had casual talks with Saudis who had never visited the West and with others who had lived in the West for some time. Many argued that the traditional institutions of family and tribe perform the political roles of interest articulation and representation that interest groups and lobbies fulfill in the West. Political parties as collective actors competing for power and forming either the government or opposition do not have counterparts in the Saudi culture. A Saudi progovernment journalist said, "It is highly destabilizing to allow political parties in the kingdom. Tribal and familial cleavages will spontaneously convert into party competition and political campaigns with a lot of agony and prejudice. In a country that is named after one family, other unsatisfied families are not going to be controllable."

Saudi political control is also cemented by religious teachings. Around 74 percent of the Saudi respondents to the survey believed strongly that democratic institutions and procedures such as political parties, parliament, and elections are incompatible with Islamic sharia as they understand it.

There are, of course, limits to government control, and the Saudi public seems quite aware of their government's shortcomings. Even though Saudi Arabia has a Shura Council, Saudis tend to consider it powerless and, according to a Saudi engineer, often refer to it with the disparaging term *manshaffa*, or towel. This is because the council offers the royal family a way to clean up or sanitize unpopular decisions. The royal family can put some distance between themselves and an unpopular ruling, despite the fact that the council is fully appointed by the king and he alone is its constituency.

The negative image that Sunnis hold of Shiites, and vice versa, and the low status of women also work against political tolerance and democracy. Around 40 percent of Saudi respondents believed women should not be enfranchised, and 34 percent preferred to limit their participation to voting in the event that Saudi Arabia adopted some form of elections. The data also show that around 35 percent of Saudi women would not think of themselves as political actors at any level, and 33 percent would limit any participation to voting—they would not expect to serve as representatives in elected councils or assume executive positions.

These attitudes can be attributed to legal restrictions on the one hand and to social and cultural traditions on the other. Legally and financially speaking, women are not considered full citizens and must therefore be dependent on men. They are declared inferior both "rationally and psychologically" and thus "always in need of man's custody" (al-Fassi 2003). The Saudi government has recently taken small steps to improve the status of women. The Saudi crown prince has openly committed himself to gradual reforms that would give women more political rights.

The most pervasive sociocultural force responsible for the oppression of women in Saudi Arabia is the educational system. A Saudi intellectual and political scientist states that most of the Islamic norms that students learn in Saudi Arabia come from *salafi* (traditionalist teachers) who do not train their students in critical thinking but rather in memorizing and blindly believing sayings that do not serve pluralism, tolerance, or relative thinking (al-Hamad 2003a). Worse, they are educated to believe that the authentic and only true Islam is the *salafi* Islam of Saudi Arabia.

Not only does this sect of Islam call for the submission of women, it identifies other Muslim (let alone non-Muslim) societies as perverted and thus to be avoided rather than examined and understood. Shiites, in particular, are treated as *bid'a* who curse the first great caliphs of Islam and attack the mother of the believers, 'Aisha, as a Saudi scholar put it. One can get a taste of the virulent intolerance prevalent in Saudi Arabia from the title of a sermon given by Shaikh Abdurrahman al-Hozzeffi:

"Wipe Out the Jews, Christians, and Shiites from Arabia" (1998). The state works in conjunction with *salafi* Islam and allows citizenship only to Sunni Muslims.

Though Yemenis, Sudanese, and Tajiks show remarkable religious tolerance toward non-Muslims (especially Christians and Jews) in terms of their rights to build their houses of worship (more than 75 percent agreed or strongly agreed), this tolerance fades away when it comes to the issue of political rights. Only 4–7 percent of the Yemeni respondents, 2–12 percent of Sudanese, and 7–11 percent of Tajiks agreed that non-Muslims or Muslims of other sects should enjoy the right to fully participate in elections and to assume top legislative and executive responsibilities.

In Yemen, the pooled data show that highly conservative attitudes toward women and Muslims from other sects are responsible for the weak support for democratic norms. Tribalism also seems to play a big part in fomenting political intolerance, despite claims that it is weakening (al-Iryani 1998; Othman 1998). Generally speaking, the combination of a heterogeneous population and deep-seated social divisions seems to breed political intolerance, especially when these divisions culminate in violence.

Civil wars are certain to explain the relatively low level of sociopolitical tolerance in Sudan and Tajikistan. The long Sudanese civil war (from 1955 until late 2004) has severely diminished trust and tolerance among northern and southern Sudanese alike, especially reinforcing cleavages that separate Arab, predominantly Muslim political elites in the north from the rest of the population in the south. Tajikistan's civil war was shorter (1992–1995) but quite bloody, with more than 100,000 casualties. The violence destroyed most reserves of trust among the many local groups and factions such as Kulob, Khujand, and Hisar, who fought on one side and later formed the government, and their opponents, the Tajiks from Qarategin and Badakhshan. Indeed, "growing localism and the lack of a national consolidation have brought the [Tajik] society and the state to the verge of collapse" (Abdoullaev 1998).

The feeble support for democratic institutions among respondents in Yemen, Sudan, and Tajikistan is largely attributed to the cynical appropriation of the rhetoric and instruments of democracy by the governments of these countries to shore up their power and legitimacy. If democracy already had an image problem because of its association with the West, the abuse of democracy by political elites tends to exacerbate this problem. Only 10 percent of the Sudanese respondents and

12 percent of the Tajiks thought that elections and referenda, respectively, are free and fair. Four Sudanese students in two different group discussions differentiated between a "democracy," referring to their own country's system of government, and real democracies. Sudanese interviewees were very critical of the phenomenon of putting all major opposition figures in jail or in exile and then having so-called free elections afterward, a phenomenon that is very common in most Muslim countries. The civil war, along with the four abrupt military coups and tensions among the political and intellectual elites, drove down the hope of real democratization in the Sudan. In the 2000 elections the Sudanese people chose to punish the government by boycotting both legislative and presidential elections, which ended up with empty ballot boxes in most counties; yet still the "elected" president Omar al-Bashir claimed a landslide victory, which encouraged the ruling party to propose a change to the constitution which allows the president to be reelected an unlimited number of times, in order to guarantee the stability of the country.[3]

Pakistani and Nigerian respondents shared with citizens of Saudi Arabia, Yemen, and the United Arab Emirates relatively low levels of political tolerance. Yet as Figure 5.1 shows, they demonstrated higher support for democratic institutions and procedures (around 55 points), which is comparable to levels of those from Indonesia and Gambia. When one examines the individual responses of participants from the two cultures, it is clear that there is a lack of trust between Nigerian and Pakistani Muslims and non-Muslims of their respective countries. Pakistani Sunni, Shiite, and Ahmadi did not hide their negative attitudes toward each other either; 73 percent of them would refuse intersectarian marriages among themselves. As would be expected from most minorities that seek coexistence with the majority, however, the Shiite and Ahmadi minorities tended to have more tolerant attitudes toward the Sunni majority. The tensions among different Pakistani ethnic groups, such as the Punjabi, the Sindhi, and the Pashtun, seem to be of secondary importance or of no significance except when they coincide with religious cleavages among different sects of Muslims and between Muslims and non-Muslims (Sunni 77 percent, Shiite and Ahmadi 20 percent, Christian, Hindu, and others 3 percent). This result actually confirms other readings of the unstable social fabric of Pakistan (Chaudhri, Ahmad, and Ahmadiyya Muslim Association 1989).

Notwithstanding Pakistan's ethnic and religious divisions, women enjoy higher status there than in the societies discussed earlier in this chapter. In Pakistan, almost 68 percent of respondents had no problem with the idea that women should participate in politics as ministers (33 percent) and members of parliament (35 percent). However, according to a Pew survey, only 52 percent of Pakistanis think that women should decide for themselves on the issue of veiling (Pew 2003a). This result does not contradict the previous finding about women's participation in politics, since *hijab* for both traditionalist and modernist Islamists is considered to be mandated by sharia rather than a matter of personal preference. Actually, for this large a percentage of Pakistanis to express willingness to give women the right to decide on this issue is quite surprising. In sum, the deficit in respondents' views on Pakistan's democratic norms can be attributed mainly to nongender religious issues.

Similarly, in Nigeria, overlapping religious and ethnic cleavages can explain the lack of sociopolitical tolerance among respondents (Suberu 1996). Though around 75 percent of Nigerian respondents agreed or strongly agreed to the right of Christians and Jews to build their own houses of worship (a right that is actually given to the people by the book of Islam), 34 percent of the Nigerian respondents believed that Christians and Jews should be disfranchised, and 32 percent thought that their participation should be limited to voting and nothing more. Commenting on this finding, a Nigerian student studying Islamic *fiqh* in Al-Azhar, Egypt, said, "[Nigerian] Christians impede Muslims from living according to Islam. Muslims of Nigeria are going to fight for sharia no matter what it costs, even if they have to have their own Islamic state in northern Nigeria."

This finding suggests that Nigeria's public culture among Muslims (50 percent of the population) poses a problem not only for the country's prospects as a sustainable democracy but more fundamentally for the unity of the country. Given Nigeria's history of electoral disputes, coupled with ethnic violence and a military coup in the 1960s, nation building seems to be both an urgent and an elusive goal (Aborisade 2002).

Unlike Pakistani respondents, Nigerians evidenced a significant gender gap, with around 17 percent of the respondents refusing to accept that women should participate in politics at all and 57 percent limiting their participation to voting; only 2 percent of them trusted women to occupy top executive positions such as ministers. Once again, a Pew survey confirms this attitude toward women from a different perspective, by showing that 53 percent of Nigerians (the highest percentage among the Muslim countries surveyed in that sample) clearly disagreed with allowing women to decide on veiling (Pew 2003a).

Negative experiences of military interventions and high levels of corruption and manipulation of elections in both countries have had an impact on the attitudes of ordinary Muslims toward elections and democratic procedures (Aborisade 2002; Jafri 2002; Jawed 1999; Ujo 2000). Only 20 percent of the pooled respondents from Nigeria and Pakistan showed some satisfaction with the performance of political parties and elected officials. A fifty-seven-year-old Pakistani respondent commented on the e-mail version of the survey: "The survey overlooked the role of the military. . . . I never voted for a government without [its] being overthrown by a coup. . . . There is no need for elections if the officers see themselves [as] better politicians."

A Nigerian respondent described elections as "an arena for bribery and corruption" that makes them absolutely undemocratic and un-Islamic. Another Nigerian and four Pakistani respondents made similar comments. Such criticism of democratic institutions is very common in both countries. Moreover, around 70 percent of the respondents in both countries were unsure whether democratic institutions such as parliaments and elections are against Islamic sharia. Indeed, religion generally compounds democracy's image problem in the more conservative Muslim world. This study found that 60 percent of the Saudis, 50 percent of the Yemenis, and 53 percent of the Omanis disagreed or strongly disagreed that "democracy" could be equivalent to the Islamic system of *shura*, which they strongly prefer. This percentage was much lower among respondents from Libya (40 percent), Tajikistan (25 percent), Pakistan (27 percent), and Nigeria (30 percent), where the word *democracy* is commonly and publicly used by Westernized intellectuals and politicians.

Democratic institutions come under suspicion not only because of fraud and religious views but because of their negative impact on deeply divided societies. In these societies, including Sudan, Pakistan, Yemen, and Nigeria, the easiest way for political competitors to win votes is by appealing to ethnic, tribal, and religious constituencies, thus deepening divisions in a way that is very destructive to the social fabric and diminishes both political tolerance and support for democratic institutions.

Democracy's image problem in the Muslim world is evidenced in low voter turnout. In three of seven countries where elections are frequent, the turnout in most elections was around 35–41 percent, according to the usually exaggerated official sources (World Bank 2001a).

What are the prospects for democratic reform in countries with low support for democratic norms and institutions? Without major cultural shifts, any elite-led democratic transitions will need to address nontolerance toward women (as in Saudi Arabia, Yemen, Nigeria, and Libya), other Muslim sects (Saudi Arabia, Yemen, Pakistan, and the United Arab Emirates), and non-Muslims (Pakistan, Nigeria, and Yemen). Holding other noncultural factors constant, one may anticipate that even if a ruling elite decides to administer a genuine democratic transition, or if occupying forces try to tilt one of these countries toward democracy, they will most likely be forced to adopt one of two strategies:

1. To adopt, at least in the short run, some form of exclusionary democracy by excluding certain sectors of society, just as most Western democracies disenfranchised women and minority groups for quite some time, until there is a higher level of support for the proceduralist aspects of democracy among those who are already enfranchised.
2. To adopt a quota system, allocating a certain number of seats to women and other minorities. Probably the number of these seats would not correspond to the actual proportion of women and minority groups within the total population, given the need to appease the illiberal majority in the short run.

These two strategies might help countries reduce the domestic tensions and even prevent a civil war that could thwart a democratic transition. Of course, they assume that well-crafted democratic institutions can coexist with poor democratic norms. The support for this assumption comes from some established democracies that have managed to survive even with a relatively low level of democratic norms. Israel is a case in point. According to a survey conducted by the Israel Democracy Institute, 57 percent of the Jewish citizens of Israel support forcing the Arabs of Israel (their de jure fellow citizens) to depart Israel, while 53 percent of them objected to giving Arabs full citizenship rights. Additionally 77 percent believe that Arabs should not take part in any "vital decisions" (*al-Hayat*, May 18, 2003). Taking these indicators together, one would put Israelis' support for democratic norms, as operationalized in this project, not far from that of Sudanese and Tajiks. Building upon the experience of Israel, a good policy recommendation to democracy builders in the above-mentioned Muslim countries is to proceed with caution and introduce democratic institutional reforms gradually, without upsetting the fragile social fabric, which is already precarious due to low levels of tolerance, equality, and trust.

Moderate Support for Democratic Norms and Institutions

The prospects for democratization increase the more one moves rightward in Figure 5.1, as the support for democratic institutions increases.

The circle in the middle of Figure 5.1 encloses what might be considered the average Muslim cultures: those that demonstrate greater tolerance of sociopolitical differences and are more accommodating to democratic institutions and procedures but have not yet reached high levels of support for democracy. These cultures include eleven groups of Muslims (including the ninety-one Iraqi respondents) and most notably two minorities: Lebanese Muslims and Muslims of European countries. Muslims of all these countries have been exposed to initial steps of a democratic transition (such as Gambia, Indonesia, and Bangladesh) or at least some liberalization process (such as Kuwait, Qatar, Bahrain, and Turkmenistan) in the past twenty years. Compared to cultures of the first group, which are less supportive of democracy on either institutional/ procedural or sociopolitical tolerance/trust bases, Muslims in these societies seem to be more ready to enter into democracy insofar as it is instituted fairly and honestly. According to a Syrian intellectual, "Syrians are ready to die for Hafez al-Assad and Bashar al-Assad on one condition: give them the right to choose that for themselves . . . through free elections."

Most of these cases, with the exception of Muslims in the European Union countries, are products of the third wave, and they are embodiments of Samuel Huntington's saying: "A general tendency seems to exist for third-wave democracies to become other than fully democratic" (Huntington 1996). All these cultures currently have some sort of public elections. Some of them are new to elections, like Qatar and Bahrain, while others have never undergone competitive multiparty elections, like Syria and Iraq until recently. A third group has had bloody experiences with elections, including Lebanon and Algeria. Among this group of societies, Kuwait stands alone as the country that fully used to disenfranchise women, in contrast to Indonesia and Bangladesh with their female heads of government. Gambia is constitutionally a presidential republic, yet despite its democratic institutions, there is no fair chance for the opposition to check the government. Turkmenistan, a country under dictatorial rule, manifested the lowest support for democratic institutions in this group (53 points). With the exception of the Muslims of Turkmenistan and of Europe, approximately 40–46 percent of respondents from other countries in this group characterize their current political system as exactly in the middle between fully free and full dictatorship; this reflects a tendency to see the pros and cons of the status quo and to compare it with what real democracy looks like. An Algerian professor of sociology, commenting on this finding, said, "Most of the people in these countries, with the exception of Iraq, Syria, and

Turkmenistan, can opine and talk freely, yet they are not politically effective. They are like one-eyed men. They cannot say that they cannot see, but they cannot say they see well like normal people either."

Despite the fact that the mode of the responses was toward the middle point of partially free and partially dictatorial, only 10 percent of respondents in Iraq, Syria, and Algeria perceived their country as free or partly free. This ratio increases dramatically to around 40 percent in the case of Muslims in European Union countries and Lebanon. Around 20–30 percent of respondents in the remaining countries considered their country to be free or partially free.

Surprisingly, the data suggest that Qatar has the highest level of support for democratic norms in this group of cultures (around 62 points). Actually Qatar, along with Bahrain, is often cited as a society in which a modernizing and liberal elite is ahead of the general population. Qatar, which is essentially a city-state, has capitalized on its homogeneity and small population to confront and address women's issues since the assumption of the Hamad Bin Khalifa al-Thani government in 1995. The number of Qatari women attending university is higher than the number of Qatari men with full political rights. Around 49 percent of Qatari respondents, the highest ratio in all Gulf states, found it acceptable for Qatari women to be voted into the parliament and assume ministerial positions. This finding suggests an answer to a question raised in the *New Yorker* in 2002. Under the title "Democracy by Decree," reporter Mary Anne Weaver asked, "Can one man propel a country into the future?" (Weaver 2000). The answer seems to be yes. Though there is no data available about Qataris' attitudes toward democracy before 1995, now Qatar currently ranks highest among all Gulf states in terms of its support for democratic norms and second only to Kuwait in terms of support for democratic institutions. In terms of democratic norms, it scores even higher than Jordan, Tunisia, Iran, Senegal, and Mali, all of which preceded it in their liberal/democratic transitions. Kuwait, on the other hand, lacks this support for women's enfranchisement, with around 45 percent of respondents refusing to support women's right to participate in politics at all.

Lebanon's, Indonesia's, and Syria's relatively clear deficits in regard for norms can hardly be attributable to the public's attitude toward women. Only 5 percent of respondents in Indonesia, 7 percent in Lebanon, and 13 percent in Syria thought that women should not be entitled to vote in public elections. A Pew project showed, moreover, that 86 percent of Muslims in Indonesia and 90 percent of Muslims in Lebanon endorsed women's right to decide on wearing *hijab*, an attitude that can be described as modernist or pluralist.

In these three countries, especially in Lebanon, however, there is a high level of intolerance and lack of trust of non-Muslims and among different sects of Islam. The effect of the Lebanese civil war on Muslims' low level of tolerance toward Lebanese non-Muslims is clear. Nevertheless, Lebanese tolerance is still high compared to that seen in other countries that experienced similar tragedies, such as Tajikistan, Nigeria, and Pakistan. Less tolerant than Indonesians, 33 percent of the Muslims of Lebanon who responded to the survey considered it right to disfranchise all non-Muslims, and only 5 percent favored the right of non-Muslims to assume top executive offices such as ministers. The shadows of the civil war are still evident in Lebanon, even during basketball games, where one hears slogans of racial and religious bigotry. In a recent basketball game, the fans of al-Riady (the "Sportive"), mostly Muslims, shouted "Syria—Syria," expressing their support of the Syrian army that backed Lebanese Muslims. In response, the fans of al-Hikma (the "Wisdom"), mainly Christians, shouted "USA" and "Hakim—Hakim," in reference to the Christian leader of the so-called Lebanese forces who was famous for killing his Muslim opponents during the civil war.

Lebanese Muslims seem to be only somewhat more tolerant in regard to inter-Islam sectarianism, with around 27 percent supporting the disfranchisement of Muslims from other sects, while only 6 percent would give them full political rights. Syrian respondents were somewhat similar to Lebanese regarding attitudes toward Muslims from other sects, but Syrians were dramatically less tolerant of non-Muslims, especially Jews, with around 70 percent supporting their total disfranchisement. The long war against Israel is the first factor to come to mind to explain this finding. However, the level of intolerance noticeably decreases to 16 percent of respondents in favor of disfranchising Christians. Only 10 percent of Syrian Muslims surveyed opined that fellow Muslims from other sects should be disfranchised. Around 17 percent of the Indonesian respondents did not believe that Christians and Jews should participate in politics at all, and only 3 percent gave them the right to fully participate as ministers. Indonesians, however, were more tolerant toward fellow Muslims from other sects; only 5 percent of the respondents asserted that Muslims from other sects should be deprived of political rights.

If other factors are not taken into account, a mass-led democratic transition appears to be a possibility in these countries that occupy the middle circle of Figure 5.1; yet it is not very likely given these respondents' halfhearted support for democratic institutions. This does not mean that there are no political demands for economic or social reforms. But these demands are likely to fall short of calling for real democratic transition. That said, an elite-led democratic transition would not meet much resistance at the mass level, provided that institutions were designed to reduce social tensions in these societies (Hadenius 2001).

The case of Iraq is significant in this regard. The ninety-one Iraqis who responded to this survey showed a level of tolerance and trust toward each other (53 points) that is actually higher than levels among respondents in Indonesia, Syria, Algeria, Lebanon, and Kuwait. Nothing in the current data shows Iraqis to be exceptionally antidemocratic. The main concern expressed by Iraqi Arab (Sunni and Shiite) respondents was the separatist tendency of Kurdish nationalists. Many Iraqi Arabs preferred the unity of their country over democracy with a divided Iraq. A 2005 survey of Iraqi college students supports this finding: "While 60% agreed with the statement that democracy is preferable to any other kind of government, a significant proportion, 27 percent, believed that there were circumstances where a non-democratic government was preferable. 13 percent of respondents were indifferent to the type of government governing them" (Latif 2005: 4). A liberal Iraqi commentator supported the coalition forces' reluctance to hold early elections in Iraq: "Iraqis have to move toward democracy cautiously and gradually. . . . Though the odds of a democratic Iraq are high, democracy needs training" (al-Qashtini 2003). This advice is consistent with my earlier conclusion that the countries in the middle circle do not necessarily manifest the level of tolerance that would make a quick resort to elections a smart move. However, as was stated by the spokesman of Ayat Allah Ali Sistani, the spiritual leader of Iraqi Shiites, "Elections is our way to achieve independence. We will show tolerance to Iraqis regardless of religion and ethnicity. We do not want to give any foreign country the pretext to determine the future of Iraq" (Al-Watan, September 15, 2004).

The circle in the middle contains as well the average of all Muslims, including the ones that were coded as "others" since the number of respondents from their countries did not meet the criterion of 480 respondents per country. On average Muslims, regardless of their land of origin, are relatively, but not highly, tolerant toward women, non-Muslims, and Muslims of other sects, with a score of 54 points. In other words, average Muslims are not as intolerant as the stereotype suggests. Moreover, average Muslims are relatively supportive of democratic institutions and procedures that are recognized as genuine: their score for support of democratic institutions reaches 60.

High Support for Democratic Institutions and Norms

The symmetry between support for democratic institutions and norms continues with the group of cases in the upper right corner of Figure 5.1, which produced the highest levels of support for democratic norms and institutions. These rankings largely confirm what was found in Pew Project surveys of 2002 and 2003, which identified Muslims of Jordan, Lebanon, Morocco, and Mali as among the most supportive of democracy (Allen 2005).

When it comes to explaining, then, why some of these countries have not already achieved stable democratic governments, the data suggest that one should search for noncultural explanations. Moroccans, for example, have the highest level of support for democratic institutions and a relatively high level of tolerance, yet their country is not a constitutional monarchy following the Westminster model (though the constitution of 1962 allows for a representative government, elected parliament, and multiparty system). The inordinate strength of the monarchy reduces the political parties to administrative units for all intents and purposes (Gillespie and Youngs 2002). However, the Moroccan respondents' support for democratic institutions such as political parties and parliament is understood given the fact that independence was achieved mainly by the efforts of the al-Istiqlal (Independence) Party founded in 1944 and through many negotiations and coalitions inside an elected parliament. The data suggest that Morocco's lack of a stable democratic system cannot be attributed to individuals' attitudes but to the role played by the king (Bourqia and Miller 1999; Layachi 1998).

Respondents from Turkey, similarly, expressed the highest level of sociopolitical tolerance in terms of culture and very high support for democratic institutions. Yet military interventions to protect and safeguard the secular system, along with a somewhat illiberal constitution, pose a great obstacle for full democratization. Both the survey data and the focus-group discussions suggest Turkey has a publicly tolerant culture that does not reflect the practices of its government, especially the government's military arm. One should recall that the public already voted a woman with *hijab* into the parliament. It was the secular government, induced and supported by the military, that disqualified her, not the Turkish people (Saktanber 2002). Even the Kurdish issue does not seem to be a battle of Turkish individuals but rather a case of the military's inducing government oppression since 1924 (Ibrahim and Gèurbey 2000). According to a Turkish student of engineering, "There is no guarantee that the military would not strip the president himself of his constitutional rights. They can change the constitution or even tear it up in an hour." This reading of Turkish culture is compatible with the finding that democracy has not been viewed as a top priority by Turkish officials and politicians (Heper and Sayari 2002). The 2002 elections reflected the Turkish people's disappointment with all the parties that have been in power since the military gave up power in early 1983 (Kedourie 1996).

Muslims in the United States seem to be more supportive of democracy than other Muslim minority groups in India, Europe, and Lebanon. For instance, 57 percent of US Muslims believe that women should be given all political rights without reservations. This ratio goes down to 51 percent for EU Muslims and 41 percent among Indian Muslims.

With the exception of Iran, almost all other societies in this group have (semi-)secularist constitutions and governmental platforms. This finding supports the arguments made by some that secularism, once introduced to Muslim societies, will increase the level of tolerance and peaceful coexistence among religions and sects (Baghdadi 1999). This position is further supported by the fact that the exception, Iran, holds the second-lowest ranking for support of democratic norms among the most democratic Muslim countries. (Only Jordan scores lower in this group.) An anonymous Iranian reformist lawyer explained that this is not because Iranians are intolerant; rather, it is because "they do not go, in terms of their tolerance, to the level of infringing upon the roots of their religion." This analysis finds support in the pooled data. In the four questions regarding the political rights of Christians, Jews, and other non-Muslims and of women and Muslims from other sects, the mode was to allow all of them to vote and to become members of the parliament. The second most supported option was to give them full political rights, including the ability to become the country's top executive, which suggests that Iranians in general are tolerant but cautious.

The relative deficit in Jordan's democratic norms is attributed mainly to polarized views regarding the political rights of women. At one end of this spectrum, 33 percent of the respondents would refuse to give women any political rights. At the other, 42 percent want to give women full political rights. Another factor that seems to be responsible for the relative deficit of democratic norms in Jordan is the attitude toward Muslims from different sects: 55 percent of the respondents would refuse to give others any political rights. As one respondent commented, this may be because of a fear of the effect of tribalism and sectarianism on the unity of the country rather than because of prejudice or bigotry.

The data also reveal attitudes about political tolerance that are shared broadly across Muslim societies. The pooled data suggest that tolerance toward Jews is much less than tolerance toward Christians in all Muslim countries, except for the case of Morocco, where Jews have always been part of the social fabric (as shown in Tables 5.1 and 5.2). In Table 5.1, given the large norm of *t* (39.3), one can reject the hypothesis that Muslims treat Christians and Jews alike and accept the alternative hypothesis that Muslims are more tolerant toward Christians than toward Jews. There was a near consensus among all the interviewees, secularists and Islamists alike, that this discrepancy in tolerance between Jews and Christians can be attributed to the Quran's clear criticisms of the Jews and to Muslims' sympathy and solidarity with their brothers and sisters in Palestine. Morocco, once again, is the exception: there was no statistical difference in the ways Moroccan Muslims perceive Christians and Jews (see Table 5.2).

As Table 5.3 shows, Muslims have a tendency to show greater tolerance toward fellow Muslims from other sects more than toward non-Muslims. This holds true for respondents from Indonesia, Gambia, Egypt, Nigeria, India, Malaysia, Turkey, Qatar, and Bangladesh. Notably, what separates these countries from many other Islamic societies is their lack of intense divisions between Islamic sects. Sectarian

Table 5.1   Attitudes Toward Jews and Christians in the Whole Sample (T-Test)

	Mean	Std. Err	Std. Dev.	T
Christians	2.799	.007	1.052	39.316
Jews	2.639	0.008	1.111	

Note: A T-ratio above 1.96 indicates that there is a statistically significant difference between the means at confidence level of 0.95. N = 20,457 and 2-tailed test.

Table 5.2   Difference in Tolerance Toward Jews and Christians in Morocco (T-Test)

	Mean	Std. Err	Std. Dev.	T
Christians	3.351	0.029	0.685	1.265
Jews	3.344	0.029	0.696	

Note: A T-ratio below 1.96 indicates that there is no statistically significant difference between the means at confidence level of 0.95. N = 558 and 2-tailed test.

Table 5.3   Difference in Tolerance Toward Muslim Minorities and Non-Muslim Minorities (T-Test)

	Mean	Std. Err	Std. Dev.	T
Non-Muslims	2.652	0.010	1.065	−8.6966
Muslim minorities	2.727	0.009	1.052	

Note: A T-ratio above 1.96 indicates that there is a statistically significant difference between the means at confidence level of 0.95. N = 11,168 and 2-tailed test.

intolerance prevails, however, in Saudi Arabia and Kuwait (where Sunni are the majority), as well as Bahrain and Iran (where Shiites are the majority). Muslims from Morocco, Senegal, Mali, Lebanon, the United Arab Emirates, Oman, Pakistan, and Sudan do not have a statistically significant difference between tolerance of Muslims of other sects and tolerance of non-Muslim minorities. As Figure 5.1 shows, however, this can mean either high tolerance of both groups or extremely low tolerance of both, as is the case in countries like Pakistan and Sudan.

Many people cite sectarian divisions in countries such as Saudi Arabia and Pakistan as a major obstacle to democratization. These divisions, no doubt, pose serious obstacles to power sharing. That said, as was demonstrated with Israel, democracies often succeed with surprisingly high levels of public intolerance of minorities. Further evidence of this is a Pew survey that revealed that nearly four out of ten American citizens "would not vote for a well-qualified Muslim for president" (2003b). Further, a significant percentage of Americans would not vote for a qualified evangelical (15 percent), a Jew (10 percent), a Catholic (8 percent), or an atheist (52 percent). Thus, inter- and intrareligious tensions are not a distinctly Muslim phenomenon, though they can be especially acute and troubling in some Muslim countries.

Rigid attitudes toward women's political efficacy in general are a male rather than a female phenomenon, as Table 5.4 suggests. That is to

Table 5.4   Difference in Tolerance Toward Women (T-Test)

	N	Mean	Std. Err	Std. Dev.	T
Male	15,476	2.696	0.008	1.050	−34.131
Female	7,738	3.176	0.010	0.909	

Note: A T-ratio above 1.96 indicates that there is a statistically significant difference between the means at confidence level of 0.95. N = 15,835 and 2-tailed test.

say, with the exception of Turkey and Tajikistan, all sampled data reveal a clear tendency among women to support their own political rights more than men do. There were no statistically significant differences between Turkish men and women in their support for women's rights; likewise, Tajik men and women both expressed relatively low support of women's political rights. Still, even in countries with little support for women's political rights, women on average are more tolerant than men.

Muslims and the "Ideal" Political System

Supporting democracy means that one has an idea about how it works in action. Likewise, the people who oppose democracy must have an idea of what the alternative is. To gauge these preferences, respondents were given a list of thirteen countries representing various political systems and asked to choose the one that comes closest to their "best/ideal/favorite" one. They were also given the option "none of the above." In the following question in the survey, they were asked in an open-ended format to state why they chose the political system they chose. After a daunting process of coding, the results are presented in Table 5.5.

The table reveals a number of intriguing trends among Muslims. The percentage of those who chose "none of the above," 40.6, is quite surprising given that the thirteen countries the respondents could choose from represent virtually every type in the modern world, from absolute monarchy (Saudi Arabia) to constitutional monarchy (Britain), from most totalitarian (Iraq) to most democratic (United States and France), and from most secular (India and Turkey) to least secular (Afghanistan under the Taliban and Iran); they could also choose a range of systems in between, such as those of Jordan, Egypt, and Sudan.

When most of the intellectuals and activists whom I interviewed learned that four out of every ten literate Muslims preferred none of the thirteen mentioned political systems, they advanced different explanations, such as lack of information about these systems, vagueness of the question, ignorance, and nostalgia for previous golden ages of Islam. The last explanation seems particularly cogent because it was primarily Islamists, whether traditionalists or modernists, who refused all current political systems. Fully 48 of the former and 14 percent of the latter fell into this category. Secularists, by contrast, were significantly more grounded: only 2 percent of statists and 1 percent of pluralists dreamed

Table 5.5 Respondents' Ideal Political Systems (percentage)

	(1)		(2)	(3)	(4)	(5)	(6)
	Freq.	Total	Selecting Own Country	Modernists	Traditionalists	Autocrats	Pluralists
Iraq	43	0.18	0	0	0	11	0
Turkey	102	0.42	12	18	1	5	22
Jordan	173	0.71	11	5	2	21	10
Pakistan	311	1.28	8	1	4	18	4
Egypt	395	1.62	3	2	1	19	6
Sudan	398	1.63	15	5	12	9	3
Saudi Arabia	401	1.65	14	1	14	1	0
UK	503	2.06	34	10	1	1	14
India	546	2.24	23	6	0	2	12
France	955	3.92	31	7	0	1	10
Afghanistan	2,989	12.27	-	3	14	2	0
Iran	3,372	13.84	27	17	3	6	6
USA	4,072	16.71	37	11	0	2	12
None	9,883	40.56	-	14	48	2	1
Total	24,365	100		100	100	100	100
Support democracy		24.93		34	1	6	48

Source: E-mail and written survey 2002.

of a system not on the list. (Though I will continue to touch upon the issue of motivation in this section, it will be explored more deeply in the following one.)

Traditionalist Islamists are known to perceive democracy as being antithetical to Islamic government; thus it makes sense that those who chose an extant political system looked to Sudan, Saudi Arabia, and Afghanistan under the Taliban. These three political systems ascribe to themselves the role of defending and abiding by Islamic sharia. Support for the Taliban was relatively high among only 14 percent of the traditionalists. A female Emirati teacher, speculating on why it was not more popular, suggested that with civil war dividing the brothers of Afghanistan, it was still not as good as the golden age of Islam. It is interesting that out of the 14 percent of traditionalists who chose Saudi Arabia as their ideal political system, only 2 percent were actually Saudis. The rest have not had direct experience with the country. Moreover, only 14 percent of Saudis generally perceive their political system to be the best one (column 2). A traditionalist Saudi shaikh, who was privately critical of the regime, attributed the lack of support for the Saudi political system to the rulers' duplicity. The Saudi regime bases its legitimacy on Islam, but the people are not convinced.

Comparatively speaking, however, the Saudi political system was considered more legitimate than the Iraqi, Egyptian, and Pakistani, with 0 percent of Iraqis (most of them were not in Iraq during the survey), 3 percent of Egyptians, and 8 percent of Pakistanis believing their own political systems to be ideal. Jordanians, Sudanese, and Turks were, surprisingly, not much more positive in their view of their political system, which lends support to the notion that legitimacy is a serious problem in many Muslim countries. In fact, the focus-group discussions made clear that most respondents could not separate their attitudes toward their country's political system from their ideas about their current government. "Once they hate the government, they hardly accept the rules and institutions of the system," a Sudanese professor noted.

The unique position Iran holds among traditionalist Islamists across the Muslim world and its own people is worthy of examination. Though a self-described Islamist country, Iran was not widely chosen by traditionalists as having an ideal political system. The twenty-seven Sunni traditionalists who were interviewed deliberately avoided Iran as their ideal system because it is a Shiite country. Capturing this sentiment, an Emirati graduate student observed, "Whoever does not adopt the Prophet and his companions' system of life and government cannot be right." The Emirati student refers to the severe criticisms, even insults, raised by some Shiites toward Prophet Muhammad's wife, Aisha, and the early three Caliphs of Islam who, according to Shiite Muslims, usurped the Caliphate from Ali, Prophet Mohamed's cousin. That said, Iranians seem to be the most satisfied with their political system of all Muslims living in Muslim countries; 27 percent think it to be the best system of government. Of these respondents, however, 90 percent were traditionalists. A twenty-one-year-old female traditionalist student from Iran said earnestly, "Allah has made Iran the refuge of all true Muslims. . . . It will never remain as such unless all true Muslims vote, write, teach, preach, and die to keep it so. . . . The West and its collaborators from other neighboring countries do not want Iran to remain as is, since it symbolizes their moral vacuum. They want us [Iranians] to be like them. But *insh'aa Allah*, this will never happen."

Traditional Iranians like this student tend to think of themselves as guardians of Allah's message against Allah's enemy. When I explored who Allah's enemies specifically are, I found that they are a vast and motley group, from West to East, with one common goal: to devour Islam. This circle of enemies includes fellow Iranians "who prefer the Western style of life, food, songs, dress, and social relationships over Allah's way of life," another Iranian student said.

Both modernists and pluralists preferred the Turkish model (18 and 22 percent respectively). Essam Al-'Eryan of the Egyptian Muslim Brotherhood praised the Turkish system and proposed it as a viable system that can allow all voices to be heard on equal footing. Of course, he lamented the role of the military in this regard. But he clearly preferred it to the Iranian model, which for him was another example of an authoritarian regime dressed in Islam. Because the Turkish system seems to be one that Islamists and secularists can agree upon, it may be the most promising model for Muslim states looking to democratize. Pluralists also appreciated the Jordanian political system (10 percent), largely because of its capacity to peacefully absorb Islamists into the political system.

Generally speaking, any efforts to democratize would seem to require an alliance between modernists and pluralists, as they, unsurprisingly, are most likely to name a democratic regime as their ideal political type. Thirty-four and 48 percent, respectively, named a democratic country as their model political system. These two figures are shown in the last row of Table 5.8 and have been calculated by adding up the percentage of the supporters of the four stable democracies in the model (italics).

Living in a democracy also seems to impart a more favorable view of democratic government among Muslims. Those Muslims who lived as minorities in democracies, even those with troubles such as in India, seemed to be more satisfied with their own political system. This satisfaction reached its peak in the United States (37 percent) and was at its lower end in the case of India (23 percent). Keeping in mind that these data were collected immediately before the new measures taken by the US government toward Muslims in the United States after September 11, one suspects that this percentage would be sharply lower were the survey to be conducted now. Generally, though, the results show that Muslims are not satisfied with their own political system and are in search of a better one.

The secular statists mostly favored Jordan, possibly because it is more stable with rare social unrest, compared to other statist regimes. One should remember that in Jordan Islamists are allowed to participate in elections and have their own political associations. Of course, the Islamists have legitimate complaints regarding their exclusion from the government, no matter how many seats they win, and of the support the king gives to his preferred political associations. According to Mustapha K. Al-Sayyid of Cairo University, Egypt is a good example of a stable, relatively liberalized country where the masses are left to mind their own business, if not to be politically active. Support for the Iraqi model appeared only among statists. (As Table 5.6 will demonstrate, support for Iraq under Saddam Hussein had no democratic or Islamic reasons.) The same can be said about statists who supported the democratic systems of the West. This support had nothing to do with democracy; rather, it was a matter of personal (not political) freedoms, economic advancement, and technology.

The respondents were asked to spell out why they made their choices. A summary of the responses is presented in Table 5.6. In the table, the respondents who chose a system are classified into one of four reasons: purely democratic reasons, purely Islamic reasons, a mix of democratic/Islamic reasons, and other reasons (such as liberating occupied territories, affection for a place, or economic advancement). Around 74 percent of Muslims who did not find any of the thirteen political systems appealing were propelled by Islamic reasons. According to an Emirati citizen who chose none of the mentioned systems, "None of these systems come close to the Islamic state established by the Prophet. They are not designed to set Allah's word above all other words" This reasoning was very common among traditionalists (around 93 percent) and some (around 6 percent) among modernists.

Such reasoning supports the secularists' argument that many

Table 5.6   Explanation of Ideal Political System

	Freq.	(1) Percent	(2) Democratic Reasons	(3) Islamic Reasons	(4) Combination	(5) Other Reasons
Iraq	43	0.18			100	
Turkey	102	0.42	32	11	21	36
Jordan	173	0.71	3	5	31	61
Pakistan	311	1.28	10	8	22	60
Egypt	395	1.62	9	15	21	55
Sudan	398	1.63	5	72	11	12
Saudi Arabia	401	1.65	1	82	3	14
UK	503	2.06	55	11	23	11
India	546	2.24	47	12	20	21
France	955	3.92	51	7	28	14
Afghanistan	2,989	12.27	0	68	0	32
Iran	3,372	13.84	5	11	78	6
USA	4,072	16.71	52	13	25	10
None	9,883	40.56	2	74	18	6
Total	24,365	100	20.9	29.9	23.2	26.0

Source: E-mail and written survey 2002.

Muslims are nostalgic for a golden past of glory and splendor; thus they lack a practical capacity to develop sociopolitical systems that would be compatible with modern life. According to a secularist intellectual, "It should be known that the dead are controlling the contemporary Arab and Muslim societies. . . . To date, we have not solved the problem between 'Ali and Moa'weya or al-Hussein and Yazeed and even failed to swallow them" (Saleh 2003). The data definitely support this claim in regard to how at least 40 percent of educated Muslims perceive the world they live in.

However, it seems that Muslims are not as uninformed as some of the intellectuals and activists whom I interviewed suggest. Rather, many of them have come up with their own synthesis of Islam and democracy. For instance, most of those who chose stable democracies as their preferred/ideal political systems were not captives of the fallacious "either Islamic or democratic" assumption. They advanced arguments based upon Islamic and democratic references at the same time, as is clear from column 4 in Table 5.6.

What is more interesting is the tendency of many modernists to argue that the British, Indian, French, and US political systems are Islamic systems of government in the way they are structured. "Had

Muslims been able to independently develop their own systems of government, they would have come up with a French system of government with the president as the caliph and the ministers as his aides while the parliament is *ahl al-hall wa al-aqd (people of knowledge and piety),*" a Tunisian respondent said.

"The colonial era distorted the natural development of the Islamic caliphate. The Ottoman Empire started political reforms in the nineteenth century, but the West did not want us to outdo them," a Malaysian respondent said.

"Islam is justice. Whatever achieves justice is Islamic. Thus democracy is as Islamic as prayer and fasting," an Iranian respondent said.

"The US system is like the Islamic caliphate system. The differences are just in names," a Malian respondent said.

"The British system is the best one to fit the modern Islamic state," a Nigerian respondent said.

The Elasticity of Demand for Democracy

From Table 4.1, one infers that around 55 percent of all pooled Muslims support democracy over incumbents who are generally undemocratically elected. However, are Muslims ready to pay the price of democracy? That is to say, assuming that the only way for Muslims to achieve democracy would be through mass-led demonstrations, strikes, and public demands following the Romanian, Georgian, or Ukrainian path toward democracy, are they ready to do that?

The phrase "elasticity of demand for democracy" is useful in this regard. It refers to the degree to which persons are willing to sacrifice for democracy. In microeconomics, the term "elasticity of demand" is used to reflect the sensitivity of quantity demand to price changes. In other words, to what extent is a person ready to sacrifice his or her money (in this case his or her freedom or even life) to gain the demanded commodity (in this case political rights)? The demand for drugs by addicts is *inelastic*: that is, no matter how expensive the drug is, the addicted person has no other choice but to pay what is needed. On the other hand, demand for flowers or perfume is very elastic. A very small increase in the price of these commodities may lead to a very sharp decline in the demand for them.

How do Muslims perceive their political rights: as necessary drugs or luxurious flowers? Two survey questions (32 and 39) can shed some light on this issue. The first reads: "To achieve their political rights (e.g.

freedom of expression and freedom of association), Muslims should
. . ." Four options are offered, ranging from violent opposition to rulers
to patience and prayer to Allah. The second asks: "There are individuals
who are killed or sent to jail because they publicly ask for their political
rights. Do you agree or disagree with what they do?" The respondents
are given five choices, starting from "strongly agree" and ranging to
"strongly disagree." Confirmatory factor analysis was run to verify that
the two questions measure the same dimension. Varimax rotation followed by Cronbach's test of reliability and internal consistency showed
that the responses expressed a high level of internal consistency
(alpha = 0.91). The responses to the two questions were standardized
and rescaled, as reflected in Table 5.7. A culture with high points would
be more ready to sacrifice for democracy, in which case the demand for
democracy is less elastic. In such societies, no matter how much one has
to sacrifice for one's political rights, many would be ready to pay the
price.

Some cultures seem to be more ready to sacrifice for democracy
than others. Composite scores from Iran, Turkey, Mali, Senegal, and
Malaysia are the highest in this regard. Arabs as a distinct group of
Muslims seem to be the least ready to sacrifice for democracy. There is
a good deal of supporting evidence for the "Arab exceptionalism" argument. Non-Arab Muslim states have been described as "overachievers"
in democracy relative to their level of economic development. Arab
Muslim states, by contrast, clearly rank as "underachievers" (Stepan
and Robertson 2003). This study suggests that the lack of democratization in the Arab world can be partially attributed to Arabs' general
unwillingness to make sacrifices for their political rights. Countries like
Morocco and Egypt, having strong public support for democratic institutions and norms as well as relatively liberal cultures, rank 16 and 24,
respectively, in a list of thirty-two countries. It seems, then, that if
Arabs are given democratic freedoms and procedures as a gift from
their rulers, they will accept them, but the chances of a mass-led democratization are relatively low compared to the chances in countries like
Iran and Turkey.

The situation in Iran is worth further examination because there a
Muslim ruler, Khomeini, actually linked political activism to religious
obligation. If, in Islam, issues and things can be classified as *wajib*
(obligatory), *mostahab* (recommended), *mandob* (acceptable), *makrouh*
(hated), or *haram* (forbidden), Iranian Muslims' political duties are
largely perceived as an obligation, like prayer and fasting. According to
an Iranian journalist, "If I die for my right to freely publish what I

Table 5.7   Muslims' Relative Elasticity of Demand for Political Rights

Elasticity	N	Mean	Std. Dev.	Min.	Max.	Scale from 28 to 100
Saudi Arabia	743	−2.27	1.53	−3.62	1.92	28.06
UAE	545	−2.20	1.95	−3.62	2.64	29.53
Yemen	396	−1.89	1.55	−3.62	2.64	35.83
Libya	512	−1.58	2.06	−3.62	2.64	41.89
Oman	458	−1.52	1.95	−3.62	2.64	43.20
Qatar	464	−1.01	1.46	−3.62	2.64	53.46
Tunisia	495	−0.86	1.74	−3.62	2.64	56.32
Tajikistan	449	−0.81	1.62	−3.62	2.64	57.48
Morocco	575	−0.69	1.70	−3.62	2.64	59.81
Turkmenistan	478	−0.68	1.64	−3.62	1.52	59.99
Jordan	634	−0.65	1.69	−3.62	2.64	60.56
Pakistan	1473	−0.60	1.77	−3.62	2.64	61.65
Syria	577	−0.55	1.48	−3.62	2.64	62.61
Kuwait	438	−0.52	1.90	−3.62	2.64	63.22
Bahrain	395	−0.51	1.80	−3.62	1.52	63.43
Sudan	532	−0.49	1.44	−3.62	1.52	63.82
Egypt	1277	−0.43	1.47	−3.62	2.64	65.03
Lebanon	430	−0.30	1.96	−3.62	2.64	67.69
Nigeria	543	−0.25	1.97	−3.62	2.64	68.64
Algeria	515	−0.06	2.42	−3.62	2.64	72.43
EU	708	0.57	1.73	−3.62	2.64	85.13
Indonesia	1208	0.61	1.66	−3.62	2.64	85.87
Bangladesh	825	0.82	1.72	−3.62	2.64	90.07
USA	984	0.85	1.46	−3.62	2.64	90.63
Albania	447	0.95	1.41	−3.62	2.64	92.74
India	1357	0.98	1.48	−3.62	2.64	93.33
Gambia	478	0.99	1.41	−3.62	2.64	93.48
Malaysia	1072	1.14	1.31	−3.62	2.64	96.43
Senegal	517	1.19	1.25	−3.62	2.64	97.60
Mali	510	1.21	1.20	−3.62	2.64	97.89
Turkey	948	1.26	1.10	−3.62	2.64	99.01
Iran	1031	1.31	1.16	−3.62	2.64	100.00

Source: E-mail and written survey 2002.

believe in, I'll die as *shaheed* [martyr]." Student demonstrations with cries of "Death to dictatorship!" and denunciations of the banning of reformist newspapers such as *Salam* are mainly an Iranian phenomenon.

Most demonstrations in the Muslim world are not for democracy or democratic rights; rather, they are anti-American or anti-Israeli, or for solving economic problems. Unfortunately, the demonstrations do not pay off. A Sudanese female student noticed that most of her colleagues demonstrate for nonpolitical issues while "the whole problem is political. . . . We are given the right to demonstrate but not to affect, to waste our time and energy shouting but not to really change anything. I gave up the habit of demonstrations."

A survey conducted by the al-Ahram Center for Strategic Studies found that around 75 percent of Egyptians pointed to democracy as their favorite political system, but when asked about their priorities, only 7 percent set political reform as their first priority compared to addressing economic and social problems, achieving Arab or Muslim unity, and the liberation of Palestine (Sa'eed 2003). Alarmed by this finding, I asked all participants in the focus groups in the countries I visited the following hypothetical question: "Would you accept a contract with a ruler like Saddam Hussein that gave him the right to rule for life on the condition that he would actually liberate Palestine?" Surprisingly, the great majority of those I questioned—around 73 percent—responded affirmatively. Arabs were more inclined to accept the Saddam/Palestine deal, around 89 percent. Roughly 61 percent of non-Arab Muslims showed support for it, which is still a solid majority. Recognizing that I had given them a loaded question, I followed up with a condition: "Lifetime Saddam Hussein means no political freedoms for all your lifetimes." This fact did not change many minds. A majority of Muslim respondents rejected the proposed contract only in Turkey, Iran, and the United States.

How should we understand this surprising response? First, the occupation of Palestine is perceived to be the number-one issue in the mind of all Arabs and most Muslims. And as if the Muslim body had a bleeding nose, it finds it very difficult to focus on anything else. Part of this commitment stems from religious obligation, as Counselor al-Bishri of Egypt explains: "In the Muslim mind, issues of personal freedom come second to the issues of *ummah*'s freedom." A similar assessment comes from a twenty-year-old female from the United Arab Emirates. Commenting on the hypothetical Palestine/Saddam deal, she argues, "At least with a free Palestine, we can say that we achieved something meaningful for our religion." Al-Bishri believes that the Muslim focus on religious duties goes a long way toward explaining why the Egyptian liberation movement, while realizing the goal of national independence, failed to achieve constitutional government, a situation common to most Muslim countries.

From the focus-group discussions, a second explanation emerged concerning Muslim support for the hypothetical pact. Simply put, Saddam Hussein is not seen as being as bad as Israel. A Pakistani engineer reasoned, "Saddam Hussein is not the enemy of Muslims. He is the enemy of Kuwait. Israel is the enemy of Muslims." When I explained to him and the other participants that Saddam Hussein had killed more Muslims than Israel had, he accused him of being a tool in the hands of Israel and the United States. Though the rest of the Pakistani interviewees disagreed with him, they agreed that Saddam was less a threat to them than was Israel. This response needs to be understood in the national context in which the respondents were situated. With the exception of the Kuwaiti and Saudi media after 1991, most government-owned Arab mass media refrain from airing the dirty laundry of other Arab governments, lest their own laundry be brought to light too. But this restraint, of course, is not applied to information about Israel's use of Western (mainly US) weapons to kill their brothers and sisters in Palestine. Statistically, Saddam Hussein did kill more Muslims than all Israeli wars with Arabs did. But who knows that?

The Muslim interviewees (27 percent) who refused to accept the Saddam/Palestine deal had interesting arguments to make. An Egyptian student of business commented, "Israel wins because it is a democracy; we will not defeat Israel with Saddam in power." Other interviewees voiced similar thoughts. With the exception of three respondents who were not particularly concerned about the liberation of Palestine, considering it a Palestinian issue, the great majority of the interviewees valued democracy as an essential means for a better life and a free state of Palestine. One inference that can be made with some degree of certainty is that most Muslims perceive national independence from non-Muslim powers to be more worthy of sacrifice and resistance than resisting their own corrupt statist rulers.

Concluding Remarks

This concluding section has two purposes: first, to discuss the country-level variation in the attitudes toward democratic institutions and norms, and second, to shed some light on the prospects for democratization in these countries based on the society-level data analyzed in this chapter and the previous one.

Explaining the Society-Level Variation

To shed light on reasons that some societies are aggregately more supportive of democracy than others, the previous analysis should be put together in a way that can reveal some regularities. Table 5.8 reveals that there is significant correlation between societies' aggregate support

Table 5.8   Variables Causing Aggregate Support for Democracy

	Norms	Institutions
% of statists and traditionalists	–0.72***	–0.76***
% of Muslims in support of status quo/incumbents	–0.69***	–0.81***
% of Muslims ready to sacrifice for political rights	0.27**	0.31**
% of Muslims choosing democracies as ideal system	0.74***	0.83***

Source: E-mail and written survey 2002.
Notes: Number of cases = 32.
*p < 0.05, **p < 0.01, *** < 0.001—2-tailed tests.

for democratic norms and institutions, on the one hand, and the aggregate attitudes of Muslims within their society. Muslim societies score highest on support for democratic institutions and norms scales when the following conditions are present:

1. The distribution of attitudes indicates that statists and traditionalists are in the minority and modernist Islamists and pluralist secularists are in the majority.
2. Muslims have negative attitudes toward undemocratically elected incumbents.
3. Muslims are ready to sacrifice for their political rights.
4. Muslims do not cherish fantastic, nostalgia-fed ideas about what government can or should be and thus accept a democratic system of government.

Prospects for Democratization

In an attempt to explain the emergence and acceptance of new norms in the international system, Martha Finnemore and Kathryn Sikkink (1998) identify a three-stage life cycle: (1) norm emergence, (2) norm acceptance, and (3) norm internalization. The logic underlying this schema helped to inspire the four types of political culture I have identified to clarify levels of democratic potential in Muslim societies. First, certain societies are at the stage of rejecting democratic norms and institutions because they are deemed either harmful or *haram*. In the second type of Muslim political culture, democracy has emerged in the discourse of some intellectuals and *ulama* but has not been widely accepted among the masses. A third type is marked by broader support for democracy, though the general public is not intensely committed to and willing to fight for it. In this instance, acceptance of democracy can be attributed to the efforts of *ulama* as well as modernist and pluralist intellectuals and activists. The fourth type reaches a higher level of democratic internalization in the sense that democracy is not a luxury for the majority of the public. Rather, it is seen as the solution to pressing problems, and this requires the public to speak out even if this involves significant risks.

To summarize, Muslim societies can be divided into four types of cultures: (1) cultures that reject the norms and institutions of democracy, (2) cultures in which democratic notions of government have emerged but have not taken root, (3) cultures in which democracy is generally accepted but not considered the top priority, and (4) cultures in which democracy has been internalized and individuals perceive it to be necessary for solving socioeconomic problems.

Persons of these cultures differ not only in the extent to which they will sacrifice for their political rights but also in their perception of the status quo. Some cultures seem to produce individuals who are relatively comfortable in their beliefs; the society manifests a state of cultural/political equilibrium. Some societies, for example, perceive themselves as nondemocratic and do not want democracy. Thus, they are classified as steady rejecters of democracy. Other cultures are in greater flux: there is strong desire for change and little support for incumbents. The form that change might take, however, is unclear: it may not be a democratic change at all. If the only clear consensus is dissatisfaction with the status quo, it can be hard to ascertain what such a society actually supports.

In Table 5.9, the thirty-two societies examined in this survey are broken down into four types of political culture, characterized (1) rejection of democratic governance, (2) emerging support for democracy, (3) broader acceptance of democracy, or (4) internalization of democratic values. Each society's classification is based on a composite measure that incorporates five indicators: (1) support for democratic norms, (2) support for democratic institutions, (3) democratizability (democratic potential), (4) elasticity of demand for democracy, and (5) ideal political system. For three of the four cultures, a further distinction is made between those societies that are firmly rooted in a particular type of political culture and those that lean toward a particular political culture but demonstrate less support for the status quo (the sixth indicator). These societies are labeled as less certain because they are not as firmly rooted in the political culture within which they are categorized.

Under category 1, five societies have a political culture characterized by a rejection of Western-style democratic government. These

Table 5.9 The Spectrum of Democratic Beliefs in Muslim Societies

	Rejection of Democratic Governance		Emergence of Support for Democracy	Broader Acceptance of Democracy		Internalization of Democratic Values	
	1 Steady	2 Less Certain	3	4 Steady	5 Less Certain	6 Steady	7 Less Certain
Societies	UAE Oman Libya	Saudi Arabia Yemen	Sudan Pakistan Nigeria Indonesia Tajikistan	Qatar Bahrain Morocco Tunisia Jordan Algeria	Gambia Lebanon Turkmenistan Kuwait Syria Egypt Bangladesh	Turkey Mali Senegal India Albania USA EU	Iran Malaysia
Support for democratic norms	M/H	L	L/M	H	M/H	H	M/H
Support for democratic institutions	L/M	L	M	M/H	M/H	H	H
Democratizability	L	L	L/M	M/H	M/H	H	H
Support for the status quo	H	L	L/M	M/H	L/M	H	L/M
Elasticity of demand for democracy	H	H	H/M	M	M/L	L	L
Ideal system	D	Not D	D	D	D	D	D

Source: E-mail and written survey 2002.
Notes: L: Low; M: Moderate; H: High; D: Democratic

countries are the United Arab Emirates, Oman, Libya, Saudi Arabia, and Yemen. However, there is a subtle difference among them. The first three societies firmly reject democracy while the other two are less certain in this rejection. This difference can be inferred when one compares the degrees of consistency among the six indicators for each society. For instance, almost all measures suggest that the United Arab Emirates will not have to deal with mass-initiated demands for democracy in the near future. It is a country with a relatively high level of sociopolitical acceptance of minorities but with very little support for what they do not have, which is democratic institutions. Furthermore, the elasticity of demand for democracy is high, meaning that Emiratis have little desire to sacrifice for democracy. Finally, they are quite satisfied with the status quo. Saudi Arabia and Yemen, by contrast, are less certain in their rejection of democracy because, in spite of the majority preference for nondemocratic systems (for religious reasons), there are only low levels of support for incumbents and the status quo.

The next type of political culture in Table 5.9, emerging democracies, deserves some explanation. Unlike the other categories, it is not broken down among those societies that are firmly rooted in the culture and those that are less rooted because of a desire for change. These societies, then, are by definition less firmly rooted. But what makes Sudan, Pakistan, Nigeria, Indonesia, and Tajikistan emerging democracies instead of less certain rejecters? The answer is that their support for democratic institutions is clearly higher than the rejecters', of both the firm and the less certain variety, and they are somewhat more willing to sacrifice for democracy, even if their commitment is not overwhelming. Beyond this, they tend to identify countries with democratic political systems as having the ideal form of government. That said, they do not demonstrate high levels of political tolerance for oppressed groups. It is possible, then, that if any of these statist governments weakened their grip, ethnoreligious tensions could erupt. On the other hand, if low levels of democratic norms did not immediately derail the democratic project, tolerance might gradually increase as democratic institutions became established.

It is important to emphasize once more that a lack of support for the status quo does not guarantee that any change will be toward democratization. It is clear, however, that the majorities of educated Muslims in most of the countries studied prefer democratic political systems, given the responses to the question about their ideal system of government.

Among countries demonstrating an emergence of support for

democracy, Indonesia seems most likely to have a successful democratic transition. The data show that Indonesians' elasticity of demand for democracy is 85 points in a 0–100 scale, which means that, relatively speaking, Indonesian Muslims are ready to sacrifice for their political rights more than Muslims from all other countries in this category. Voter turnout in the first round of the Indonesian presidential elections in July 2004 attested to the Indonesian commitment to democracy. An impressive 78 percent of the population voted, which indicates how important this election was to the average Indonesian citizen, despite the socioeconomic and political problems of the country.

Thirteen cultures broadly accept democratic norms and procedures yet do not perceive them to be of highest priority. Six of these cultures seem to be relatively firm in their acceptance due to their relatively high levels of support for democratic norms and institutions and their preference for a democratic political system. Yet because of their relative support for the status quo, they are likely to advance toward democracy only if elites take the initiative. When such initiative is taken, often it is seen primarily as a way to defuse public anger or to gain greater international acceptance. If elites are not inclined to push for reform, however, there is little chance that they will be forced out. Ahmad Yusuf of the Arab League describes the people residing in societies with this type of political culture as "happy slaves."

The countries in column 5 are not as stable, due to their lower elasticity of demand for political rights combined with a moderate to low support for the status quo. Despite their lower tolerance of minorities and women, these cultures seem more inclined to advance toward democracy because of their willingness to sacrifice for it and their relative dissatisfaction with the status quo.

There are nine other societies that show great support and appreciation for democracy, including seven stable cultures and two less certain ones. All the societies that appear in column 6 have witnessed some sort of peaceful transfer of power in the past decade or so. This observation may suggest that there is a dialectic relationship between democracy and culture. In other words, once democracies are in place they tend to create the culture conducive to democracy. Such a theory rings true given the fact that Muslims in these countries express a very high level of support for democratic norms and institutions, have generally liberal attitudes toward "other" ideologies, and voice relative support for the status quo and election mechanisms; further, the elasticity of their demand for democracy is low. Another common factor among the societies that internalize democracy is that none is Arab.

Muslims of Iran and Malaysia share almost all the characteristics of steady democratic internalization except for their lower level of democratic norms (and, of course, their lower level of support of the status quo). This means that these two countries have democratic potential if internal divisions can be overcome or at least temporarily put aside. If not, democracy will not be the only game in town.

Notes

1. Appendix 4 has a technical description of how the two scales were developed.
2. www.aljazeera.net/news/arabic/2003/3/3-4-7.htm.
3. www.aljazeera.net/news/arabic/2000/12/12-25-1.htm.

6

Conclusion:
What Can Be Done?

It's strange for me to say it, but this process of change has started because of the American invasion of Iraq. I was cynical about Iraq. But when I saw the Iraqi people voting, 8 million of them, it was the start of a new Arab world. The Syrian people, the Egyptian people, all say that something is changing. The Berlin Wall has fallen. We can see it.

—Lebanese politician Walid Jumblatt,
Washington Post, February 23, 2005

Although there are few points of consensus in modern social science, the incompatibility of Islam and democracy is a candidate for one of them. Many students of Islam and the Middle East operate from the implicit if not explicit assumption that Muslims have one creed (Islam), and thereby one culture, and collectively share a disdain for modernity, rejecting democracy as a formula of governance. A thorough reading of the scholarship on Islam and democracy in the West suggests that most students of Islam and the Middle East resort to theological, juristic, and philosophical arguments to link Islam to autocracy. This scholarship relies mainly on secondary sources when addressing this relationship and arguably assumes that Muslims are prisoners of an eternal and uniform culture. In most cases, it is either implicitly or explicitly assumed that this culture hardly changes or evolves since it is genuinely associated with Muslims' creed. This resistance to change has been suggested as the core affinity between Islam and autocracy.

This book has addressed this by empirically analyzing contemporary Muslims' attitudes rather than ancient jurists' contributions and thus seeks to shift attention from Islamic texts to contemporary Muslims' mindsets. Ultimately, it finds ample evidence to demonstrate that literate Muslims are heterogeneous enough to defy any one-size-fits-all cultural explanation. Moreover, they are heterogeneous for heterogeneous reasons. This does not mean that Muslims do not have some common cultural traits and deficiencies. Muslim intellectuals and *ulama* have been partly responsible for the lack of democratization in most Muslim societies, due to their uncompromising readings of Islam and democracy and a lack of consensus on the urgency of democratic reforms.

That said, the variation I found in individual Muslims' religious beliefs within countries serves to refute Fish's assertion that "religious traditions are usually constant within societies [and vary] only across societies" (Fish 2002). In fact, this project demonstrates significant variation both across and within societies. A quick look at Tables 5.6, 5.7, 5.8, and 5.9 readily shows that inside each Muslim society, no matter how democratic or undemocratic, there are representatives of each of the four main schools of thought: traditionalists, modernists, pluralists, and statists. This finding also reminds us that not all secular Muslims are pluralists, since some are statists, and not all Islamists are antidemocratic traditionalists, since some are modernists.

At the society level, a Muslim society would score highest on the democratic institutions and norms scales and thus have democratic potential if several conditions are in place:

- The distribution of attitudes indicates that statists and traditionalists are in the minority and modernist Islamists and pluralist secularists are in the majority.
- There is a majority of Muslims who have negative attitudes toward the undemocratically elected incumbents.
- There is a majority of Muslims who do not harbor utopian ideas about what government can or should be and thus who accept a democratic system of government.
- There is a majority of Muslims who are ready to publicly demand and sacrifice for their political rights.

The traditionalist narrative is but one narrative and is actually in the minority in most Muslim societies. Saudi, Yemeni, Sudanese, Pakistani, and Nigerian societies are the most plagued by this inherently antidemocratic belief system. Thus, these societies' political cultures are definite obstacles to democratization. While not all traditionalists are ready to use violence against their societies or rulers, the danger of violent traditionalists lies in the fact that, no matter how few they are, they can put the whole democratic transition and demands for democracy on hold. In Muslim countries such as Algeria, Lebanon, Egypt, Indonesia, Pakistan, Nigeria, and Sudan, where democratic praxis and norms are still nascent, violence gives the statist governments of the region the pretext for tightening freedoms, imposing martial law, violating basic rights, and claiming an incompatibility between democracy and their society. Yet the necessity of this approach is certainly debatable. It is indeed possible that democratization can help to lessen tension and violence. Spain, for example, was able to press on with its democratization process despite all the violence committed by Euskadi Ta Askatasuna or ETA (Linz and Stepan 1996).

Moreover, it is clear that Muslim societies can achieve high levels of support for democracy. Societies (or Muslim minorities within societies) that have a majority of modernist Islamists and/or pluralist secularists are Turkey, the United States, the European Union, Albania, India, Malaysia, Mali, Senegal, Tunisia, Iran, Egypt, and Morocco. In regard to these societies, it is difficult to argue that citizens' values stand as an obstacle to democracy. Indeed, for those that are still under statist governance, the evidence suggests that one should search for noncultural reasons for why they do not democratize.

In some Muslim societies, despite the existence of a relatively strong traditionalist discourse, there have been some pluralist and modernist intellectual elites who have injected debates about democratic norms into the public arena. The evidence suggests that some societies are moving toward greater acceptance of democratic norms but have yet to fully internalize them. They include Qatar, Bahrain, Morocco, Tunisia, Jordan, Algeria, Gambia, Lebanon, Turkmenistan, Kuwait, Syria, Egypt, and Bangladesh. However, others, such as Sudan, Pakistan, Indonesia, and Tajikistan, are still in a state of "norm-emergence."

Where democracy does emerge in the Muslim world, it is likely to have a strong religious component. In twenty-six of the thirty-two societies studied, the absolute majority of respondents supported an active role for Islam in politics (Table 2.3). The exceptions are Tajikistan, Turkmenistan, Mali, Tunisia, Albania, and Turkey. This result holds two important lessons: (1) At least in the short to medium run, no democracy can emerge with the marginalization of Islam as a source of political ideology or of Islamists as political actors. (2) Free and fair elections in most Muslim countries would bring Islamists to power, if other variables remain constant. This study confirms the assertion that Islamists will be among the beneficiaries of democratization in the short term (Feldman 2003).

The latter point should be understood within the context of the gigantic gap between Muslim rulers and publics, as shown in Table 4.1. What seems to be emerging is a legitimacy crisis in the Muslim world. Indeed, most Muslims, if given the opportunity to change their ruler, would do so. Other surveys confirm the same results. A Pew survey found that 90 percent, 85 percent, 85 percent, and 72 percent of citizens of Morocco, Jordan, Palestine, and Kuwait, respectively, disagree with their government's official positions (Borting 2003). Dissatisfaction, however, does not necessarily lead to revolt. On average, Arabs are less ready to sacrifice for their political rights than are non-Arab Muslims in countries such as Iran, Turkey, and Mali.

My individual-level analysis aims at explaining why Muslims who live in the same society adopt different and even contradictory attitudes toward democracy. Below I summarize how certain variables affect individuals' support for democracy across societies, ceteris paribus.

1. Except for citizens of Saudi Arabia and the United Arab Emirates, the more educated Muslims are, the more they support democracy, as long as other variables remain constant.
2. Muslim women are more supportive of democracy than men in all Muslim societies, as long as other variables remain constant.
3. Muslims who have resided in a democracy for a year or longer endorse democracy more than Muslims who did not have this experience, as long as other variables remain constant.
4. Modernist and pluralist Muslims who believe in the compatibility between *shura* and democracy strongly support democracy compared to those who have doubts about this compatibility, as long as other variables remain constant.
5. Muslims who are not satisfied with incumbent rulers tend to be more supportive of democracy, as long as other variables remain constant.
6. In most cases, the more Muslims have experience with political participation through voting, the more they support democratic institutions and norms, as long as other variables remain constant.

Many of the relationships listed above seem to be solidly rooted in particular experiences and preferences of Muslim individuals. It is, then, more accurate and helpful to understand Muslims as rational actors seeking to satisfy their widely varying preferences than as a monolithic group driven primarily by passions.

This study also showed that certain variables had contradictory effects across Muslim societies. This was true of income, age, and religiosity. Further country-specific research should be undertaken to shed light on the causes of these contradictions.

Another important finding is that blaming the West for the continuation and spread of dictatorships in the Muslim world, and thus refusing it as a credible agent of democratization, is so common among pro- and antidemocratic Muslims alike that it ended up having no statistical effect on the attitudes of Muslims toward democracy, except in the cases of the United States and Albania.

What Can Be Done?

If one wants to summarize the whole cultural map of Muslim societies regarding the issue of democracy and autocracy, it is safe to say that there are two broad types of subcultures in the Muslim world: the culture of "dictatorship, but . . ." and the culture of "democracy-as-a-must." The former is the subculture of two groups of Muslims: (1) traditionalist Islamists who argue that a just statist ruler who abides by sharia and defends its tenets is the most legitimate ruler of all and (2) statist secularists who argue in favor of a Hobbesian ruler who maintains the state's sovereignty and defends it against its foreign and internal enemies. In both cases, Muslims behave as rational actors who find that the advantages of having a statist ruler outweigh having a democratically elected one.

The "democracy-as-a-must" subculture is the one that is adopted by modernist Islamists and pluralist secularists. Modernist Islamists treat democracy, insofar as it does not contradict the clear-cut taboos of Islam, as a vehicle to fight dictatorship and ensure pluralism in society. Pluralist secularists argue that democracy is the core component of modernity and should be adopted on secular grounds. Democracy has no future in Muslim societies unless the "democracy-as-a-must" subculture becomes the dominant culture. "Democracy must triumph in theory before it can be realized in practice. Muslims must widely and unambiguously accept that Islam and democracy are compatible and that meaningful faith requires freedom" (Khan 2003).

For those who wish to help make the "democracy-as-a-must" subculture prevail, there are some practical lessons to be learned from this project. First, advocates of democracy in the Muslim world should make more efforts to Islamize democracy rather than democratizing Islam.

Islamizing democracy is a philosophical, theological, and juristic endeavor that aims at finding Islamic roots for democratic norms and praxis. Many sayings and actions of the Prophet Muhammad can be endorsed as the Islamic roots of majority rule, the moral and political equality of women and non-Muslims, obligatory *shura*, and the eradication of apathy and the "dictatorship, but . . ." culture. This is one of the main conditions for "pluralist democracies [to] surely grow" (Aslan 2005).

Islam is widely known to be more pluralistic than many other religions. Muslim democrats need to rediscover their religion and reassess where the problems lie. My research has shown that the same verse from the Quran means different things to different people, to the extent that in most cases the balance of political power in a society determines the outcome of any religious debate. Modernists and pluralists should talk to each other, learn from each other, and teach each other. Secularists, for their part, need to reexamine their self-defeating strategy to democratize/secularize Islam through distorting Islamists' image, debunking *ulamas'* roles, copying Western experiences, implanting secular solutions, and heightening the intellectual civil war. This approach has been perceived by many Muslims as a Western attack on their legacy and identity. Using Islamic teachings to reform Muslims' culture seems the most feasible strategy in most of the societies studied in this project.

Rachid al-Ghannouchi, founder of the Tunisian Islamic movement al-Nahda, believes that "once the Islamists are given a chance to comprehend the values of Western modernity, such as democracy and human rights, they will search within Islam for a place for these values, [and will] implant them, nurse them, and cherish them just as the Westerners did before, when they implanted such values in a much less fertile soil" (al-Ghannouchi 1996). The process of Islamization of democracy is based on three assumptions.

First, democratic norms and praxis are not entirely Western. They are humankind's shared efforts to fight despots and tyrants anywhere and anytime. Muslims have made significant contributions to democratic philosophy by emphasizing the values of unity, respect for order, equality, peaceful coexistence, and pluralism and have also worked for the abolition of slavery and the emancipation of humanity throughout Islam's history.

Second, "wisdom is the goal of the believer—wherever he or she finds it, he or she should learn it," as most Muslims believe that Prophet Muhammad said.[1] Early Muslims did not find it anti-Islamic to learn systems of administration from the Persians, irrigation from the Egyptians, and philosophy from the Greeks. They can learn from others what they lack without necessarily finding it anti-Islamic.

Third, many Muslims' setbacks in the form of poor governance have their roots in the Ottoman Empire and European colonialism. Democratic impulses began to escalate in Europe in the early eighteenth century onward, but this was also the period during which most Muslim countries began to fall under the colonial control of the Europeans, who distorted the class structures and cultural priorities of Muslim societies. Thus, the best way to correct this historical lapse is to catch up and learn what Muslims would likely have invented or developed if left to their own devices.

Up to this point, I have focused on changing the public mindset to create fertile soil for democracy. Another important component of democratization is getting the backing of political elites. As much as the public and institutions matter for democratization, one should not underestimate the importance of elites who have the commitment and skills to redistribute power in society without endangering the unity of the nation or the sustainability of democracy. This study suggests that political actors and opinion leaders have specific tasks to carry out in laying the foundation of a "democracy-as-a-must" culture.

Role of Ulama

There have always been lively debates within the Islamic tradition on who has the historical right to interpret Islam and its teachings (Wright 1992). This historical, and possibly eternal, debate is settled in the minds of most literate Muslims, who trust *ulama* over intellectuals. Muslims who perceive democracy as an extension of *shura* tend to also trust that the *ulama* are important agents for democratization.

The effort of the eighty-year-old shaikh Yusuf al-Qaradawi of Egypt is one of the most successful attempts to Islamize democracy. His book *On the Fiqh of the Islamic State* (2001) is a notable attempt to demonstrate the Islamic underpinnings of democracy in the Sunni Muslim world. This book is often quoted by other modernist *ulama* and intellectuals in their books, booklets, and sermons. It has given informal permission to many *ulama* to use the originally alien word *democracy*.

Al-Qaradawi's attempt, along with those of others, has made democracy acceptable to many Muslims, but it is still not perceived as a must, as many modernists perceive waging jihad against Israel or US troops in Iraq or Afghanistan to be.[2] A Muslim who dies while waging this type of jihad believes that she or he will go to heaven, but no such reward is promised for waging jihad against dictatorships.

Take another example, Ayatollah Ali al-Sistani, an Iraqi Shiite communal leader who adopted nonviolent attitudes toward the coalition troops in Iraq, advocating countrywide elections rather than the US-proposed regional caucuses. Al-Sistani is widely believed by Iraqis to be a tactful leader. When asked, "What should we do when foreign soldiers talk to us or want to buy from us?" al-Sistani's fatwa was not to use violence but "Be kind and nice, yet always ask the foreign troops: when are you leaving?" Al-Sistani issued another fatwa likening voting to jihad for a better Iraq. He established the principle of one Iraq for all religions and ethnicities. He engaged non-Shiite Iraqis rather than negating them. For many, he is the opposite of Saddam Hussein. He did not want to wage a war against the coalition troops that would lead to civil war or another version of dictatorship (al-Saffar 2005).

Syria, by contrast, has seriously lacked *ulama* who will get behind calls for democracy. In 2000, ninety-nine Syrian intellectuals published a demand for greater democracy and freedom of expression in a rare direct appeal for political reform in their country. The petition calls the Syrian government to join the world's "common language" of democracy "by expanding civil liberties, liberalizing press freedoms and releasing political prisoners" (Schneider 2000). One might argue, based on the findings of the current research, that if this petition for democracy had been signed and aggressively endorsed by *ulama*, popular pressure on the Syrian government would have been substantially augmented. Without aggressive support on the part of the *ulama*, such petitions for democracy will be perceived by most Muslims as elitists' demands for their own narrow interests.

Out of 7,829 audiotapes available at islamway.com and islamweb.net,[3] I found only fifteen tapes that attack dictatorship in the Muslim world. One tape, by al-Qaradawi with the title *Democracy in Islam*, explicitly defends democracy, universal suffrage, elections, voting, and representative government as a full package. Another tape, by Shaikh Sa'id Marrawi (a Syrian most likely), criticizes democracy but contends that it is better than dictatorship: "No Islam and no freedom is worse than no Islam with freedom." Unfortunately, the attempts of *ulama* to Islamize democracy are still few in number and shallow in effect.

The scarcity of audiotapes that seek to Islamize democracy may be partially explained by the positions of statist governments. Such governments contend that these tapes are part of the Islamists' strategy to cynically use democracy to secure power. However, optimistic researchers perceive the attempts to Islamize democracy as a gradual *aggiornamento* (to borrow a term from Vatican II) to reform Islamic discourse (Ansary 2003). Such a process must be gradual as a greater number of *ulama* and Islamic thinkers do not try to discard traditional religious doctrines but to reinterpret them in the light of modern needs.

John Esposito characterizes the challenge ahead for Muslim *ulama* and intellectuals with eloquence: "A major issue in democratization in Muslim societies is whether or not scholars and leaders have successfully made the transition from listing 'democratic doctrines of Islam' to creating coherent theories and structures of Islamic democracy that are not simply reformulations of Western perceptions in some Muslim idioms" (1996).

The Role of the United States

After the events of September 11, understanding Islam and Muslims has become a matter of national security for the United States, especially considering that many Muslims perceive the war on terrorism as a US crusade against Muslim countries. More than 70 percent of Muslims in Turkey, Indonesia, Pakistan, Lebanon, Jordan, Morocco, and Palestine were disappointed that the Iraqi people did not fight the US invasion and did not show enough support to military operations against American troops in Iraq (Borting 2003). Shibley Telhami's 2004 survey confirms the deep distrust Muslims feel toward the United States. Asked to rank five of eight possible motivations for the Iraq War, four cited by the Bush administration and four cited by critics, as Washington's most likely real motivations, majorities in every country except Saudi Arabia (ironically) named "controlling oil" as one of the top motivations, along with "protecting Israel." The next most highly rated motive—chosen by two-thirds of all respondents—was "weakening" or "dominating" the Muslim world (OneWorld 2004). The Egyptian foreign minister asks: "What model are you talking about in Iraq? Bombs are exploding everywhere, and Iraqis are killed every day in the streets? Palestinian elections? There were elections seven years prior" (Williams 2005). Indeed, distrust of the United States cuts across all ideological, demographic, and social divisions in the Muslim world.

Yet despite the difficulty of transplanting Madisonian democracy into the Muslim world without a thorough and thoughtful understanding of Muslim culture, the war on terrorism does seem to be ushering in, or at least hastening, changes in the Muslim world. It has put pressure on leaders of the Muslim world to, at a minimum, mount democratic window dressing, and it has given Muslim intellectuals and activists more grounds for criticizing the status quo and those responsible for it. As Kanan Makiya forcefully put it, "Instead of recognizing our own fallibility and frailty, we Arab intellectuals—secular and non-secular alike—have, on the contrary, been perfecting in the last quarter of a century a different kind of language, one that is constantly preoccupied with blaming others for problems that are largely—although not completely—of our own making" (Makiya 2002).

Muslim rulers, for their part, are only too aware that any Muslim country can be Iraq if it challenges US interests (al-Khouri 2003). One intellectual has likened the US invasion of Iraq in 2003 to Napoleon's invasion of Egypt in 1798. The French invasion of Egypt awakened Egypt and the Middle East from the mentality of the Middle Ages. Likewise, the US invasion of Iraq poses another challenge to the embattled totalitarian ideologies of the region, mainly pan-Arabism and Islamic fundamentalism (Saleh 2004).

Some Muslims who had given up hope that democracy could emerge without foreign pressure now hope that the United States will not diminish its pressure for democracy in the Muslim world because of some tactical gains. Autocratic rulers will try to trick the United States through deceptive constitutional amendments, giving up their weapons of mass destruction, being more cooperative in the war on terrorism, and maintaining diplomatic relations with Israel. They will do these things only to save their positions in power (Darwish 2005).

The United States is also likely to learn its own lessons from the war in Iraq. First, it can prevent Muslims from doing certain things, but it cannot force them to do others. For instance, the United States exerted enough pressure on the Pakistani government to stop the 20,000 self-funded madrassas (or religious schools), but it cannot force the Pakistani population to be tolerant toward each other. True democracy will not take hold without local agents of democratization. These agents cannot be manufactured and exported to the Muslim world. Fake democracy needs only fake democrats, while liberal democracy needs liberal democrats. Liberal democrats exist in the Muslim world but could use international protection and support. "Moral, public support from the international community and the United States can have the effect of strengthening the movement for democracy. Direct intervention and manipulation can only be counterproductive" (Harb 2005).

The experience of recent years indicates that the United States cannot create real democrats on the ground, but it can put statist Muslim regimes on the defensive. It has moved from an attitude of "do nothing" to correct for the misgovernance of "our" allies to that of "something should be done." Yet tough choices still must be made: "Between the realist's option of 'do nothing' and the romantic's option of 'elections now' lies a third path—gradual yet persistent liberalization" (Mustafa and Makovsky 2003).

The larger US strategy, then, should involve both pressure on autocrats and dialogue with pluralist secularists and modernist Islamists who can themselves pressure the rulers for democratization. A worldwide commitment to democracy in the Muslim world empowers Muslim democrats. As an Egyptian Nasserist put it during the anti-Mubarak demonstration in March 2005, "The police forces did not hit us as they usually do. . . . A lot of foreign TV cameras were there. They [the government] do not want to look bad."

Yet the United States should also take a clear stand: its invasion of Iraq was an exceptional decision that will not occur in any other cases. Muslims in general will not accept democracy under the US flag. The United States should also resist involving itself in the creation of artificial "made in the USA" Muslim democrats. One certain way of discrediting any politician in the Muslim world is to associate him with the Central Intelligence Agency. Louay of Sudan tellingly referred to such sponsored politicians as "intellectual marines."

Finally, the United States has the capacity to pose challenges to Muslim nondemocratic rulers, but it does not have much control over what will happen should these rulers lose power. The situation in Iraq is very telling in this regard. The United States did not have control over most of the actors in the region. Things could have deteriorated very easily, had not the players acted in an unexpectedly responsible manner. If eventually a democracy emerges in Iraq, one should not hastily attribute that to US plans. Many mistakes were made and the outcome could have been catastrophic, but "God is merciful," as Ibrahim Hassoun of Iraq put it.

Miles to Go in the Marathon of Democratization

Islam is 600 years younger than Christianity and is just beginning to confront the very thorny issues of church and state that Christians faced with the Reformation and wars of religion. Like Christians, Muslims will need time to come up with a new version or reading of their religion to accommodate democratic mechanisms. Not only is Islam a relatively young religion, but most Muslim countries achieved their national independence only in the last half-century. Britain, by contrast, took seven centuries after the Magna Carta to shape its democratic political system, and it took the United States 150 years to give women the right to vote. Though Muslim countries have a long way to go to become established democracies, literate Muslims are increasingly aware of their "autocratic dilemma" and refuse what a student from Morocco called the "tricks of tyranny" used by Muslim rulers.

In a very rich focus-group discussion among eleven Arab students studying in the Arab League's Institute of Arab Research, each of the group members suggested a list of "tricks" played by their rulers to remain in power. They showed great awareness that these tricks had actually deluded their ancestors. There was consensus that the rulers prioritize goals such as Arab unity, economic development, fighting colonialism, and liberating occupied lands over the political rights of Arab/Muslim citizens and the government's constitutional accountability. More important, Handeyya of Palestine expressed the conviction that these tricks will not be sufficient to silence the new generations of Arabs and Muslims as they silenced older generations. Several other participants concurred.

Such attitudes offer some hope that the future is going to be different from the past. The focus-group participants articulated other reasons that political reform might be on the horizon. They repeatedly pointed to what I call the biological, geological, theological, ideological, and technological challenges that are likely to press Muslim leaders into granting Muslim citizens more political rights. Awareness of these challenges among young literate Muslims indicates that the democracy-as-a-must mindset is spreading throughout the Muslim world.

The "biological challenge" refers to the generation gap between old rulers and the majority youth, which stems from the relatively high birth rate (around 2.7 percent on average) for newer generations of Muslims. Around 60 percent of Muslims are now under thirty years old, and they do not have the historical memories of their parents. According to Ahmad Shaker of Egypt, "People my age have a different set of priorities from my parents. My father is crazy about Gamal Abdel Nasser. I was born in 1976 (six years after Nasser's death). I remember him from movies." Like Ahmad, most Egyptians who were born in the 1970s have not lived the dream of pan-Arabism, socialism, and Nasserism. It is not enough to reason that President Mubarak was the leader of the Air Force in 1973 (during the Yom Kippur War) and therefore has a right to govern Egypt longer. Lamia of Jordan said, "Yes, I want to see a free, independent Palestinian state, but I do not think that this means the [dictatorial] status quo should perpetuate." In a different focus-group discussion, Nasser of Saudi Arabia, age twenty-five, stated that "political change does not necessarily mean Western-democracy, but definitely we [Saudis of his age] do not want their 'tomorrow' to be a replication of their 'today.'" This analysis also seems to explain why, in Lebanon and Egypt, an increasing number of educated young men and women are joining the movement called Keffayah—the Arabic word for "enough." Clearly, the new generations throughout the Muslim world want to see economic, political, and social change.

The second challenge many Muslim leaders face could be called "geological." This refers to the fact that control of primary resources such as oil, phosphates, or geostrategic waterways has declining importance for preserving the power of the ruling elites.[4] As was discussed earlier, these resources bought the rentier and semi-rentier states some legitimacy in the 1970s through the 1990s (Korany 1994). Important changes, however, are making these resources less relevant. Drastic increases in the Muslim population have effectively served to reduce the perks that any given citizen will receive from the rentier state. Take Saudi Arabia as an example. Data show that in spite of the surge in its oil income in the early 2000s, the Saudi government continues to face serious long-term economic challenges, including high rates of unemployment (17 percent), one of the world's fastest population growth rates (2.4 percent per year), and a consequent need for increased government spending. In addition to this, there is an increased demand on the part of the new generations for free education, healthcare, and jobs. With mass expectations exceeding what the government can deliver, the rentier formula, which Salman Ra'ie of Indonesia characterizes as producing economic supercitizens who are content to be political nobodies, cannot work in the future.

The present data show that with the exception of the United Arab Emirates and Oman, most interviewed literate Muslims, including citizens of the countries with greatest oil-based wealth, blame their rulers for their plight. Their resentment of their rulers can be understood if one looks at the rise and fall of GDP per capita. "Oil is not enough to buy the necessary legitimacy any more," as a Kuwaiti respondent said. For instance, in the early 1970s, the GDP per capita in the Arab Gulf states was less than $1,000, but it jumped to $12,000 in the late 1970s due to a sharp increase in oil prices. This increased the expectations of the citizens. Nowadays, per capita GDP is around $10,000 (but the discrepancy among states has increased: $20,000 in the United Arab Emirates versus less than $10,000 in Saudi Arabia). A quick comparison with South Korea, Taiwan, and Singapore shows that their GDP per capita increased from $740, $1,132, and $3,040 to $15,530, $20,500, and $22,300 respectively during the same periods (World Bank 2001b). Primary resources alone have proved ill-suited to establish stable economies. More important, they have been used by political autocrats to control society.

There is compelling evidence that the model of a government-controlled economy is not appealing to most young Muslims. Surprisingly, resentment toward government-controlled economies was apparent among Muslim participants from oil-rich countries. This lack of satisfaction among the citizens of countries that have achieved higher levels of spending because of the geological virtue of oil is striking. Emran of Pakistan, who lived in Saudi Arabia with his family for five years before traveling to the United States, said, "Most people in the Muslim world thought that Saudi Arabia has the best political and economic system because of Islam. [But] with the increasing number of non-Saudis who went home and told stories about injustices and corruption, most of us do not want to live there unless no other opportunities are available." Emran's perception is not peculiar to him. During an interview, Ahmed Yusef of the Arab League observed that Egyptians who have not visited Saudi Arabia have more positive attitudes about it than Egyptians who have worked there.

The increasing globalization of economies is making ruler control and legitimation even more difficult. As state industries are privatized, there are fewer government resources to distribute. Moreover, as the private sector increases, it redistributes political power within society (Zakaria 2001), further weakening the capacity of ruling elites to rely on "the grace of geology" to buy legitimacy.

Third, there is a new "Islam-related" challenge facing Muslim autocrats, which I call the "theological challenge." Some Islamists have proved that they are more committed to democracy than some secular autocrats. The "theological/theocratic" card used by autocratic rulers to defame Islamists is losing credibility due to the fact that many Islamists have proved to be less violent or radical than their own rulers. Modernist Islamists have been consistently seeking to establish their commitment to peaceful democratic participation in Indonesia, Bahrain, Malaysia, Pakistan, Egypt, Morocco, Yemen, Kuwait, and Jordan, where they are powerful opposition forces in Parliament. "Islamists in Turkey, for example, have demonstrated their impressive ability to adapt to social and political realities—in the process becoming poster-boys for

Islamic moderation . . . and the Islamic-leaning Justice and Development party . . . has sought active engagement with the West, particularly the European Union" (Hamid 2005).

As noted by Ibtissam of Bahrain, "It is becoming more difficult to claim that all Islamists are followers or students of Al-Qaida leaders." Tareq of Jordan proudly thinks of the Muslim Brotherhood as more democratic than the secular government supported by the king: "We do not use violence against them [the government]. We do not detain anybody. We do not prevent anybody from voting. We are more democratic than they are. Even Osama [bin Laden] and Zarqawi, they were made by those who used them to fight the Soviets, not by us."

Sa'eed of Morocco agrees. "If the Muslim Brotherhood were followers of Zawahri, no Muslim ruler would have been in office. The Muslim Brotherhood has a huge number of followers. If they decide to use violence, [I swear by Allah] there will be civil wars in all Muslim countries. But we are peaceful people. We want Islam by *da'wa*."[5]

Hajjaji of Libya asserts, "I do not pray much, but I know that Islam is the solution. I'd vote for Islamists if we had elections." When I asked him if he feared that radical Islamists would take over, he argued that "radical Islamists should not be allowed to run for elections. But moderate Islamists should be encouraged to run." Based on the German experience, in which extremists both on the right (Nazis) and on the left (communists) are banned from participating in elections, Hajjaji has a point. There are constitutional mechanisms available to protect democracy from its enemies. However, one should be extremely cautious. The lessons of history tell us that the collapse of an old dictatorship is usually succeeded by a period of moderate rule; following this, radical rule frequently prevails: "The Jacobins in the French Revolution, Lenin in the Russian Revolution, Mao in China, Khomeini in Iran, and the Taliban in Afghanistan all came to power after more-moderate provisional governments, which came to power immediately after regime collapse, failed" (McFaul 2003).

Most of the respondents readily distinguish between Islamists who want to participate in politics through democratic means and others who reject democracy altogether, while most governments do not recognize the distinction. In adopting democratic discourse and disassociating themselves from violent radical Islamists, modernist Islamists debunk the theology/theocracy pretext for postponing democratization.

The fourth challenge involves technology. All the developments surveyed here would not have been possible but for the technology that has connected Muslims in unprecedented ways to the larger world. Satellite dishes and the Internet show Muslims what is happening in Georgia, Ukraine, Iraq, and other countries. Advances in communication technologies have facilitated a demonstration effect. The US secretary of state described it this way: "Once you have populations that are looking around—and one of the really remarkable impacts out there has been satellite TV where people watch Afghans vote or they watch Iraqis vote or they watch the Lebanese in the streets or they watch as far away as Ukraine or Georgia, today Kyrgyzstan—and they say 'well, why not us?' (Rice 2005).

As Abo Lamaa of Saudi Arabia put it: "Saudi TV is like a 'one-man show.' It always emphasizes that there is nothing wrong with the government. . . . But once one watches al-Jazeera or other non-Saudi media networks, we know the truth." He said, "In Saudi TV, there is democracy only regarding criticizing the players, referees, and trainers of soccer teams."

Talal of Syria thinks of himself as "Internet guy." Following government-owned media makes "one stupid"; thus he gave up this bad habit. A Tunisian student stated that "when we listen to the Tunisian TV, we find it glorifies the president. Switch to a non-Tunisian channel, you will hear something different. I do not trust the Tunisian TV. It is the president's TV." Siddiqqa of Malaysia summarized the impact of the Internet on his personality in this way: "I am still Malaysian but with a bigger eye. I see more and know more."

Satellite and communication technology has ended the era of "one-man-show" media. Opposition figures, parties, and movements have websites with detailed audio and visual material that traditionally would have been censored. Even when some governments censor some of this antiregime material, opposition members can send it out by e-mail. Yusuf Ugur of Turkey noted, "Every person can create a website and become a publisher and an opinion leader." Thanks to the revolution in communication technology, rulers are increasingly losing control over what their citizens watch, read, and listen to. As Mohamed Maqdoni of Iraq put it: "No more Big Brother's media."

The fifth challenge has to do with ideology—specifically, the fading allure of nondemocratic ideologies of the 1950s and 1960s (Qablan 2005). Most Muslim regimes adopted some form of socialism to justify state-controlled economies and one-party systems to achieve (nondemocracy-related) goals such as liberating land, achieving national unity, or simply guaranteeing self-survival. In the judgment of Ihssan Zameel of Indonesia, a diplomat who lived in Iraq and the Arab Gulf area for six years, "this was the worst mistake ever. . . . The revolutionary officers of the 1950s and 1960s made the wrong choices by adopting socialism and one-party systems. They nationalized the political and economic spheres. . . . We pay for that now."

Most of the ideologies adopted by the first generation of liberators in the Muslim world, including socialism and one-party systems, lost their credibility after decades of formal independence, widespread corruption, and the collapse of the Soviet model. Take pan-Arabism as an example. Hamza of Algeria lost faith in pan-Arabism "because of what Arabs do to each other," as he put it. Further, he said, "Nasserists are in the minority in Egypt and throughout the Arab world. Ba'thism is a notorious party throughout the Arab world. The Arab League cannot be weaker. The goal of liberating Palestine has come down to the dream of a semiindependent state in the Gaza strip and West Bank. . . . Pan-Arabism is a dream that will never come true because of our mistakes. . . . We have to understand the world [outside] ideological lenses."

Only Syria and Iran remain committed to nondemocratic ideologies. Turkey, even under Islamist government, is trying to join the European Union for economic reasons. The Arabs of Maghreb (Morocco, Algeria, and Tunisia) aspire to closer ties with the Europeans. Southeast Asian Muslim countries (Indonesia and Malaysia) have joined the Association of Southeast Asian Nations (ASEAN) in order to share in its economic promises and have committed themselves to periodic elections. Pakistan, Egypt, Jordan, and Arab Gulf states seek closer economic ties with the United States, which has put the issue of democracy on its foreign-policy agenda.

In sum, biological, geological, theological, technological, and ideological challenges have all negatively affected the legitimacy of most incumbents. In response, pseudodemocratic steps have been taken by statist elites as public relations maneuvers to deflect the pressure. However, there is an increasing awareness among literate Muslims that they are worse off under current regimes.

This analysis should not lead to the hasty conclusion, however, that getting rid of the statist rulers will instantly have a positive effect. Although statist rulers in most Muslim countries are illegitimate in the eyes of their own people, one should not assume that their sudden absence would mean an automatic transition to democracy. The United States made this mistake in assuming that Iraq's plight was attributable to Saddam Hussein and Afghanistan's problems to the Taliban, and that once Saddam and the Taliban were ousted, Iraq and Afghanistan would become democracies. The experiences of Afghanistan and Iraq teach us that Saddam was Saddam because of Iraq and that the Taliban was the

Taliban because of Afghanistan. The Bush administration thought it would be doing the work of John Locke.[6] Instead, it found itself doing the work of Thomas Hobbes.[7]

Will a ruler be more likely to succeed in holding a country such as Iraq or Afghanistan together if he is like Saddam Hussein or if he is like James Madison? While most incumbents are not legitimate and can be removed from power rather easily, they are often functional in holding together their societies, which are plagued with reinforcing social cleavages. The collapse of state institutions in Afghanistan, Iraq and, for that matter, Somalia, after the Taliban, Saddam, and President Muhammad Siad Barre were ousted, was not a mere coincidence. There are structural and cultural factors behind these three cases. In most Muslim countries, the authority of individual rulers, the legitimacy of regimes, and the sovereignty and unity of states are inextricably interwoven. In almost any country in the region, an abrupt shift in power would not only diminish the authority of the ruler but also threaten the legitimacy of the regime and imperil the unity of the state itself. It is relatively easy to remove from power unpopular autocrats who are suppressing separatist tendencies. It is considerably more difficult to bring to power true democrats who can appease separatist tendencies. The complexity of the problem was evident in Somalia immediately after the overthrow of President Barre in January 1991, after the overthrow of the Taliban in 2001, and in Iraq after Saddam was forced out of office in 2003. The absence of Saddam Hussein meant no Ba'thist regime and endangered the unity of Iraq as a state. If the United States were to press for a similarly abrupt shift in power in Saudi Arabia, for instance, this would likely affect not only the persons who currently hold power but the whole legitimacy of the Saudi family and the unity of the Saudi state. Save for Egypt and Tunisia, which have a very solid social fabric, this analysis can be applied to almost all other Muslim countries.

That is why pressure on Muslim regimes from outside and inside is good. Take Saudi Arabia. The Saudi kingdom has been known for having one of the most rigid political and social systems in the Muslim world. In post–September 11 Saudi Arabia, "the word *Islah* [reform] has been on all lips" (al-Fassi 2003). Saudi officials declared specific steps toward allowing public participation in the kingdom. Prince Sultan bin Abdel-Aziz, deputy prime minister of Saudi Arabia, promises real political reforms. He states that he refuses the notorious 99 percent election results of other Arab countries; according to him, "manipulating elections is the easiest thing the kingdom can do."

His brother Crown Prince Abdullah has promised to expand the role of the Shura Council and to raise the bar of accountability and transparency and renewed this promise after becoming the king in 2005. The Saudi royal family promised and carried out the first local elections in early 2005. A national dialogue under the auspices of the crown prince has started in response to many written and oral petitions by Saudi academicians, modernist Islamists, liberal intellectuals, businessmen and women, and leaders of tribes. Two famous petitions signed by 100 and 450 Saudi public figures in January and April 2003 specifically asked for political, bureaucratic, and economic reforms, including the crafting of a written constitution for the kingdom and rejecting the claim that the Quran is the constitution. The local elections of 2005 did not represent a drastic departure from authoritarian rule, as women were not allowed to participate and half of the local council seats were appointed. Thus the election did not result in any redistribution of political power in the kingdom. Still, it has had a huge and significant impact as an example of how democratic reforms may be introduced to a country that has a long tradition of dismissing modernity on religious pretexts. Significantly, now the shaikhs and *ulama* of Saudi Arabia are urging all Saudis to participate in elections on the grounds of serving the Muslim *ummah* and cooperating for the interest of the country. When asked afresh if voting is *bid'a*, many Saudi scholars have retreated from their previous fatwas asserting that it was. One scholar who was known for advocating reforms but not on democratic grounds now perceives voting in local elections as an example of the "*massleh morssala* [unbounded interests] that can be used for the benefit of Islam and Muslims." He said the traditionalists who boycotted the elections because voting is *bid'a* were "entitled to their *ijtihad*." Yet he encouraged all Saudis to vote.[8]

Many, though still not the majority, of Saudis participated in the local elections. Some of their comments prove that a portion of the Saudi population is hungry for more reforms. This is not surprising, since the majority of young Saudis are well educated and have access to the Web and satellite dishes. A female Saudi physician encapsulated in her own family's experience the changes that have overtaken Saudi society: "My mother didn't go to any school, because then there were no girls' schools at all. My older sister, who is 20 years older than me, she went up to the sixth grade and then quit because the feeling was that a girl only needs to learn to read and write. Then I went to college and medical school on scholarship to the States. My daughter, maybe she'll be president, or an astronaut" (Kristof 2002b).

Take another country that has been described in this project as a stable nondemocracy, the United Arab Emirates. Emirati intellectuals are asking, "Why not here?" An Emirati female intellectual wrote, "The UAE is the only country in the Gulf area where nobody takes the issue of political participation seriously. . . . Even Saudi Arabia, which was traditionally known for its rigid political system, has witnessed the first local elections. . . . We should start our political reforms. We should not wait until reform is imposed upon us from abroad."[9] The president of UAE has just ordered a modest but promising step toward allowing UAE citizens to elect half of the powerless consultative council in December 2005. In Kuwait, there are threats that if parliament does not vote for women's rights, the government will dissolve it. Modernist *ulama* issued a new fatwa stating that enfranchising women is a matter that should be left to the ruler to decide. Many Kuwaiti liberals are pleased that Kuwaiti women will finally be able to vote in the parliamentary elections of 2007. The same can be said about many other countries that have been facing change and challenges. Turkey, with an Islamist party in power, is introducing a new model that is gaining more appeal in the Muslim world. This model, which has been labeled "religious or pious secularism," is suggested to be the exemplar for Iraq and other Muslim countries (Gawad 2003).

Muslims are on the path of democracy. Some countries will take longer than others to arrive. But for the previous delineated biological, theological, geological, technological, and ideological reasons, the culture of "dictator, but . . ." is fading away. Pressures from inside and outside are making the cost of oppression extremely high.

Notes

1. Actually, this is not an authentic hadith, but it is widely attributed to the Prophet.

2. Pacifist traditionalists and modernists would not use violence against their own rulers or societies but can do so against colonial powers.

3. These two websites have been identified by many respondents as their main sources of religious knowledge. Besides, they are among the richest Islamic websites, offering free audiotapes and books in seven languages.

4. Ten of the eleven members of the Organization of Petroleum Exporting Countries (OPEC) are Muslim countries.

5. *Da'wa* means inviting Muslims and non-Muslims into a better understanding of Islam.

6. John Locke (1632–1704) was an English philosopher and author of *Two Treatises of Government*. His writings have influenced most advocates of political rights and democracy.

7. Thomas Hobbes (1588–1679), another English philosopher, authored *Leviathan,* aimed at curbing civil wars even at the expense of personal and political liberties.

8. Shaikh A'ed al-Qarni of Saudi Arabia, Interview, *al-Sharq al-Awssat,* February 9, 2005.

9. Aaesha Al-Murri, The Union Council Between Elections and Appointment, *Wajhat,* March 16, 2005.

Appendix 1
Glossary

ahl al-hall wa al-aqd. The people who have the power of contract with the ruler. Theoretically, these people should be the most pious and powerful. However, the vast majority of Muslim jurists have argued, more pragmatically, that *ahl al-hall wa al-aqd* are those who possess the necessary *shawka* (power or strength) to ensure the obedience or the consent of the public.

al-Muraja'at. A sect of Islam that was known for postponing the final verdict on a sinner until the Day of Judgment.

al-salaf al-salih. The pious predecessors. *Al-salaf al-salih* is used to refer to the early companions of the Prophet, but traditionalists tend to extend it to all ancient scholars who spent their lives studying and preaching Islam.

al-Tawheed. Monotheism.

al-wala' wa al-bara'a. Alliance with Muslims and disloyalty toward non-Muslims.

'aqeeda. Creed.

bay'a (or bay'ah). An oath of allegiance to the ruler on the condition that he obeys Allah's sharia.

bid'a. Humanly generated practices introduced in the religion of Allah. The Prophet stated that "every *bid'a* is a deviation from the true path and every deviation leads to hellfire."

caliph (or khalif). Successor: a title formerly given to a Muslim political leader of the *ummah*.

da'wa (or dawa). Inviting Muslims and non-Muslims into a better understanding of Islam.

fatwa. Religious verdict, or legal verdict given on a religious basis. Fatwas are based on the Holy Quran and hadiths.

fiqh. Islamic jurisprudence, or the science of ascertaining the precise terms of the sharia.

fitnah. Internal divisions or civil strife.

hadith. A saying of the Prophet Muhammad. After his death, the hadiths were tested for accuracy and collected into organized bodies of material. Hadiths of the Prophet are second in authority only to the Quran.

hudud. The legal and criminal limits ordained by Allah and Islamic penal code.

ijma'. A consensus view among Muslims, especially among Muslim *ulama* on any Islamic principle.

ijtihad. Independent reasoning or original interpretation of problems not directly addressed by the Quran or the hadiths.

ikhtlaf. Differences and divisions of opinion on religious matters. Such diversity is permissible as long as the basic principles of Islam are not affected. The opposite of *ijma'*.

imam. A person who leads prayers, a Muslim caliph, or a famous Muslim scholar in *fiqh*.

jahilliyya (or jahiliyyah, jahiliyah). A state of ignorance, such as the ignorance that prevailed in the eras that preceded the revelation of the Quran.

kharijite (or kharijies). Dissidents or outsiders. Historically the term was applied to a group of Muslims who turned against Ali, the fourth caliph, and killed him while he was praying.

khateeb (or khatib). Preacher at a mosque.

khiraj (or kharaj). Tax imposed on a conquered land.

madhab. Subtradition and school of *fiqh*.

Mutazila (or Mutzilah). Members of a theological school that flourished in Basra and Baghdad in the eighth to tenth centuries. The Mutazila were the first Muslims to use the categories and methods of Hellenistic philosophy to derive their dogma.

Qiyas. Analogical reasoning, considered by most Sunni *ulama* to be the fourth source of *fiqh* (after the Quran, hadiths, and *ijma'*). Shiite scholars accept the first three, but instead of the Qiyas, they employ *'aql* or reason (i.e., cost-benefit analysis).

sadd al-dhari'ah. Blocking the means to illegality. According to this principle, a lawmaker or *ulama* can claim that a certain act that is lawful ought to be considered unlawful because it leads to the commission of illegal acts.

shaikh (or sheikh). A title or a nickname for an elderly person or a religious leader in a community. This title is also given to a wise person. It is used here to refer to the leaders of prayers. See also *imam*.

sharia (or shariah). Islamic legislation. The revealed and the canonical laws of the religion of Islam.

shura. Mutual consultation. Islamist modernists consider it Islam's equivalent to Western democracy.

taqlid. Imitating and emulating the *salaf*, or the predecessors, in their praxis and opinions.

ummah. The Islamic nation or community, regardless of political borders, languages, or ethnicities.

waqf. Endowment: a charitable trust in the Name of Allah, usually in perpetuity and usually for the purposes of establishing the religion of Islam, teaching useful knowledge, feeding the poor, or treating the sick.

zandaqqa. Heresy. The use of the term can be traced back to the early Abbasid era to refer to any deviation from the authentic orthodoxy of Islam as understood during the Prophet's life and the forty years after his death.

Appendix 2
The Survey: Islam and Politics

Part 1

In this section, you will be asked to give us some information about your age, education, nationality, etc.

1. How did you learn about this survey?
2. What is your gender?
   [ ] female (girl/lady)
   [ ] male (boy/gentleman)
3. What is your age?
4. How far did you go in school?
   [ ] less than high school diploma
   [ ] high school diploma
   [ ] some college
   [ ] received undergrad degree (e.g., bachelor)
   [ ] received an advanced degree (e.g., master's or Ph.D.)
   [ ] no response
5. What is your annual personal income level in your own currency (if you are still supported by your parents, indicate their income)?
   [Ten ranked options were provided.]
6. What currency did you have in mind while answering the previous question?
   [Selections were provided based on country.]
7. Do you think that the elections or referenda (parliamentary, presidential, or syndicates) that occur in your country, if any, are free and fair?

[ ] very fair and free
[ ] somewhat fair and free
[ ] not fair or free at all
[ ] my country does not have elections or referenda

8. If you have the nationality (citizenship) of a Muslim country, select it from the following list. (If you are not from a Muslim country, go to the next question. If you are from a Muslim country, answer this question and skip the next one.)

9. If you are a Muslim who has the citizenship of a non-Muslim country, what is it?

10. What is your country of birth?

11. What is your original/native language?

12. Which one of the following would best describe your status? (Check all that apply).
[ ] I am an Arab Muslim
[ ] I am an African (non-American) Muslim
[ ] I am a white American Muslim
[ ] I am an African American Muslim
[ ] I am a Muslim of a European nationality
[ ] I am an Asian non-Arabic-speaking Muslim
[ ] I am a Muslim who does not fit into the previous categories
[ ] I am not a Muslim
[ ] other, please specify:

13. Which one of the following best describes your status?
[ ] Sunni Muslim
[ ] Shiite Muslim
[ ] other, please specify:

14. Name three *non*-Muslim countries in which you resided (stayed) for one year or more. If there are none, leave the space empty (blank):

15. How many times do you pray (make *salat*) daily?
[ ] I pray 5 times a day without delay.
[ ] I pray 5 times a day but not necessarily on time.
[ ] I pray from 2 to 4 times a day.
[ ] I pray once a day.
[ ] I rarely pray.
[ ] I do not pray at all.
[ ] other, please specify:

16. Are you satisfied with the performance of the political parties (if any) and (elected) representatives (if any) in your country of origin?

[ ] very satisfied
[ ] satisfied
[ ] not sure
[ ] unsatisfied
[ ] very unsatisfied

17. How many times have you voted in public elections or referenda (parliamentary, presidential or syndicates)?
    [ ] my country has elections, but I never voted
    [ ] voted only once
    [ ] twice or more
    [ ] never voted because my country does not have elections

18. How many times have you had any sort of alcoholic beverages or wine (*khamr*)?
    [ ] never in my lifetime
    [ ] only once in my lifetime
    [ ] twice in my lifetime
    [ ] sometimes
    [ ] once a week or more
    [ ] other, please specify:

Part 2

In this section, you will be asked to tell us what the best form of government looks like from your own perspective. For questions 19 to 29, please indicate whether you agree or disagree with the statements in each question.

19. Non-Muslims (e.g., Christians, Jews, or Hindus) should be allowed to build churches or temples to practice their religion in Muslim countries.
    [ ] [five-point scale from "strongly agree" to "strongly disagree"]

20. Islamic sharia gives non-Muslims (Christians, Jews, or Hindus) the right to have their own houses of worship in Muslim countries.
    [ ] [five-point scale from "strongly agree" to "strongly disagree"]

21. Democracy is very close to *shura* (consultation) and can be adjusted to suit the Islamic sharia.
    [ ] [five-point scale from "strongly agree" to "strongly disagree"]

22. By allowing people to make their own laws, democracy replaces the will of Allah with the will of the people; that is why it is some type of disbelief (*kofr*).
    [ ] [five-point scale from "strongly agree" to "strongly disagree"]

23. Islamic movements should be allowed to form political parties (*ahzab*) and run for elections (*intikhabat*).
    [ ] [five-point scale from "strongly agree" to "strongly disagree"]
24. Political participation (for example, voting in elections) is some type of enjoining the good and forbidding the evil (*amr bi-al ma'roof and nahii a'an al-monkar*).
    [ ] [five-point scale from "strongly agree" to "strongly disagree"]
25. If we let Muslims elect their rulers, these elections will lead to homosexuality (*shozoz*), drinking alcoholic beverages (*shorb al-khamr*), and secularism (*'almania*).
    [ ] [five-point scale from "strongly agree" to "strongly disagree"]
26. One popular saying is that "Islam is both religion and state" (*deen wa dawla*). Do you agree?
    [ ] [five-point scale from "strongly agree" to "strongly disagree"]
27. If Islamists reach government through elections in Muslim countries, they will stay in power (government) in the future even if people do not want them in power.
    [ ] [five-point scale from "strongly agree" to "strongly disagree"]
28. Political institutions and processes such as elections, parliament, and political parties are against Islamic sharia.
    [ ] [five-point scale from "strongly agree" to "strongly disagree"]
29. The West (USA and its allies such as Britain and others) does not want Muslims to freely elect their rulers.
    [ ] [five-point scale from "strongly agree" to "strongly disagree"]
30. Which one of the following countries comes closest to your best (ideal/favorite) political system?
    [A list of thirteen countries of the world, plus "none of the above"]
31. Why have you chosen this country to be the closest to your best (ideal/favorite) political system?
32. To achieve their political rights (e.g., freedom of expression and freedom of association), Muslims should:
    [ ] challenge their authoritarian rulers *violently* even if they may be killed or jailed
    [ ] challenge their authoritarian rulers *peacefully* even if they may be killed or jailed
    [ ] express their negative feeling towards their rulers but *not* publicly
    [ ] be patient and pray to Allah to grant them better rulers
33. Regarding the Arab-Israeli conflict, whose opinions do you trust most?
    [ ] your Muslim government

[ ] official religious scholars (shaikhs appointed by the government)

[ ] unofficial religious scholars (independent shaikhs)

[ ] the intellectuals (independent press)

[ ] none

[ ] other, please specify:

34. Some Muslim countries have Christian (*massehi*) minorities that want to participate in the political process as voters, members of parliament, and/or ministers. If you had the ultimate say in this regard, what would you allow them to do?

[ ] They should not be allowed to be part of the political process at all.

[ ] They should be allowed to vote in public elections only.

[ ] Beside voting, they should be allowed to be members of the parliament.

[ ] Beside voting and parliament membership, they should be allowed to be ministers.

35. Some Muslim countries have Jewish minorities (*yahood*) that want to participate in the political process as voters, members of parliament, and/or ministers. If you had the ultimate say in this regard, what would you allow them to do?

[ ] They should not be allowed to be part of the political process at all.

[ ] They should be allowed to vote in public elections only.

[ ] Beside voting, they should be allowed to be members of the parliament.

[ ] Beside voting and parliament membership, they should be allowed to be ministers.

36. Do you think that Muslim women should be allowed to participate in the political process as voters, members of parliament, and/or ministers? If you had the ultimate say in this regard, what would you allow them to do?

[ ] They should not be allowed to be part of the political process at all.

[ ] They should be allowed to vote in public elections only.

[ ] Beside voting, they should be allowed to be members of the parliament.

[ ] Beside voting and parliament membership, they should be allowed to be ministers.

37. Please mention the names of three *ulama*, intellectuals, or politicians who have the most influence on your political knowledge and positions.

38. On a scale of political freedom from 1 to 5, where 1 is a non-democracy/dictatorship (*istibdad*) and 5 is a free political system, how free do you consider your country of origin?
    [   ] 1 (full dictatorship)
    [   ] 2 (partial dictatorship)
    [   ] 3 (in between/in the middle)
    [   ] 4 (partially free)
    [   ] 5 (fully free)

39. There are individuals who are killed or sent to jail because they publicly ask for their political rights. Do you agree or disagree with what they do?

40. Based on Islamic shari'a, where would you put your country of origin on the following scale?
    [   ] 1 full non-Islamic government
    [   ] 2 partial (to some extent) non-Islamic government
    [   ] 3 in between
    [   ] 4 partial (to some extent) Islamic government
    [   ] 5 full Islamic government

41. If you were allowed to choose among three political rulers for your country of origin, which one of the following would you prefer?
    [   ] a religious Muslim ruler who establishes the *hudud* of Islam in which his citizens cannot disagree with him or question his actions
    [   ] a religious Muslim ruler who establishes the *hudud* of Islam in which his citizens may disagree with him and hold him accountable for his actions
    [   ] a good ruler who is not necessarily a good Muslim but willing to give up power if he loses public support

42. Which of the following reasons can best explain why democracy has not emerged in most countries of the Muslim world? (Check all that apply and designate each of these as very important reason, somewhat important reason, not a reason at all, or do not know.)
    [   ] *the West* (by supporting authoritarian rulers)
    [   ] *the individuals* (who are not ready for democracy)
    [   ] *the rulers* (who do not leave their positions)
    [   ] *Islam and democracy* contradict each other
    [   ] *the scholars* (shaikhs who are opposed to democracy)

43. Do you think that Muslim countries should have democratic rulers instead of the current political rulers?
    [   ] yes
    [   ] no
    [   ] I am not sure

44. Would you accept that your son/brother gets married to a woman from another religion (Christian, Jewish, etc.)?
    [ ] yes
    [ ] no
    [ ] I am not sure
    [ ] other, please specify:
45. Would you allow a Sunni and Shiite to get married to each other?
    [ ] yes
    [ ] no
    [ ] I am not sure
    [ ] other, please specify
46. Muslims who adopt Western ideologies such as liberalism, socialism, or communism should be allowed to form political parties (*ahzab*) and run for elections (*intikhabat*).
    [ ] [five-point scale from "strongly agree" to "strongly disagree"]
47. In your opinion, what is democracy?
    [open ended]
48. In your opinion, what is Islam?
    [open ended]
49. Some Muslim countries have Muslim minorities (e.g., Shiite and Ahmadi) that want to participate in the political process as voters, members of parliament, and/or ministers. If you had the ultimate say in this regard, what would you allow them to do?
    [ ] They should not be allowed to be part of the political process at all.
    [ ] They should be allowed to vote in public elections only.
    [ ] Beside voting, they should be allowed parliament membership.
    [ ] Beside voting and parliament membership, they should be allowed to be ministers.
50. Please feel free to add comments if you wish.
    [open ended]

Notes

1. Respondents had the option of responding to the survey in English, Arabic, Farsi, French, or Urdu.
2. Some questions were not allowed in some countries, so there were some modifications of the survey from country to country.

Appendix 3
Data Collection

Collection of the data analyzed here was funded mainly by the Middle East Research Council of Beirut, Lebanon, and logistically supported by the Center for the Study of Developing Countries and the Center of Political Research and Studies, Cairo, Egypt. The survey, conceived in 2002, was designed to tap into the opinion of Muslims on political issues.

It was limited to literate Muslims because of the extreme logistical difficulties that would have faced researchers in surveying noneducated Muslims. If illiterate Muslims had been included, I would have been forced to drop the idea of the survey and obtain secondary sources, or to administer a survey that represented all Muslims but excluded all of the more sophisticated questions.[1] Consultation with some researchers and area experts revealed a preponderant preference to target the "political class" that comprises mainly literate Muslims in order to keep politically sensitive questions. This, however, was more than a practical consideration. Because literate Muslims are more politically engaged than the illiterate, they are more likely to influence political changes in the Muslim world, and their opinions thus would offer a better gauge of future trends. For these reasons, then, information obtained from illiterate Muslims, though rare, was discarded.

I also had to think carefully about how to approach literate Muslims. Though mail and telephone surveys are the most common means for surveying people in open societies, many researchers I consulted in the Muslim world raised concerns that these two tools would adversely affect the reliability and response rates of the survey, given the sensitivity of the questions asked. My consultations led me to conclude that face-to-face written surveys were to be preferred over telephone and mail surveys for two reasons: First, there would be the possibility of explaining any of the survey questions and assuring confidentiality to the respondents. Second, this would open up the possibility of having focus-group discussions with some of the respondents to add depth to the survey findings. While observers and participants in the pilot study expressed their concern that in some countries respondents might be worried that they were actually being monitored by government agents, a promise of strict anonymity and oral assurances of confidentiality before surveys were handed in seemed to help in convincing respondents to cooperate. I also sought to increase trust by having native academicians and research centers administer the surveys whenever and wherever possible. Both are considered trustworthy and highly unlikely to act as government agents.

For the purpose of systematically checking for the impact of the suspicion of governmental surveillance, another survey was developed. It was administered through the Web by e-mailing Muslims the URL of a website and asking them to respond to the same questions as those on the written survey. Technically, this kind of e-mail survey is drawn from a nonprobabilistic controlled-quota sample in the sense that there is no known probability for the possibility of including all Muslims who have access to the Internet in the frame of respondents. However, some nonprobabilistic surveys can be more representative than others if there are known possible sources of biases (Scheaffer 2005).

Obtaining survey responses from two different tools poses a methodological challenge and provides a methodological opportunity to examine the efficiency of the two tools as well. The e-mail survey adopted a nonprobabilistic sampling technique that does not ensure the elements are selected in a random manner. It is difficult then to guarantee that certain portions of the population were not excluded from the sample, since elements do not have an equal chance of being selected. Note that it is entirely possible that the elements that were not selected did not differ from the selected elements, but this could be determined only through an examination of both sets of elements. Thus, either of two broad scenarios may be the case: (1) The two tools are in conflict mainly due to the fact that Muslims who have access to the Internet are a homogeneous group of Muslims who think alike and thus are not representative of the broader population of literate Muslims. (2) The two tools are complementary in gauging Muslims' attitude since the two pooled samples are drawn from the same population.

To test these two broad scenarios, a question about how many times a week the respondents have access to the Internet was added to the written survey. Contrary to my initial expectations, the analysis of variance (ANOVA) did not demonstrate significant differences between the means of those who have regular access to the Internet and of those who do not (significance level 0.90). To confirm the previous finding, ANOVA was used again to compare the responses from the two samples regarding the questions relevant to the purpose of this project. Again, no statistical difference was found in any case (significance level 0.90). As a third step to confirm the complementary nature of the tools, preliminary regression analysis was used to make sure that the demographics did not differ between the two groups of respondents. Except for age, there was no difference between the coefficients obtained from the e-mail survey and the written survey. The previous precautionary statistical tests suggest that the sampling technique did not produce a systematic bias in the data, which is a necessary condition for relying on the data regarding the relationship between Muslims' attitudes toward democracy and the factors that might be influencing these attitudes. This finding supports a similar inference made based on a survey in eight Arab countries, which showed that "in the aggregate, Internet access appears to make little difference in the personal concerns of Arabs. Even where rankings and ratings do differ, the differences are slight" (Zogby 2002).

It has been stated that "the relationships expressed in theoretical propositions are presumed to be universally present . . . both in representative and non-representative samples. To disprove or demonstrate their existence is hence possible in any kind of sample—biased or unbiased" (Zetterberg 1963). However, when using a biased sampling for a verification, "we must have assurance that the relationship we want to prove is not introduced into our data by selective sampling. . . . Also, when using a biased sample for verification, we should realize that we have no knowledge of the population to which the result can be safely generalized" (Zetterberg 1963).

This survey's lack of significant discrepancies can be explained by the fact that the two tools (the e-mail and face-to-face surveys) targeted almost the same population of mostly urban, literate, and nonpoor Muslims. Yet ANOVA suggests that some respondents exhibited less self-restraint in criticism of their governments and support for elected accountable governments in the e-mail survey than respondents did in the face-to-face one. This discrepancy can be explained by the freedom of expression that respondents enjoy in cyberspace as compared to face-to-face surveys. This finding has been confirmed by the fact that with the exception of question 43, "Do you think that Muslim countries should have democratic rulers instead of the current political rulers?" the respondents to the e-mail survey were more critical of their rulers than were respondents to the face-to-face survey and the focus-group discussions in Saudi Arabia, Sudan, and Libya.

Survey Administered by E-mail

A lengthy process of four steps was undertaken to collect the e-mails of the potential respondents and then to stratify them.

1. Collecting the convenience sample. The initial pool of e-mails was selected from more than 200 public websites (e.g., chat rooms, petitioning sites, e-mail groups, commentary on articles and news from various newspapers) in the same five languages in which people provided their e-mail addresses. The initial process resulted in approximately 49,400 e-mailed responses. The process of collecting these e-mails took around nine months (July 2001–March 2002).[2]

2. Expanding the frame of the network sample. These people were e-mailed in the first week of May 2002 with an invitation to participate anonymously in a worldwide survey of Muslims on political issues. Upon their agreement, they were asked to visit a webpage where they could provide anonymous preliminary information regarding demographics (gender, age, income, and education), country of origin, citizenship, and residence (if different), and religious denomination (Sunni, Shiite, Ahmadi) in any of the following languages: Arabic, English, French, Farsi, and Urdu.

Additionally, they were asked to forward the initial e-mail to other Muslims aged eighteen and above. By the end of May 2002, around 61,700 e-mails from sixty-four countries around the world had been sent by Muslims expressing interest in participating in the survey. These 61,700 e-mails have become the network or snowball sampling frame. The main advantage of network sampling is to increase the diversity, yet it may produce nonrepresentative samples. That is why stratifying the e-mails according to known characteristics within each country was essential.

3. Stratification of the network sample. The 61,700 e-mails represented diverse individuals in diverse Muslim and non-Muslim societies; nonetheless, representativeness technically remains unknown. Since statistical tests are appropriate only for probability samples, the seemingly unrelated regressions and multiple logistic regressions that are employed in this book should be understood as approximate guides.

Following many suggestions found in the literature to partially cope with the problem of nonprobability, however, I subgrouped the e-mails by country of citizenship or origin, if different. I eliminated the e-mails for countries from which the total number of responses was fewer than 480 (a convenient cutoff). The remaining list included thirty-nine countries where Muslims have a notable presence. Upon consulting with many area specialists, I decided to deal with each country separately. I drew stratified proportionate random samples from the e-mails, based upon the three known national demographics of the population of each society. The consensus among the area specialists was to use the level of education, income, and religious sect (Sunni, Shiite, and Ahmadi) as the three strata. These national demographics were obtained from national censuses, the indexes of the World Bank, International Monetary Fund, CIA factbook, and human development reports.[3]

When the e-mails of each country had been stratified according to their demographics and Islamic sect into homogeneous discrete strata (with heterogeneity between subsets), the pooled respondents were found to represent literate Muslims of middle and/or upper classes of only thirty-three countries. Thus, on the basis of the relative proportion of the population, I randomly selected the e-mails to represent literate Muslims between eighteen and fifty-five. The main advantage of this technique is to ensure the proper representation of the stratification variables, which in turn "enhances the representation of other variables related to them" (Babbie 2004: 206).

4. Sending the final survey.   Around 55,100 e-mails were sent out to represent the stratified samples from the thirty-nine countries. Responses numbered 24,681 (45 percent response rate). The sample size of each society is provided in Table A3.1. Again, I discarded the e-mails from countries with fewer than 480 respondents. This left the final sample of 32 countries with 480 respondents or more. Although Iraq did not meet the cutoff sample size criterion, it is included in the aggregate analysis for its relevance. The respondents to the e-mail version had to respond to the same fifty questions as were in the written survey during the same period. Comparing the income gap between the average citizen (measured by GDP per capita) and the average income of the respondents to the survey indicates that the respondents are relatively richer than average. I take this gap to imply that the respondents belong to the

Table A3.1 Respondents to the Survey

Country	Written Sample	E-mail Sample	Total N	College Access (%)[a]	Literacy Rate (%)[b]	$ GDP per Capita[c]	$ Sample Mean Income	% GDP per Capita Gap	% of Female
Albania		500	500	15	85	760	921	121	52
Algeria	198	570	768	15	60	5,900	7,050	119	43
Bahrain	102	530	632	21	86	15,100	16,300	108	42
Bangladesh	196	935	1,131	7	39	1,750	3,141	179	42
Egypt	1,617	1,346	2,963	38	53	2,900	4,139	143	45
EU	118	774	892	40	99	24,000	25,149	105	49
Gambia		489	489	NA	33	1,450	6,769	467	43
India		1,497	1,497	11	57	2,500	3,690	148	44
Indonesia	154	1,331	1,485	15	85	3,000	6,492	216	47
Iran	342	1,138	1,480	21	77	6,000	8,399	140	45
Iraq		91	91	14	58	1,600	6,921	433[a]	41
Jordan		687	687	31	88	3,800	8,012	211	43
Kuwait	113	533	646	21	82	18,100	18,919	105	42
Lebanon		534	534	45	86	4,400	5,505	125	42
Libya	266	597	863	58	80	6,000	7,609	127	37
Mali		521	521	29	46	760	1,919	516[a]	45
Malaysia	683	1,177	1,860	28	88	8,500	9,721	114	45
Morocco	125	627	752	10	50	3,800	7,035	185	51
Nigeria	138	579	717	27	64	650	2,889	444[a]	47
Oman		494	494	11	72	13,000	13,231	102	43
Pakistan	872	1,685	2,557	5	45	2,000	3,398	170	44
Qatar		568	568	27	81	20,000	20,441	102	43
Saudi Arabia	182	942	1,124	22	73	11,000	11,692	106	36

(continues)

Table A3.1 continued

Country	Written Sample	E-mail Sample	Total N	College Access (%)[a]	Literacy Rate (%)[b]	$ GDP per Capita[c]	$ Sample Mean Income	% GDP per Capita Gap	% of Female
Senegal	187	569	756	4	39	1,300	6,501	500[a]	43
Sudan	447	583	1,030	7	53	1,500	2,306	154	34
Syria		613	613	18	75	3,000	3,991	323[a]	44
Tajikistan		497	497	15	99	1,000	4,492	449	42
Turkmenistan		504	504	NA	98	5,000	5,898	118	41
Tunisia	119	546	665	23	73	6,300	7,489	119	45
Turkey	264	1,058	1,322	25	85	6,500	7,749	119	46
UAE	185	595	780	12	76	21,000	21,139	101	41
USA	223	1,083	1,306	71	97	37,000	36,649	99	51
Yemen	168	488	656	11	50	850	3,271	385[a]	32
Total	6,699	24,681	31,380						
Average				22.487	70.7	7,285	8,921		43
Stand. Dev.				15	19	8,415	7,667		4.3

Notes: By comparing the statistics of GDP per capita, college access, and literacy rates between the pooled data, and upon consulting with area specialists in most of these countries, one should argue that the available data are drawn from upper-class literate Muslims only in the cases of Yemen, Tajikistan, Nigeria, Syria, Iraq, Gambia, Senegal, and Mali (italic in the table). The rest of the data are drawn from middle- and upper-class literate Muslims in the other countries.

a. UNESCO report on global education is available at www.uis.unesco.org/TEMPLATE/html/Exceltables/education/enrol_tertiary.xls.

b. World Bank, *Human Development Report,* 2002.

c. This entry shows GDP on a purchasing-power parity basis divided by population as of July 1 for the same year. World Bank, *Human Development Report,* 2002, and CIA, *The World Factbook.*

middle and upper classes. But there is a difference in degree. For instance, the Albanian respondents to the survey, as indicated in the last column of Table A3.1, are 21 percent richer than average Albanians. However, the economic gap along with the literacy ratio increases dramatically in the cases of Gambia, Iraq, Mali, Nigeria, Senegal, Syria, Tajikistan, and Yemen. This large gap indicates that the pooled data can speak only for the *upper class*.

Though admittedly imperfect, combining the data from the e-mail survey and the written surveys serves three desired purposes. (1) It provides a larger sample size with wider representation of a greater number of Muslim countries and thus ensures more diversity in Muslims' sects, ages, genders, and political ideologies. (2) It strikes a balance between the advantages of a written survey followed by deeper focus-group discussions and the e-mail survey in which researchers distanced themselves from any influence on the respondents (Smith 2002; Solomon 2001). (3) It controls for the effect of fear from responding to very politically sensitive questions, given the fact that the e-mail survey does not meet the same level of self-censorship that face-to-face surveys may encounter.

That said, I do not find statistically significant attitudinal differences between literate Muslims who have access to the Internet and literate Muslims who do not have access to the Internet. With all these measures to ensure the reliability and validity of data, one should deal with these data and the results stemming from them as an attempt to provide baseline data that will help in exploring an empirical puzzle that has for so long been tackled only from theological and historical perspectives.

A technical note should be made about the unknown representativeness of the e-mail survey. According to Christine B. Smith, "Perhaps the most critical problem with Internet-based research is the practical impossibility of probability sampling, so that one can only tentatively generalize to a very specific population, if at all" (Smith 2002). After discussing different accounts of this problem, she concludes that "we do this all the time," whether we use e-mail, telephone-based, or paper-based surveys. None of them is completely random. The solution that Smith advances is to "learn more about [the respondents'] demographics," which will enable "generalizability to well-studied segments of the overall population." Others suggest that nonprobabilistic samples are better for understanding relationships between variables than for making descriptive estimates about target populations (Allen 2002; Babbie 2004; Lehtonen and Pahkinen 2004; Sampath 2001; Wingard-Nelson

2004). Two econometricians examined five decades of sampling mathematically and theoretically and suggested that the great majority of the sampling methods that social scientists use do not actually produce random samples unless we ignore the impracticality of most of the underlying assumptions (Ullah and Breunig 1998).

Face-to-Face Survey

The same questions on the e-mail survey were used in a face-to-face written survey in Egypt, United Arab Emirates, Pakistan, Algeria, Libya, Malaysia, Iran, and Turkey, as well as among Muslim students who studied at three American universities (Western Michigan University, Colorado University, and the University of Michigan) and Muslims who attended four Islamic centers in Michigan in mid-April 2002. An attempt to administer a face-to-face survey in Saudi Arabia failed mainly because of security concerns on the part of the Saudi academicians who volunteered to help in administering the survey. Egypt and the United States were particularly important for this study, given the diversity of non-native Muslims who live in both of them.

The sample is of a multistage design. The first level of stratification was the most obvious: we divided the entire population to be studied into the eight countries. Hence each country represents a stratum in the design. Within each country, the urban area was defined. We sought to narrow our definition of "urban area" to the areas of high population concentration. Country samples were of area probability design. In each country, the most recent population census data were used to stratify the urban areas into lower, middle, and upper socioeconomic status (SES). The sample size assigned to each stratum was based on these SES estimates. The failure to interview Muslims of lower SES led the team to redesign the sample to reflect Muslims of middle and upper SES. Within each stratum, census maps were used to select, at random, an appropriate number of political subdivisions (e.g., districts and counties), and within each subdivision, census maps were used to select an appropriate number of segments from which to draw the interviews. In Libya and Sudan, I made subjective judgments (which were cross-checked by regional specialists) concerning the best estimate of which cities, towns, areas, schools, and colleges should be chosen to be representative of each country.

As always, the target population (the population for which information is required) and the survey population (the population actually covered) differ for practical reasons, even though they should in theory be the same. It was extremely difficult to obtain a balanced sample of all literate Muslims from all parts of each country. That is why it was necessary to impose geographical and career limitations excluding certain parts of the target population because they were inaccessible. Thus, the respondents to the face-to-face survey were mainly college students and graduates, with an undersampling of Muslims with a high school degree or less.

Table A3.1 lists the number of participants who responded to the written survey. Further information about the survey is available from the author. As noted above, one question was added to the written survey, asking respondents to indicate how frequently they surf the Internet, to help control for the effect of the Internet and to examine the demographic and attitudinal characteristics of the individuals who have access to the Internet. The three main traits that are common among regular Internet users are maleness, affluence, and youth.

The written survey is used not only to check the consistency and reliability of the email survey but also to expand the generalizability of the results to people who do not necessarily have access to the Internet.

The Gallup Organization, World Values Survey, Pew survey project, and Zogby International also ran face-to-face surveys in different Muslim societies in the years 2002 and 2003 (Gallup 2002; Inglehart 2003; Pew 2003a; Pew 2003b; Tessler 2002b; Zogby 2002). Comparing the demographics of the respondents to e-mail and written surveys of this project with the literate Muslim respondents to these other surveys indicates a clear oversampling of the relatively affluent over the relatively less advantaged and individuals under 40 over older people. These surveys indicated that they oversampled men and the urban literate.

Since I make no attempt at any descriptive estimation of *all* Muslims who support or oppose democracy, it matters little whether the pooled data are a representative sample of all Muslims of the world or not. It is enough that it is representative of the literate Muslims of the middle and upper classes who potentially pay some heed to political matters.

Focus-Group Discussions

An important part of this project was to randomly select groups of three to eleven of the respondents to the written survey and conduct focus-group discussions with them. These discussions took place among Muslims in eight societies: Egypt, Libya, the Sudan, the United Arab Emirates, Iran, Turkey, Algeria, and the United States.

Subjects were selected randomly. They were introduced to the purpose of the survey and the possible benefits. The respondents were given the opportunity to express their opinions for around thirty minutes in a friendly get-together with beverages provided. The number of individuals invited to participate in the focus-group discussions was more than 600, but only 188 accepted.

Three advantages have been gained from conducting intensive interviews and focus-group discussions.

1. This research method permitted respondents to reveal their convictions and uncertainties, their processes of drawing conclusions, their emotional reactions, their foci for passion and indifference, and their expertise and ignorance. With the interviews, it was possible to evaluate the content, complexity, and strength of individual beliefs about democracy, and this definitely added depth to the survey analysis.

2. The survey produced some findings that were substantiated during the focus-group discussions. For instance, female support of democracy was better understood in light of statements given by the female interviewees who believed that democracy promotes their sociopolitical position. Intensive interviews permitted discussion with female respondents of what they expect and how they would feel about the effect of democracy on their life. Because the same conclusions derive from different types of data collected in different ways, we can have greater confidence in their reliability.

3. The intensive interviews and focus-group discussions also permit attention to certain data that are overlooked by quantitative tools. For instance, what if a Shiite Muslim woman makes a novel argument against democracy? Regression analysis will simply ignore her position if there is statistically enough evidence that most educated Shiite women are prodemocracy. Intensive interviews and focus-group discussions bring these potential anomalies to the researcher's attention.

The main disadvantage of the focus-group discussion is that it is not as diverse and representative as the survey. However, this disadvantage is of little concern for the purposes of this project, given my primary reliance on the pooled survey data for drawing inferences. The focus-group discussions were used solely to put flesh on the bones of the statistical tests.

Elite Interviews

Five to nine elite interviews with *ulama*, activists, and intellectuals were conducted during visits to each of the previously listed eight countries, as well as Saudi Arabia. The interviewees were selected on the basis of two criteria: to represent diverse ideological positions toward democracy and because they had been identified either in the written survey or during the focus-group discussions as influential opinion leaders in their country. The interviewees were asked to comment and reflect upon the descriptive graphs of the e-mail surveys. Some of them asked for the results to be sent to them ahead of the interview and had extensive comments on them. Others interpreted the findings and used them in later references to defend their political causes.

Selection of Countries

There were four main determinants for selecting the countries in which the written survey, focus-group discussions, and elite interviews would be conducted. They should

1. represent the geographical and religious diversity of the Middle East and Muslim world,
2. represent a wide array of experiences to reflect how Islam and democracy are perceived from both the masses' and the elites' points of view,
3. yield a high number of responses in pilot tests of the e-mail survey from citizens of those countries, and
4. offer the researcher reliable connections to assist in gaining access to potential focus-group and survey respondents.

Notes

1. Most other surveys, such as the Pew and the World Value Survey, ask very broad questions such as whether one prefers a democracy versus a government with strong leadership. These kinds of questions, though standard, do not capture which aspects of democracy a Muslim respondent advocates and which he or she does not. Further, they do not capture the impact of Islam on respondents' political attitudes.

2. I am indebted to Ghada Sharaf of Egypt, Abdulhaq al-Jundi of Syria, Mohamed al-Ameen of Senegal, Hafez Noa'man and Ateeq Mumtaz of Pakistan, Hameed Siddiqi of Malaysia, Hussain Mahdi and Ezzat Mansouri of Iran, and Mai Somany of Indonesia for their indispensable effort to collect these e-mails and to lead the teams that translated and tested the translated versions of the surveys.

3. I am highly indebted to Susan Carlson (Sociology Department), Kevin Corder (Political Science Department), and Matthew Higgins (Economics Department) of Western Michigan University. These three methodologists offered valuable advice and thorough guidance throughout the process of stratification.

Appendix 4 Principal Component Factor Analysis

Q #	Religiosity (2 questions)	Democratic Institutions (3 questions)	Democratic Norms (4 questions)	Elasticity of Demands for Political Rights (2 questions)
15	1. How many times do you pray (make *salat*) daily?			
18	2. How many times have you had any sort of alcoholic beverages or wine (*khamr*)? *Alpha = 0.926*			
24		1. Voting is some type of enjoining the good and forbidding the evil.		
25		2. Public elections of rulers will lead to taboos.		
28		3. Democratic institutions and procedures are against sharia. *Alpha = 0.875*		
34			1. Attitude toward participation of Christian minorities in the political process	
35			2. Attitude toward participation of Jewish minorities in the political process	
36			3. Attitude toward participation of Muslim women in the political process	
49			4. Attitude toward participation of Muslim minorities in the political process *Alpha = 0.763*	
32				1. The risk Muslims take to express their demands for their political rights
39				2. Appreciation for people killed or jailed because of their political rights *Alpha = 0.91*

Note: Principal component factor analysis was used with Varimax rotation and Kaiser normalization. The total model predicts 78.8 percent of cumulative variance. The religiosity and support for democratic institutions scales were reversed, so that a positive response expresses more religiosity and greater support for democratic institutions.

Cronbach's estimate of reliability and internal consistency is reported as Alpha.

Appendix 5
Data Processing
and Regression Models

Preparing Individual-Level Data

Using the standard statistical procedures, I checked for missing data, outliers, perfect collinearity among variables, and nonnormality of variables. Regarding the missing data, using the SAS 8.2 command of PROC MI shows that there are certain variables that contain high percentages of missing responses. The missing responses were clearly missed at random (MAR assumption).

To handle this problem of missing data, the researcher opted to use the technique of *multiple imputation*. Instead of filling in a single value for each missing value, Rubin's multiple imputation procedure replaces each missing value with a set of plausible values that represent the uncertainty about the right value to impute (Rubin 1987). These multiply-imputed data sets are then analyzed by using standard procedures for complete data and combining the results from this analysis. No matter which complete-data analysis is used, the process of combining results from different imputed data sets is essentially the same. This results in statistically valid inferences that properly reflect the uncertainty due to missing values. SAS 8.2 has the MI procedure that creates multiply imputed data sets for incomplete p-dimensional multivariate data. It uses methods that incorporate appropriate variability across m imputations. Once the m complete data sets are analyzed using standard SAS/STAT procedures, PROC MIANALYZE can be used to generate valid statistical inferences about these parameters by combining the results. I averaged parameters across data sets to get single point estimates and calculated standard errors using variation within and

173

between data sets. For scalar point estimate, the following formula was used:

$$\bar{q} = \frac{1}{M} \sum_{j-1}^{M} q_j$$

where q could be regression or logit coefficients, M is the number of data sets, and q_j is the parameter estimate from the jth data set.

For the scalar standard error estimate, the following formula was used:

$$se_q = \sqrt{\frac{1}{M} \sum_{j-1}^{M} se_j^2 + \left(1 + \frac{1}{M}\right)\left(\frac{1}{M-1}\right) \sum_{j-1}^{M} (q_j - \bar{q})^2}$$

where se_j is the standard error estimate for the jth parameter; q_j is the jth parameter estimate; and M is the number of data sets.

M in this project = 5, and the MI was conducted for each country separately.

Since I used multiple indicators to gauge the same variables, the problem of collinearity was noticeable. The factor analysis helped to combine collinear indicators. There was no real outlier or influential case, which is unlikely to happen in survey research.

Heteroskedasticity

Almost all the models used in this project are plagued by heteroskedasticity (HSK), a violation of the "equal variance of error term" assumption in OLS regressions. HSK does not lead to biased coefficients but tends to interfere with standard errors, thus disordering t-values and potentially masking the significance of a regressor. This is called "loss of efficiency" in econometrics. To solve this problem, I used the White robust estimation of standard errors in both the SUR and multiple logistic regressions.

Seemingly Unrelated Regression and Multiple Logit Regressions

Arnold Zellner's idea of combining several equations into one model to improve estimation efficiency ranks as one of the most successful and lasting innovations in the history of econometrics (Greene 2000). Thus, Zellner's seemingly unrelated regression (SUR) was used to account for the contemporaneous correlation between error terms in the two equations of democratic institutions and norms for each society (Srivastava and Giles 1987).

To provide more certainty about the robustness of the SUR analysis, multiple logistic regressions (MLR) were run as well. The logistic regressions serve to examine the robustness of the SUR coefficients. That is why the asterisks in Table 3.1 reflect the common results between the two types of regressions (SUR and MLR). For instance, the logistic regression in the cases of USA, Libya, and Bahrain showed a positive relationship between Muslims who support political Islam and those who support democratic institutions. Since this result was not supported by the SUR system and does not have a theoretical basis, Table 3.1 does not report the relationship.

Using the logistic regression as a check mechanism has the important advantage of dropping some of the most controversial assumptions of OLS and SUR, such as the linear relationship between the dependent and independent variables, multivariate normality, and homoskedastic residuals for each level of the independent variables.

References

'Aawa, Mohamed S. al-. 1989. *On the Political System of the Islamic State* (Arabic). Cairo: Dar-Alshorouk.

AbdelGalil, Maher. 2003. "Emerati Women: Education Is the Only Path to Freedom." *Al-Hayat*, May 3.

Abdelrazeq, Hussain. 2003. "Forum on Democracy in the Arab World" (Arabic: "Al-Democrateya fi al-Watan al-Arabi"). Jazeer.net, available at www.aljazeera.net/programs/opinions/articles/2001/11/11-29-6.htm.

Abdoullaev, Kamoloudin. 1998. "The Civil War in Tajikistan." *Peace and Policy: TODA Institute for Global Peace and Policy Research* 3, no. 1.

'Abeykan, Abdelmohsen al-. 2003. "Suicide Operations." *Al-Sharq al-Awssat*, July 6.

Abo al-Magd, Kamal. 1988. *Dialogue, Not Confrontation: Studies on Islam and Modern Times* (Arabic). Cairo: Dar Al-Shorouq.

Abootalebi, Ali R. 2000. *Islam and Democracy: State-Society Relations in Developing Countries, 1980–1994.* New York: Garland.

Aborisade, Oladimeji. 2002. *Politics in Nigeria.* New York: Longman.

Abou El Fadl, Khaled. 2001. "Islam: Images, Politics, and Paradox." *Middle East Report* 221 (Winter).

———. 2003. "Islam and the Challenge of Democracy." *Boston Review*, April/May.

Abrahamian, Ervand. 1993. *Khomeinism: Essays on the Islamic Republic.* Berkeley: University of California Press.

Abu Odeh, Adnan. 2003. "Interview with Anthony Shadid: Restrictive Arab Nations Feel Pressure from Within." *Washington Post*, February 27.

Abul Khair, Ali. 2003. "Political Islam and Democracy" (Arabic). *Al-Wafd*, February 2.

'Affifi, Mayadda al-. 2002. *Al-Ahram al-Arabi*, January 5.

Ahmad, Akbar, and Lawrence Rosen. 2002. "Islam, Academe, and Freedom of the Mind." *Chronicle of Higher Education*, February 8.

Ahmed, Ali al-. 2002. Interview. *Frontline*, PBS, March 19.

Ahmed, Leila. 1992. *Women and Gender and Islam.* New Haven, CT: Yale University Press.

Ahmed, Rafiuddin. 2001. *Understanding the Bengal Muslims: Interpretative Essays.* New Delhi: Oxford University Press.

'Alem, Galal al-. 1975. "Leaders of the West Say: Destroy Islam, Annihilate Its People" (Arabic: "Kaddat al-Gharb Yakoloon: Damero al-Islam wa Abeedo Ahlaho"). Transcript. Tripoli, Lebanon.

Ali, Ausaf. 2000. "Can Fundamentalist Islam and Democracy Coexist in a Country? *Los Angeles Times*, March 20.

Allen, Jack. 2002. *Randomness and Optimal Estimation in Data Sampling.* Rehoboth, NM: American Research Press.

Allen, Jodie. 2005. "Iraqi Vote Mirrors Desire for Democracy in Muslim World." In *The Pew Global Attitudes Project.*

'Alyan, Lubna Solayman al-. 2003. Interview. *Al-Sharq al-Awssat*, June 7.

Amirahmadi, Hooshang. 2002. "Iran, Islam, and the Perceived Threat." Worlddialogue.org.

Anderson, Lisa. 1997. "Fulfilling Prophecies: State Policy and Islamist Radicalism." In *Political Islam: Revolution, Radicalism, or Reform?* edited by John L. Esposito. London: Lynne Rienner Publishers.

Ansari, Abdelhamid al-. 2003. "A Woman Invades the Household of Shaikhs" (Arabic). *Al-Sharq al-Awssat*, November 23.

Ansary, Abou Filali. 2003. "The Sources of Enlightened Muslim Thought." *Journal of Democracy* 14, no. 2.

Anwar, Ibrahim. 1995. *The Need for Civilizational Dialogue.* Washington, D.C.: Georgetown University, Center for Muslim-Christian Understanding, History and International Affairs.

Arabeyat, Abdel Latif. 1998. "Contemporary Political Islamic *Fiqh*" (Arabic: "Al-Fiqh al-Islami al-Mo'asser"). Al-Jazeera.net, available at www.aljazeera.net/programs/shareea/articles/2002/7/7-27-5.htm.

Arkoun, Mohamed. 1994. *Rethinking Islam: Common Questions, Uncommon Answers.* Edited and translated by Robert D. Lee. Boulder: Westview.

Armstrong, Karen. 2000. *Islam: A Short History.* Modern Library Chronicles. New York: Modern Library.

———. 2002. Interview by Max Garrone. Salon.com.

Asfoor, Gaber. 2003. "Awareness of the Future and the Prerequisites of Progress (Arabic)." *Al-Ahram*, March 31.

Aslan, Reza. 2005. "From Islam, Pluralist Democracies Will Surely Grow." *Chronicle Review*, March 11.

Assad, Hafez al-, and Mustafa Talas. 1990. *That Is What Assad Said* (Arabic: *Ka-dhalika qala al-Asad*). Dimashq, Syria.

'Azm, Sadek J. al-. 1969. *Critique of Religious Thought* (Arabic). Beirut: Dar al-Qalam.

Azzam, Abdullah. 1984. *Interpretation of Surat al-Tawba* (Arabic: *Fi Zelal Surat al-Tawba*). Peshawar, Pakistan: Markez al-Shaheed Azzam.

Babbie, Earl R. 2004. *The Practice of Social Research.* 10th ed. Belmont, CA: Thomson/Wadsworth.

Badry, Abdel Azeez -al. 1983. *Islam's Verdict on Socialism* (Arabic: *Hokm al-Islam Fi al-Eshtrakyya*). Al-Madeena al-Monawara, Saudi Arabia: Al-Makttabba al-'Elmmyya.

Bagabeer, Abdullah. 2003. "Cultural Indicators" (Arabic: "Mo'asserat Thaqqfeyya"). *Al-Sharq al-Awssat*, June 22.

Baghdadi, Ahmad. 1999. *Renovation of Religious Thought* (Arabic: *Tagdid al-Fikr al-Dini*). Damascus: Al Mada.

Barakah, Iqbal. 2002. "Democracy and Freedom of Women" (Arabic: "Al-Democratia and Horreyat al-Mara'a"). *Al-Ahram*, June 12.

Barakah, Iqbal, and Malak Hifni Nasif. 2001. *Muslim Women in the Lifetime of the Prophet* (Arabic: *Al-Mar'ah al-Muslimah fi Sira*). Cairo: Dar Qaba'.

Barnett, Tracy. 2003. *Oman, Modern Middle East Nations, and Their Strategic Place in the World*. Philadelphia: Mason Crest.

Basham, Patrick. 2004. "Can Iraq Be Democratic?" *Policy Analysis*, January, no. 505.

Bayes, Jane H., and Nayereh Esfahlani Tohidi. 2001. *Globalization, Gender, and Religion: The Politics of Women's Rights in Catholic and Muslim Contexts*. New York: Palgrave.

Beasant, John. 2002. *Oman: The True-Life Drama and Intrigue of an Arab State*. Edinburgh: Mainstream.

Beblawi, Hazem, and Giacomo Luciani (eds). 1987. *The Rentier State*, vol. 2 of *Nation, State, and Integration in the Arab World*. London: Croom Helm.

Berberoglu, Berch. 1999. *Turmoil in the Middle East: Imperialism, War, and Political Instability*. Albany: State University of New York Press.

Bermeo, Nancy. 1997. "Transitions to Democracy: A Special Issue in Memory of Dankwart A. Rustow." *Comparative Politics* 29, no. 3: 305–322.

Bianci, Steven. 2003. *Libya: Current Issues and Historical Background*. New York: Nova Science.

Binder, Leonard. 1988. *Islamic Liberalism*. Chicago: University of Chicago Press.

Bollen, Kenneth A. 1980. "Issues in the Comparative Measurement of Political Democracy." *American Sociological Review* 45.

Boroujerdi, Mehrzad. 1994. "Can Islam Be Secularized?" In *In Transition: Essays on Culture and Identity in the Middle Eastern Society*, edited by M. R. Ghanoonparvar and F. Farrokh. Laredo: Texas A&M International University.

Boroumand, Ladan, and Roya Boroumand. 2002. "Terror, Islam, and Democracy." *Journal of Democracy* 13, no. 2.

Borting, Meg. 2003. "Muslims Lament Israel's Existence." *International Herald Tribune*, June 3.

Bourqia, R., and Susan Gilson Miller. 1999. *In the Shadow of the Sultan: Culture, Power, and Politics in Morocco*. Harvard Middle Eastern Monographs 31. Cambridge, Mass.: Harvard University Press and Center for Middle Eastern Studies of Harvard University.

Buraiq, Sa'd al-. 1993. "The Rights of Rulers" (Arabic audio: "Hoqoq Wolat al-Amr"). Islamweb.net.

————. 1994. "The Intellectual Invasion" (Arabic audio: "Al-Ghazow al-Fikri"). Islamweb.net.

Burma, Ian. 2004. "An Islamic Democracy for Iraq?" *New York Times*, December 5.

Bush, George W. 2003. "Freedom and the Future." Speech at the American Enterprise Institute's annual dinner, February 27.

Byman, Daniel L., and Jerrold D. Green. 1999. "The Enigma of Political Stability in the Persian Gulf Monarchies." *Middle East Review of International Affairs* 3, no. 3.

Chaudhri, Rashid Ahmad, Shamim Ahmad, and Ahmadiyya Muslim Association. 1989. *Persecution of Ahmadi Muslims and Their Response.* London: Press and Publication Desk, Ahmadiyya Muslim Association.

Dahl, Robert. 1971. *Polyarchy: Participation and Opposition.* New Haven, CT: Yale University Press.

————. 1989. *Democracy and Its Critics.* New Haven, CT: Yale University Press.

————. 1998. *On Democracy.* New Haven, CT: Yale University Press.

Darwish, Adel. 2005. Relevant Numbers for Iraq and the Region. *Al-Sharq al-Awssat*, March 26.

Diamond, Larry Jay, Marc F. Plattner, and Daniel Brumberg. 2003. *Islam and Democracy in the Middle East.* A *Journal of Democracy* Book. Baltimore: Johns Hopkins University Press.

Din, Mohamed Mahdi Shams al-. 2001. *The Jurisprudence of Military Violence in Islam* (Arabic: *Fiqh al-'onf al-Mossalah fi al-Islam*). Beruit: Al-Mo'assassa al-Dawleyah Leldrassat wa al-Nashr (International Institute for Studies and Publications).

Downs, Anthony. 1956. *An Economic Theory of Democracy.* New York: Harper.

The Economist. 1998. "Country Report, Oman." London: Intelligence Unit, Great Britain. Available at: http://store.eiu.com/cart

Eickelman, Dale F. 1992. "Mass Higher Education and the Religious Imagination in Contemporary Arab Societies." *American Ethnologist* 19, 4: 1–13.

————. 1999. "The Coming Transformation of the Muslim World." *Middle East Review of International Affairs* 3, no. 3.

Engineer, Asgharali. 2001. *Islam, Women, and Gender Justice.* New Delhi: Gyan.

Eraqi, 'Atef al-. 2002. "Ethical Values Between Scientific Progress and the Achievements of Civilization" (Arabic). *Al-Ahram*, December 29.

Esposito, John L. 1992. *The Islamic Threat: Myth or Reality?* New York: Oxford University Press.

————. 1996. *Islam and Democracy.* New York: Oxford University Press.

Etienne, B. 1987. *L'Islamisme radicale.* Paris: Hatchette.

Faisal, Togan al-. 2003. Interview, *Al-Sharaq al-Awssat*, December 7.

Faki, Mostafa. 2003. "Interview with Anthony Shadid: Restrictive Arab Nations Feel Pressure from Within." *Washington Post*, February 27.

Fandy, Mamoun. 1999. *Saudi Arabia and the Politics of Dissent.* New York: St. Martin's.

Farjani, Nadir. 2002a. *The Arab Human Development Report 2002: Creating Opportunities for Future Generations*. New York: United Nations Development Programme Regional Bureau for Arab States.

———. 2002b. Interview. *Al-Sharq al-Awssat*, November 25.

Fasi, All'al. 1972. *Defending Sharia* (Arabic: *Difa' 'an al-Shariah*). Rabat, Morocco: Muassasat 'Allal al-Fasi.

Fassi, Haton al-. 2003. "Saudi Woman: New Arguments and Reforming Visions." *Al-Sharq al-Awssat*, June 14.

Fattah, Moataz A. 2006. "Educated Muslims and the Elasticity of Demand for Democracy." Available at http://personal.cmich.edu/fatta1ma/islam/sur.pdf.

Feldman, Noah. 2003. "Islamist Democracies: The West's Worst Nightmare?" *Globalist*, November 23.

Finnemore, Martha, and Kathryn Sikkink. 1998. "International Norm Dynamics and Political Change." *International Organization* no. 52: 887–917.

Fish, M. Steven. 2002. "Islam and Authoritarianism." *World Politics* no. 55:4–37.

Fisher, Yoshka. 2002. "German Minister of Foreign Affairs." *Al-Sharq al-Awssat*, April 26.

Fisk, Robert. 2002. *Pity the Nation: The Abduction of Lebanon*. 4th new American ed. New York: Thunder's Mouth / Nation Books.

Fouda, Farag. 1993. *A Dialogue on Secularism* (Arabic). Cairo: Dar Al-Fikr for Research and Studies.

Fuller, Graham. 2001. The Future of US Hegemony over the World. *Al-Jazeera*, November 28.

Gallup editors. 2002. *The 2002 Gallup Poll of the Islamic World*. Princeton, NJ: Gallup Press.

Gardels, Nathan. 2003. "Osama Bin Laden Has Given Common Identity Back to the West." *New Perspectives Quarterly* 20, no. 2.

Gawad, Ghanim. 2003. "Religious Secularism as a System of Government in Iraq." *Al-Sharq al-Awssat*, July 30.

Gazza'eri, Abo Bakr al-. 1984. *Who Is Responsible for the Loss of Islam?* (Arabic). Cairo: Maktabet al-Kolleyat al-Azhareya.

Gellner, Ernest. 1991. "Islam and Marxism: Some Comparisons." *International Affairs* 67, no. 1.

———. 1992. *Postmodernism, Reason and Religion*. London; New York: Routledge.

Gerges, Fawaz. 2001. Quoted in Margot Patterson, "Islam on the Defensive." *National Catholic Reporter*, December 14.

Ghannouchi, Rachid al-. 1993. *Public Freedoms in the Islamic State* (Arabic). Beirut: Center for Arab Unity Studies.

———. 1996. Lecture at Chatham House, London (May 9, 1995), in Robin Wright, "Two Visions of Reformism." *Journal of Democracy,* vol. 7, no. 2: 64–75.

———. 2003. Interview. Jazeera.net, December 19.

Ghazali, Mohamed al-. 1985. "Muslims' Halal Choices" (Arabic: "Kheyarat al-Muslim al-Halal"). Qatar National Radio, March 15.

————. 1997. *Constitution of Unity Among Muslims* (Arabic: *Dustor al-Wehda al-Thaqqafeya Bayn al-Muslmeen*). Cairo: Dar al-Shorouq.

Gillespie, Richard, and Richard Youngs. 2002. *The European Union and Democracy Promotion: The Case of North Africa.* Democratization Studies. Portland, OR: Frank Cass.

Gilsenan, Michael. 1982. *Recognizing Islam: Religion and Society in the Modern Arab World.* New York: Pantheon Books.

Greene, William H. 2000. *Econometric Analysis.* 4th ed. Upper Saddle River, N.J.: Prentice-Hall.

Hadenius, Axel. 2001. *Institutions and Democratic Citizenship.* Oxford Studies in Democratization. Oxford: Oxford University Press.

Hamad, Turki al-. 2003a. "Beyond Brainwashing" (Arabic). *Al-Sharq al-Awssat,* May 12.

————. 2003b. "The Winner and the Losers in Today's World" (Arabic). *Al-Sharq al-Awssat,* June, 9.

Hamid, Shadi. 2005. "Democracy Also Means That Islamists Are Allowed to Vote." *Daily Star,* March 12.

Harb, Osama El-Ghazali. 2005. "Inside and Out." *Al-Ahram Weekly,* April 6.

Hariq, Elya. 2001. *Democracy and the Challenges of Modernity Between the East and the West* (Arabic: *Al-Democratyya wa Tahdeyat al-Hadatha*). Beirut: Dar Al Saqi.

Hassan, Riaz. 2002. *Faithlines: Muslim Conceptions of Islam and Society.* New York: Oxford University Press.

Hayat Newspaper, May 18, 2003.

Heper, Metin, and Sabri Sayari. 2002. *Political Leaders and Democracy in Turkey.* Lanham, MD: Lexington.

Hijab, Nadia. 1988. *Woman Power: The Arab Debate on Women at Work.* Cambridge: Cambridge University Press.

Hochschild, Jennifer L. 1981. *What's Fair? American Beliefs About Distributive Justice.* Cambridge, MA: Harvard University Press.

Holyoake, George J. 1860. *The Principles of Secularism Briefly Explained.* 2nd ed. N.p.: n.p.

Howaidi, Fahmi. 1999. *Confirming the Truth* (Arabic: *Ihqaq al-Haq*). Cairo: Dar al-Shorouq.

————. 2003a. "The Message of the Elections of the Egyptian Syndicate of Journalism." *Al-Sharq al-Awssat,* August 4.

————. 2003b. Encouraging Moderates is the Best Mechanism to Fight Extremists. *Al-Sharq al-Awssat,* June 2.

Howaini, Abu Is'haq al-. 1998. "Alliance and Clearance" (Arabic: "Al-Wala' wa al-Bara'a"). Islamway.com.

Hozzeffi, Abdulrahman al-. 1998. *Wipe Out the Jews, Christians, and Shiites from Arabia.* Available at: http://www.alsalafyoon.com/ArabicPosts/RawafedHuthiefy.htm.

Huntington, Samuel. 1984. "Will More Countries Become Democratic?" *Political Science Quarterly* 99: 193–218.

————. 1996. "Democracy for the Long Haul." *Journal of Democracy* 7, no. 2: 3–13.

Hussein, Saddam. 1988. Interview by Kuwaiti press. Dar al-Mamun, Baghdad, February 20.

Ibn Baaz, Abdelaziz. 1992. *The Obligation of Enjoining the Good and Forbidding the Evil.* Riyadh: Dar al-Essma.

Ibn Baaz, Ahmad. 2002. "Dialogue with Extremists" (Arabic). *Al-Sharq al-Awssat*, April 19.

Ibrahim, Ferhad, and Gèulistan Gèurbey. 2000. *The Kurdish Conflict in Turkey: Obstacles and Chances for Peace and Democracy.* New York: St. Martin's.

Ibrahim, Saad Eddin. 1980. "Anatomy of Egypt's Militant Islamic Groups." *International Journal of Middle East Studies* 12:423–453.

———. 1984. *The Crisis of Democracy in the Arab World* (Arabic: *Azmat al-dimuqratiyah fi al-watan al-'Arabi*). Beirut: Markaz Dirasat al-Wahdah al-'Arabiyah.

———. 2002. *Egypt, Islam, and Democracy: Critical Essays, with a New Postscript.* Cairo: American University in Cairo Press.

———. 2003. *Democracy and Human Rights in the Middle East Today.* Washington, DC: Center for the Study of Islam and Democracy.

Ibrahim, Somaya. 2002. "Female Justices." *Al-Sharq al-Awssat*, November 25.

Inglehart, Ronald. 1997. *Modernization and Postmodernization: Cultural, Economic, and Political Change in Forty-three Societies.* Princeton, NJ: Princeton University Press.

———. 2000. "Political Culture and Democratic Institutions: Russia in Global Perspective." Paper read at the annual meeting of the American Political Science Association, August 31–September 3.

———. 2003. *Islam, Gender, Culture, and Democracy: Findings from the World Values Survey and the European Values Survey.* International Studies in Social Science 4. Willowdale, ON: De Sitter.

Iqbal, Anwar. 2003. "Mastering the Madrassas." *Washington Times*, August 17.

Iryani, Abd al-Karim al-. 1998. "The Role of the State in a Traditional Society." *Yemen Gateway.* Available at: http://www.al-bab.com/yemen/gov/iryani1.htm.

Ismail, Salwa. 2003. *Rethinking Islamist Politics: Culture, the State and Islamism.* London: I. B. Tauris.

Jafri, A. B. S. 2002. *The Political Parties of Pakistan.* Karachi: Royal Book.

Jahanbegloo, Ramin. 2003. *Iran Between Tradition and Modernity.* Lanham, MD: Lexington Books.

Jawed, Nasim. 1999. *Islam's Political Culture: Religion and Politics in Predivided Pakistan.* Austin: University of Texas.

Jawziyah, Ibn Qayyim al-. 1969. *A'lam al-Muwaqqi'in.* Cairo.

Jayal, Niraja Gopal. 2001. *Democracy in India.* Themes in Politics Series. Oxford: Oxford University Press.

Johnson, Paul. 2001. "Relentlessly and Thoroughly: The Only Way to Respond." *National Review*, October.

Karatnycky, Adrian. 2002. "The 2001 Freedom House Survey: Muslim Countries and the Democracy Gap." *Journal of Democracy* 13, no. 1: 99–112.

Karl, Terry Lynn. 1990. "Dilemmas of Democratization in Latin America." *Comparative Politics* 23, no. 1: 1–21.

Kassem, Maye. 1999. *In the Guise of Democracy: Governance in Contemporary Egypt.* London: Ithaca.

Kaufman, Stephan, and Robert R. Haggard. 1997. "The Political Economy of Democratic Transitions." *Comparative Politics* 29, no. 3: 263–283.

Kechichian, Joseph A., and Gustave E. von Grunebaum. 2001. *Iran, Iraq, and the Arab Gulf States.* New York: Palgrave.

Keddie, Nikki R. 1972. "Intellectuals in the Modern Middle East: A Brief Historical Consideration." *Daedalus* no. 44.

Kedourie, Sylvia. 1996. *Turkey: Identity, Democracy, Politics.* London: Frank Cass.

Khalaf Allah, Mohamed. 1984. *The Quranic Foundations of Progress* (Arabic). Cairo: Ketab al-Ahali.

Khaledi, S. al-. 1987. *America from Inside Through the Lenses of Sayyid Qutb* (Arabic). Jeddah: Dar al-Manar.

Khalidi, M. al-. 1984. *Criticism of the Democratic System* (Arabic: *Naqdh al-Nizzam al-Democratie*). Beirut: Dar Al-Jeel.

Khan, Muqtedar. 2003. "The Priority of Politics." *Boston Review.* Available at: http://www.bostonreview.net/BR28.2/khan.html.

Khazen, Jihad al-. 2003. "Ahl Mecca Adra Be-She'abbeha." *Al-Hayat*, June 4.

Khouri, Ragih al-. 2003. "Ghodo al-Democratya Sa-yessel." *Al-Sharq al-Awssat*, June 13.

King, Stephen J. 2003. *Liberalization Against Democracy: The Local Politics of Economic Reform in Tunisia.* Indiana Series in Middle East Studies. Bloomington: Indiana University Press.

Kinross, Albert. 1920. "Islam." *Atlantic Monthly*, November.

Korany, Bahgat. 1994. "Arab Democratization: A Poor Cousin?" *Political Science and Politics* 27, no. 3: 511–513.

Kristof, Nicholas D. 2002a. "Can This Marriage Be Saved?" *New York Times*, November 1.

———. 2002b. "Saudis in Bikinis." *New York Times*, October 25.

Kutty, Faisla. 1998. "Algerian Islamist Sheikh Mahfoud Nahnah Addresses ISNA Conference." *Canadian Chronicle*, July, 75–76.

Latif, Ali. 2005. *Iraqi Constitution: Attitudes Towards Democracy.* Baghdad: Iraqi Prospect Organization.

Layachi, Azzedine. 1998. *State, Society and Democracy in Morocco: The Limits of Associative Life.* Washington, DC: Center for Contemporary Arab Studies, Edmund A. Walsh School of Foreign Service, Georgetown University.

Lehtonen, Risto, and Erkki Pahkinen. 2004. *Practical Methods for Design and Analysis of Complex Surveys.* 2nd ed. Hoboken, NJ: John Wiley.

Lewis, Bernard. 1988. *The Political Language of Islam.* Chicago: University of Chicago Press.

———. 1993. "Islam and Liberal Democracy." *Atlantic Monthly*, February.

———. 1999. *The Multiple Identities of the Middle East.* 1st American ed. New York: Schocken.

Linz, Juan J., and Alfred Stepan. 1996. *Problems of Democratic Transition and Consolidation: Southern Europe, South America and Post-communist Europe*. Baltimore: Johns Hopkins University Press.

Lipset, Seymour Martin. 1983. *Political Man: The Social Bases of Politics*. London: Heinemann.

Luciani, Giacomo. 1995. "Resources, Revenues, and Authoritarianism in the Arab World: Beyond the Rentier State." In *Political Liberalization and Democratization in the Arab World*, edited by R. Brynen, B. Korany, and P. Noble. Boulder: Lynne Rienner Publishers.

Ma'moon, Khalil. 2003. "Islamic Fundamentalism in Mauritania" (Arabic). *Al-Sharq al-Awssat*, June 14.

Maddy-Weitzman, Bruce. 1997. "The Islamic Challenge in North Africa." *Middle East Review of International Affairs* 1, no. 2.

Mahathir bin, Mohamad, and Makaruddin Hashim. 2000. *Politics, Democracy and the New Asia: Selected Speeches*. Subang Jaya, Selangor Darul Ehsan, Malaysia: Pelanduk, for the Prime Minister's Office of Malaysia.

Mahmoud, Mostapha. 2001. "The Tale of September the 11th." *Al-Ahram*, December 22.

Makiya, Kanan. 2002. "Can Tolerance Be Born of Cruelty in the Arab World?" *New Perspectives Quarterly*, Winter.

Marsot, Afaf Lutfi al-Sayyid. 1972. "The *Ulama* of Cairo in the Eighteenth and Nineteenth Century." In *Scholars, Saints, and Sufis*, edited by N. Keddi. Berkeley: University of California Press.

Martinez, Luis. 2000. *The Algerian Civil War, 1990–1998*. CERI Series in Comparative Politics and International Studies. New York: Columbia University Press and Centre d'Etudes et de Recherches Internationales.

Mawdudi, Abo Al-A'laa. 1977a. *Concepts of Islam Regarding Religion and State*. Kuwait: Dar al-Qalam.

———. 1977b. *Islam and Modern Civilization* (Arabic). Cairo: Dar al-Anssar.

———. 1980. *Islam Facing Modern Challenges* (Arabic). Kuwait: Dar al-Qalam.

Mazrui, Ali. 1990. *Cultural Forces in World Politics*. Portsmouth, NH: Heinemann.

Mazyanni, Hamza. 2005. Interview. *Al-Hayat*, June 18.

McCain, John. 2002. Talk on State-sponsored Terrorism. American Jewish Committee, New York, May 10.

McFaul, Michael. 2003. "War with Iraq: Tinderbox." *Hoover Digest*, Spring, 2.

Mernissi, Fatima. 1991. *Can We Women Head a Muslim State?* Lahore, Pakistan: Simorgh, Women's Resource and Publications Centre.

———. 1992. *Islam and Democracy: Fear of the Modern World*. Reading, Mass.: Addison-Wesley.

———. 2003. *The Forgotten Queens of Islam*. Karachi, Pakistan: Oxford University Press.

Mohamed, Mahathir. 1989. "Islamization of Knowledge and Future of Islamic *Ummah*." In *Toward Islamization of Disciplines*, edited by International Institute of Islamic Thought. Herndon, VA: International Institute of Islamic Thought.

Mubarak, Hosni. 1992. Speech on the G-15. Cairo: Ministry of Information, State Information Service.

Murri, Aaesha al-. 2005. The Union Council Between Elections and Appointment, *Wajhat*, March 16.

Musharraf, Pervez. 1999. *Speeches.* Islamabad: Directorate General of Films and Publications.

Mustafa, Hala, and David Makovsky. 2003. "Building Arab Democracy." *Washington Post*, November 18.

Nadwi, Abo Al-Hassan al-. 1985. *The Coming Western Civilization* (Arabic). Cairo: Dar al-Sahwa.

Nefessi, Abdullah al-. 2002. Interview. Al-Jazeera, available at www.aljazeera.net/programs/opinions/articles/2002/11/11-27-1.htm.

Nehnah, Mahfouz. 1999. *The Desired Algeria* (Arabic). Algiers: Dar Annaba'.

Nettler, Ronald L., Mohamed Mahmoud, and John Cooper. 2000. *Islam and Modernity: Muslim Intellectuals Respond.* London: I. B. Tauris.

Neusner, Jacob. 1996. *Religion and the Political Order: Politics in Classical and Contemporary Christianity, Islam, and Judaism.* Atlanta: Scholars.

No'amani, Mohamed Said. 2002. "The Feasibility of Dialogue Among Cultures" (Arabic). Al-Jazeera.net.

No'man, Mustapha. 2003. "Scholars of Satellite Networks and the Explosions of Riyadh." *Al-Sharq al-Awssat*, May 17.

Norris, Pippa, and Ronald Inglehart. 2002. "Islam and the West: Testing the 'Clash of Civilizations' Thesis." Available from the authors: pippa_norris@harvard.edu or www.pippanorris.com.

Obeidi, Amal. 2001. *Political Culture in Libya.* Richmond, UK: Curzon.

Omara, Mohamed. 2002. "Facing the Western Modernist Model." *Al-Sharq al-Awssat*, February 2.

OneWorld. 2004. "Iraq War Deepens Hostility to U.S. Policies in Arab World." www.wbai.org/index.php?option=content&task=view&id=3114&Itemid=2.

ORI (Oxford Research International). 2003. "Iraqis Welcome 'Fall of Saddam.'" BBC, December 1. Available at http://news.bbc.co.uk/2/hi/middle_east/3254028.stm.

Othaimeen, Mohamed. 1998. *Fatawa* (Arabic audio). Binothaimeen.com.

Othman, Abdo Ali. 1998. "Tribe and Society in Yemen." *Yemeni Times* 8:23.

Ottaway, Marina. 2003. "Thinking Big: Democratizing the Middle East." *Boston Globe*, January 5.

Ottaway, Marina, Thomas Carothers, Amy Hawthorne, and Daniel Brumberg. 2002. "Democratic Mirage in the Middle East." *Carnegie Endowment Policy Brief,* no. 20.

Pew Research Center. 2003a. *Views of a Changing World 2003.* Washington, DC: Pew Research Center.

———. 2003b. *Religion and Politics: Contention and Consensus.* Washington, DC: Pew Research Center.

Pipes, Daniel. 1995. "There Are No Moderates: Dealing with Fundamentalist Islam." *National Interest*, Fall.

———. 2002. "God and Mammon: Does Poverty Cause Militant Islam?" *National Interest*, Winter.

———. 2003 "After Saddam? Remaking of the Mideast." *New York Post*, February 11.

Potter, David, et al., eds. 1997. *Democratization*. London: Open University.

Przeworski, Adam. 1992. "The Games of Transition." In *Issues in Democratic Consolidation: The New South American Democracies in Comparative Perspective*, edited by S. Mainwaring, G. O'Donnell and J. S. Valenzuela. Notre Dame, IN: University of Notre Dame Press.

Qablan, Marawan. 2005. "Ba'athism and State." *Al-Hayat*, March 28.

Qaradawi, Yusuf al-. 1980. *The Islamic Solution and the Imported Solutions* (Arabic: *Al-Hal al-Islamy wal-Holol al-Mustawrada*). Beirut: Mu'assat al Risalah.

———. 1984. *Ijtihad in Islam* (Arabic: *Al-Ijtihad in Islam*). Cairo: Dar al-Shorouq.

———. 2000. *Our Nation Between Two Centuries* (Arabic: *Omatona Bayen Qarnayen*). Cairo: Dar al-Shorouq.

———. 2001. *On the Fiqh of the Islamic State* (Arabic: *Min Fiqh al-Dawla Fil-Islam*). Cairo: Dar al-Shorouq.

———. 2003. "The Relationship with Non-Muslims" (Arabic: "Al-'Elaqqa ma'a Ghayer al-Moslemeen"). Al-Jazeera.net. Available at www.aljazeera.net/programs/shareea/articles/2003/6/6-25-1.htm.

Qarni, A'ed. 2005. Interview. *Al-Sharq al-Awssat*, February 9.

Qashtini, Khaled al-. 2003. "Step by Step, Move by Move." *Al-Sharq al-Awssat*, June 22.

Qutb, Sayyid. 1989. *Signposts* (Arabic). Cairo: Dar al-Shuruq.

Rahman, Fazlur. 1982. *Islam and Modernity: Transformation of an Intellectual Tradition*. Publications of the Center for Middle Eastern Studies 15. Chicago: University of Chicago Press.

Rashid, Abdulrahman al-. 2001. "Arab Representatives and Their Shameful Attitude" (Arabic). *Al-Sharq al-Awssat*, December 30.

Rawabda, Abdelraouf al-. 2003. "Forum on Democracy in the Arab World" (Arabic: "Al-Democrateya fi al-Watan al-Arabi"). Jazeera.net. Available at www.aljazeera.net/programs/opinions/articles/2001/11/11-29-6.htm.

Rice, Condoleezza. 2005. Interview. *Washington Post*, March 25.

Rikabi, Zain al-'Abedin al-. 2003. "Source of Violence: Distortion of 'Jihad'" (Arabic). *Al-Sharq al-Awssat*, May 24.

Rosen, Lawrence. 2002. *The Culture of Islam: Changing Aspects of Contemporary Muslim Life*. Chicago: University of Chicago Press.

Ross, Michael Lewin. 2001. "Does Oil Hinder Democracy?" *World Politics* 53, no. 3: 325–361.

Rouleau, Eric. 2001. "Politics in the Name of the Prophet." *Le monde diplomatique*, November.

Roy, Olivier. 1994. *The Failure of Political Islam*. Cambridge, MA: Harvard University Press.

Rubin, Donald B. 1987. *Multiple Imputation for Nonresponse in Surveys*. Wiley

Series in Probability and Mathematical Statistics. Applied Probability and Statistics. New York: Wiley.

Sachs, Susan. 2001a. "The Despair Beneath the Arab World's Growing Rage." *New York Times*, October 14.

———. 2001b. "In One Muslim Land, an Effort to Enforce Lessons of Tolerance." *New York Times*, December 16.

Sa'eed, Abdelmone'm. 2003. "Egypt the Democratic State" (Arabic). *Al-Ahram*, August 18.

Sa'eed, Ref'at al-. 2001. *Secularism Between Islam and Fake Islamization* (Arabic: *Al-'Alamnya Bayyeen al-Islam Wa al-Ta'sloum.*). Cairo: Al-Tagou' Party in Egypt.

Saffar, Hassan Moussa al-. 2005. "Shiite Between Religion and Politics." Al-Jazeera.net.

Saktanber, Ayse. 2002. *Living Islam: Women, Religion, and the Politicization of Culture in Turkey.* London: I. B. Tauris.

Salamah, Ghassan. 1994. *Democracy Without Democrats? The Renewal of Politics in the Muslim World.* New York: I. B. Tauris.

Saleh, Hashem. 2003. "Arab Intellectuals Between Zionism and Fundamentalism" (Arabic). *Al-Sharq al-Awssat*, September 5.

———. 2004. "2004 Spurs a New Revolution." *Al-Sharq al-Awssat*, January 9.

Sampath, S. 2001. *Sampling Theory and Methods.* New Delhi: Narosa.

Sartori, Giovanni. 1962. *Democratic Theory.* Detroit: Wayne State University Press.

Sawaf, Mohamed Mahmoud al-. 1979. *No Socialism in Islam* (Arabic). Cairo: Dar al-Anssar.

Scheaffer, Richard L. 2005. *Elementary Survey Sampling.* 6th ed. Belmont, CA: Wadsworth Thomson.

Schedler, Andreas. 2002. "Elections Without Democracy: The Menu of Manipulation." *Journal of Democracy* 13, no. 2: 36–50.

Schneider, Howard. 2000. "Syrian Intellectuals Call for Democracy." *Washington Post*, September 28.

Schofield, James. 1996. *Silent over Africa: Stories of War and Genocide.* Sydney, NSW: HarperCollins.

Schumpeter, Joseph A. 1976. *Capitalism, Socialism, and Democracy.* New York: Harper and Row.

Semali, Ladislaus. 1995. *Postliteracy in the Age of Democracy: A Comparative Study of China and Tanzania.* San Francisco: Austin & Winfield.

Shah, Aqil. 2002. "Democracy on Hold in Pakistan." *Journal of Democracy* 13, no. 1: 67–75.

Shahidian, Hammed. 2002. *Women in Iran.* Contributions in Women's Studies 197. Westport, CT: Greenwood.

Sharabi, Hesham. 1970. *Arab Intellectuals and the West: The Formative Years, 1875–1914.* Baltimore: Johns Hopkins University Press.

———. 1988. *Neopatriarchy: A Theory of Distorted Change in Arab Society.* New York: Oxford University Press.

Sharawi, Mohamed Motwali al-. 1980. *Al-Shura and Legislation in Islam* (Arabic). Cairo: Dar Thabet.

Shariati, Ali, and Farhang Rajaee. 1986. *What Is to Be Done: The Enlightened Thinkers and an Islamic Renaissance.* Houston: Institute for Research and Islamic Studies.

Sharot, Stephen. 2001. *A Comparative Sociology of World Religions: Virtuosos, Priests, and Popular Religion.* New York: New York University Press.

Sherman, Martin. 1998. "Paradigms of Peace for the Middle East." *Ariel Center for Policy Research* 19.

Sivan, Emmanuel. 1997. "Constraints and Opportunities in the Arab World." *Journal of Democracy* 8, no. 2: 103–113.

Smith, Christine B. 2002. "Casting the Net: Surveying an Internet Population." Available at www.ascusc.org/jcmc/vol3/issue1/smith.html (02/22).

Soekarno. 1959. *Guided Democracy: A Volume of Basic Speeches and Documents.* New Delhi: Unity Book Club of India.

Solomon, D. J. 2001. "Conducting Web-Based Surveys." *Practical Assessment, Research, and Evaluation* 7, no. 19.

Srivastava, Virendra K., and David E. A. Giles. 1987. *Seemingly Unrelated Regression Equations Models: Estimation and Inference.* Statistics, Textbooks, and Monographs 80. New York: Dekker.

Stepan, Alfred, and Graeme Robertson. 2003. "An Arab More Than Muslim Electoral Gap." *Journal of Democracy* 14, no. 3. Available at journalofdemocracy.org.

Stern, Jessica. 1999. *The Ultimate Terrorists.* Cambridge, MA: Harvard University Press.

———. 2003. *Terror in the Name of God: Why Religious Militants Kill.* New York: Ecco.

Suberu, Rotimi T. 1996. *Ethnic Minority Conflicts and Governance in Nigeria.* Ibadan, Nigeria: Spectrum / French Institutes for Research in Africa (IFRA).

Tabetba'i, Basseri. 2002. "Kuwait Women: Deputy Minister, Ambassador and University Director but Not Allowed in Parliament" (Arabic). *Al-Sharq al-Awssat*, February 6.

Taheri, Amir. 2003. "Democracy in Arabia." *Wall Street Journal Europe*, January 20.

Tahir, Umar, and Muammar Qaddafi. 1996. *Al-Qaddhafi wa-al-Thawrah al-Faransiyah, 1789–1969.* Beirut: Al-Multaq lil-Tibaah wa-al-Nashr.

Tamimi, Azzam. 2001. *Rachid Ghannouchi: A Democrat Within Islamism, Religion and Global Politics.* Oxford; New York: Oxford University Press.

Tarah, Ali al-. 2005. Kuwait and the Ramifications of the Greater Middle East Project, *Wajhat*, March 16.

Tessler, Mark. 2002a. "Do Islamic Orientations Influence Attitudes Toward Democracy in the Arab World? Evidence from Egypt, Jordan, Morocco, and Algeria." *International Journal of Comparative Sociology* 43, no. 3–5: 229–249.

————. 2002b. "Islam and Democracy in the Middle East: The Impact of Religious Orientations on Attitudes Toward Democracy in Four Arab Countries." *Comparative Politics* 34, no. 3: 337–354.

Tibi, Bassam. 1998. *The Challenge of Fundamentalism: Political Islam and the New World Order.* Berkeley: University of California Press.

Tilly, Charles. 1995. *Popular Contention in Great Britain, 1758–1834.* Cambridge, Mass.: Harvard University Press.

Turabi, Hassan al-. 2003. *Politics and Governance* (Arabic: *Al-Seyassa wal Hokm*). London: Dar al-Saqqi.

Ujo, A. A. 2000. *Understanding Political Parties in Nigeria.* Kaduna, Nigeria: Klamidas.

Ullah, Aman, and Robert V. Breunig. 1998. Econometric Analysis in Complex Surveys. In *Handbook of Applied Economic Statistics*, edited by A. Ullah and D. E. A. Giles. New York: Marcel Dekker.

Vakili, Valla. 1996. *Debating Religion and Politics in Iran: The Political Thought of Abdolkarim Soroush.* New York: Council on Foreign Relations.

Weaver, Mary Anne. 2000. "Democracy by Decree: Can One Man Propel a Country into the Future?" *New Yorker*, November, 54–61.

White, Jenny B. 2002. *Islamist Mobilization in Turkey: A Study in Vernacular Politics.* Studies in Modernity and National Identity. Seattle: University of Washington Press.

Williams, Daniel. 2005. "Egyptian Diplomat Rebuts Bush's Views on Mideast." *Washington Post*, March 9.

Wingard-Nelson, Rebecca. 2004. *Data, Graphing, and Statistics.* Math Success. Berkeley Heights, NJ: Enslow.

Wolfowitz, Paul. 2002. *Interview*, Al-Jazeera.net.

World Bank. 2001a. *Engendering Development: Through Gender Equality in Rights, Resources, and Voice.* New York: World Bank.

————. 2001b. *World Development Report.* Washington, DC: World Bank.

Wright, Robin. 1992. "Islam, Democracy, and the West." *Foreign Affairs* 71: 131–145.

Yamani, Mai. 2000. *Changed Identities: The Challenge of the New Generation in Saudi Arabia.* London: Royal Institute of International Affairs.

Zakaria, Fareed. 1997. "The Rise of Illiberal Democracy." *Foreign Affairs* 76:22–41.

————. 2001. How to Save the Arab World. *Newsweek.* December 24.

Zaman, Muhammad Qasim. 2002. *The Ulama in Contemporary Islam: Custodians of Change.* Princeton Studies in Muslim Politics. Princeton, NJ: Princeton University Press.

Zartman, I. William. 1982. *Political Elites in Arab North Africa: Morocco, Algeria, Tunisia, Libya, and Egypt.* New York: Longman.

Zawahri, Ayman al-. 2001. *The Final Will* (Arabic: *Al-Wasseyya al-Akheera*). N.p.: n.p.

————. 2002. "Alliance and Clearance" (Arabic: "Al-Wala' wa al-Bara'a"). *Al-Quds al-Arabi*, December 25.

————. n.d. *The Bitter Harvest of Muslim Brotherhood in Sixty Years* (Arabic: *Al-Hassad al-Mor: Al-Ekhwan al-Moslmoon fi Seteen 'Amah*). N.p.: n.p.

Zetterberg, Hans L. 1963. *On Theory and Verification in Sociology.* Totowa, NJ: Bedminster Press.

Zogby, James J. 2002. *What Arabs Think: Values, Beliefs, and Concerns.* New York: Zogby International.

Index

Abdullah, Crown Prince, 142–143

Afghanistan: choosing the ideal political system, 108(table), 112(table); democratization failure, 141–142

Age: as biological challenge to autocracy, 136–137; factors explaining attitudes toward democracy, 34(table); regard for democratic norms and institutions, 41–43

Ahl al-hall wa al-aqd, 147

al-Ahram Center for Strategic Studies, 116

Albania: aggregate spectrum of democracy, 120(table); elasticity of demand for democracy, 115(table); factors explaining attitudes toward democracy, 34–35(table), 36; income influencing support for democratic norms, 38; Muslim view of US role in fostering autocracy, 73; people's trust in government opinion of Arab-Israeli conflict, 80(table); percentages of the four cultural categories, 29(table); previous political participation influencing support for democracy, 48–49; prodemocratic and proincumbent stance, 66(table); survey respondents, 164(table)

Algeria: aggregate spectrum of democracy, 120(table); antidemocratic rule, 56–57; elasticity of demand for democracy, 115(table); factors

explaining attitudes toward democracy, 34–35(table); ideological challenge to autocratic rule, 141; Islamist mentality refusing democratic norms, 27–28; modernist attitudes, 18; people's trust in government opinion of Arab-Israeli conflict, 80(table); percentages of the four cultural categories, 29(table); premature democracy, 23; prodemocratic and proincumbent stance, 66(table); religiosity, 56; secularization, 59; survey respondents, 164(table); traditionalist beliefs, 127

Al-Qaida, 16

Al-salaf al-salih, 147

Al-wala' wa al-bara'a, 13, 17–18, 147

'Aqeeda, 147

Arab exceptionalism, 114

Arkoun, Mohamed, 32(n17)

al-Ashmawi, Said, 32(n15)

al-Assad, Hafez, 23

Association of Southeast Asian Nations (ASEAN), 141

Autocratic discourse, 23

Autocratic regimes: causing lack of democracy, 71; choosing the ideal political system, 108(table); emptiness of elections in, 49–51; global statistics on Muslim countries, 1–2; Islam's affinity with, 125; Muslim view of US role in fostering, 73–78;

About the Book

———

Is Islam compatible with democracy? Amid the seemingly endless debate on this issue, Moataz Fattah's study is a rare investigation of actual Muslim beliefs about democracy across numerous and diverse Islamic societies.

Fattah's survey analysis of more than 31,000 Muslims in thirty-two countries (including three countries in which Muslims live as minorities), enhanced by focus-group discussions, offers a nuanced portrait of the link between Islam and democracy. His work advances discussion on this critical topic to a new, more sophisticated level.

Moataz A. Fattah is assistant professor of political science at Cairo University and Central Michigan University.

He is also the research manager of the Partners in Development Think Tank based in Cairo, Consultant to the Arab League's Arab Women Organization, and Senior Researcher at Cairo University's Program for Dialogue among Civilizations.